Investigating Srebrenica

Studies in Contemporary European History

Editors:
Konrad Jarausch, University of North Carolina, Chapel Hill
Henry Rousso, Institut d'histoire du temps présent, CNRS, Paris

Volume 1
Between Utopia and Disillusionment: A Narrative of the Political Transformation in Eastern Europe
  Henri Vogt

Volume 2
The Inverted Mirror: Mythologizing the Enemy in France and Germany, 1898–1914
  Michael E. Nolan

Volume 3
Conflicted Memories: Europeanizing Contemporary Histories
  Edited by Konrad H. Jarausch and Thomas Lindenberger with the Collaboration of Annelie Ramsbrock

Volume 4
Playing Politics with History: The Bundestag Inquiries into East Germany
  Andrew H. Beattie

Volume 5
Alsace to the Alsatians? Visions and Divisions of Alsatian Regionalism, 1870–1939
  Christopher J. Fischer

Volume 6
A European Memory? Contested Histories and Politics of Remembrance
  Edited by Małgorzata Pakier and Bo Stråth

Volume 7
Experience and Memory: The Second World War in Europe
  Edited by Jörg Echternkamp and Stefan Martens

Volume 8
Children, Families, and States: Time Policies of Childcare, Preschool, and Primary Education in Europe
  Edited by Karen Hagemann, Konrad H. Jarausch, and Cristina Allemann-Ghionda

Volume 9
Social Policy in the Smaller European Union States
  Edited by Gary B. Cohen, Ben W. Ansell, Jane Gingrich, and Robert Henry Cox

Volume 10
A State of Peace in Europe: West Germany and the CSCE, 1966–1975
  Petri Hakkarainen

Volume 11
Visions of the End of the Cold War
  Edited by Frederic Bozo, Marie-Pierre Rey, Bernd Rother, and N. Piers Ludlow

Volume 12
Investigating Srebrenica: Institutions, Facts, Responsibilities
  Edited by Isabelle Delpla, Xavier Bougarel, and Jean-Louis Fournel

Volume 13
Samizdat, Tamizdat, and Beyond: Transnational Media During and After Socialism
  Edited by Friederike Kind-Kovács and Jessie Labov

Volume 14
Shaping the Transnational Sphere: Experts, Networks, and Issues from the 1840s to the 1930s
  Edited by Davide Rodogno, Bernhard Struck, and Jakob Vogel

Volume 15
Tailoring Truth: Politicizing the Past and Negotiating Memory in East Germany, 1945–1990
  Jon Berndt Olsen

INVESTIGATING SREBRENICA

Institutions, Facts, Responsibilities

Edited by
Isabelle Delpla, Xavier Bougarel,
Jean-Louis Fournel

Published by

Berghahn Books

www.berghahnbooks.com

© 2012, 2014 Isabelle Delpla, Xavier Bougarel, Jean-Louis Fournel

First paperback edition published in 2014

All rights reserved.
Except for the quotation of short passages
for the purposes of criticism and review, no part of this book
may be reproduced in any form or by any means, electronic or
mechanical, including photocopying, recording, or any information
storage and retrieval system now known or to be invented,
without written permission of the publisher.

Library of Congress Cataloging-in-Publication Data

Investigating Srebrenica : institutions, facts, responsibilities / edited by Isabelle Delpla, Xavier Bougarel, Jean-Louis Fournel.
  p. cm.
  Includes bibliographical references and index.
  ISBN 978-0-85745-472-0 (hardback : alk. paper) — ISBN 978-1-78238-672-8 (paperback : alk. paper) — ISBN 978-0-85745-473-7 (ebook)
  1. Yugoslav War, 1991–1995—Atrocities—Bosnia and Hercegovina—Srebrenica. 2. Srebrenica (Bosnia and Hercegovina)—History—20th century. I. Delpla, Isabelle. II. Bougarel, Xavier. III. Fournel, Jean-Louis.
  DR1313.32.S68I68 2012
  949.703—dc23

                                                                2011041083

British Library Cataloguing in Publication Data

A catalogue record for this book is available from the British Library.

Printed on acid-free paper

ISBN 978-0-85745-472-0 hardback
ISBN 978-1-78238-672-8 paperback
ISBN 978-0-85745-473-7 ebook

Contents

List of Maps   vii

Acknowledgments   viii

List of Abbreviations and Acronyms   x

List of the Srebrenica Reports and Websites   xi

Chronology   xiv

Introduction
    The Judge, the Historian, and the Legislator   1
        Isabelle Delpla, Xavier Bougarel, and Jean-Louis Fournel

Chapter 1
    The ICTY Investigations   23
        Jean-René Ruez

Chapter 2
    Introduction to the "Report-Form": Characteristics and
    Temporalities of a Production of Public Truth   40
        Jean-Louis Fournel

Chapter 3
    Reassessing the French Parliamentary Fact-Finding Mission
    on Srebrenica   56
        Pierre Brana

Chapter 4
    A Tale of Two Commissions: Dutch Parliamentary Inquiries
    during the Srebrenica-Aftermath   67
        Christ Klep

Chapter 5
    Reflecting on the Dutch NIOD Report: Academic Logic and the
    Culture of Consensus   86
        Pieter Lagrou

Chapter 6
    Reopening the Wounds? The Parliament of Bosnia-Herzegovina
    and the Question of Bosniak Responsibilities   104
        Xavier Bougarel

Chapter 7
    The Long Road to Admission: The Report of the Government of
    the Republika Srpska   131
        Michèle Picard and Asta Zinbo

Chapter 8
    Facts, Responsibility, Intelligibility: Comparing the Investigations
    and Reports   148
        Isabelle Delpla

Bibliography   177

Notes on Contributors   186

Name Index   189

Subject Index   194

MAPS

Map 1. The former Yugoslavia   xix

Map 2. Bosnia-Herzegovina   xx

Map 3. The frontlines in Bosnia-Herzegovina (April 1992–March 1993)   4

Map 4. The frontlines in Bosnia-Herzegovina (April 1993–March 1994)   5

Map 5. The frontlines in Bosnia-Herzegovina (April 1994–October 1995)   8

Map 6. Srebrenica: Execution sites and mass graves   24

Acknowledgments

This book is part of a long-term, collective, and interdisciplinary research project, over the course of which its editors have become indebted to many people and institutions.

We first thank the institutions that have funded this research: the Action concertée incitative for young researchers (ACI 67110 "Morale, politique et justice internationale au prisme des sciences humaines: concepts, discours, représentations"), coordinated by the University Montpellier 3 (research unit EA 738 "Crises et frontières de la pensée européenne"), from 2002 to 2006; the research network GDR CNRS 2651 "Crises extrêmes," which also greatly influenced the project of this book; the mixed research unit UMR CNRS 5206 "Triangle" (Ecole Normale Supérieure de Lyon – University of Lyon); and the UMR CNRS 8032 Centre d'études turques, ottomanes, balkaniques et centrasiatiques (CETOBAC) for their lasting support.

This book first appeared in French under the title *Srebrenica 1995, Analyses croisées des enquêtes et des rapports,* in *Cultures & Conflits,* no. 67 (Spring 2007); we wish to thank the editors of this journal and the publisher, L'Harmattan, for authorizing its translation into English. We are indebted to Didier Bigo, Estelle Durand, and Pauline Vermeren for their help. The French version of this book would not have been possible without the additional support of the Office of International Relations of the University Paris 8 and the Department of Philosophy of the Ecole Normale Supérieure de Paris, in the person of Francis Wolff.

The present book is an updated and enriched version of the French original, with additional chapters and new sections on historical developments. It has also benefited from the funding of the ACI 67110, of the EA 738, of the UMR 5206, of the UMR 8032, and of the GDR 2651 and from the support of Romain Descendre via the Institut Universitaire de France (IUF).

We are also immensely grateful to David Harland for his invaluable input about the Srebrenica events and the writing of the UN report. Likewise, the General Hervé Gobillard and Edward Joseph greatly contributed to our understanding of the fate of Žepa. For the enriching discussions that led to this book, we are particularly indebted to Pierre Bayard, Magali Bessone, Devrim Boy, Rony Brauman, Dejan Dimitrijevic, Ger Duijzings, Claude Gautier, Christian Ingrao, Yann Jurovics, Christopher Lucken, Frédéric Rousseau, Henry Rousso, Johanna Siméant, Thierry Tardy, and Arnaud Vaulerin.

A great thanks to Ethan Rundell for the translation of most chapters and to Peter Burk for his immense help in the editing process of several chapters.

Finally, we wish to express our warm thanks to all the people in Bosnia, including acquaintances and dear friends from Srebrenica and elsewhere, who gave us the desire to carry out this project and helped us in doing so. Over the years, they have shared much more with us than just information, offering us an all too rare encounter with humane presence and dignity.

Abbreviations and Acronyms

ARBiH: Army of the Republic of Bosnia-Herzegovina (*Armija Republike Bosne i Hercegovine*)

BiH: Bosnia-Herzegovina (*Bosna i Hercegovina*)

Dutchbat: Dutch Bataillon of blue helmets present in the Srebrenica enclave

HRC: Human Rights Chamber

ICJ: International Court of Justice

ICMP: International Commission for Missing Persons

ICRC: International Committee of the Red Cross

ICTY: International Criminal Tribunal for the former Yugoslavia

NIOD: Netherlands Institute for War Documentation (*Nederlands Instituut voor Oorlogsdocumentatie*)

RS: Republika Srpska

SBiH: Party for Bosnia-Herzegovina (*Stranka za Bosnu i Hercegovinu*)

SDA: Party of Democratic Action (*Stranka demokratske akcije*)

SDP: Social Democratic Party (*Socijaldemokratska partija*)

SDS: Serb Democratic Party (*Srpska demokratska stranka*)

UNPROFOR: United Nations Protection Force

VRS: Army of the Republika Srpska (*Vojska Republike Srpske*)

SREBRENICA REPORTS AND WEBSITES

(last updated 8 December 2011)

Assemblée nationale (président: François Loncle, rapporteurs: René André and François Lamy), *Evénements de Srebrenica. Rapport d'information déposé par la Mission d'information commune sur les événements de Srebrenica,* Paris, 22 November 2001:

http://www.assemblee-nationale.fr/11//dossiers/srebrenica.asp

Human Rights Chamber for Bosnia-Herzegovina:
http://www.hrc.ba

Human Rights Chamber for Bosnia-Herzegovina, *Decision on Admissibility and Merits: The "Srebrenica Cases" (49 Applications) against the Republika Srpska (case nos. CH/01/8365 et al.),* Sarajevo, 7 March 2003:

http://www.hrc.ba/database/decisions/CH01-8365%20Selimovic%20Admissibility%20and%20Merits%20E.pdf

International Commission on Missing Persons (ICMP):
http://www.ic-mp.org

International Court of Justice, *Application of the Convention on the Prevention and Punishment of the Crime of Genocide (Bosnia and Herzegovina vs. Serbia and Montenegro),* The Hague, 26 February 2007:

http://www.icj-cij.org/docket/files/91/13685.pdf

International Criminal Tribunal for the former Yugoslavia (ICTY):
http://www.icty.org

For the judgment of Radislav Krstić, see:

http://www.icty.org/x/cases/krstic/tjug/en/krs-tj010802e.pdf and
http://www.icty.org/x/cases/krstic/acjug/en/krs-aj040419e.pdf

For the judgment of Vujadin Popović, Ljubiša Beara, Drago Nikolić, Ljubomir Borovčanin, Radivoje Miletić, Milan Gvero, and Vinko Pandurević, see:

http://www.icty.org/x/cases/popovic/tjug/en/100610judgement.pdf

For the other indictments, transcripts, and judgments related to the Srebrenica massacre, see the rubric entitled "The Cases":

http://www.icty.org/action/cases/4

For a precise description of the exhumation process, see Dean Manning, *Srebrenica Investigation: Summary of Forensic Evidence – Execution Points and Mass Graves*, The Hague, 16 May 2000:

http://www.domovina.net/archive/2000/20000516_manning.pdf

Nederlands Instituut voor Oorlogsdocumentatie (NIOD), *Srebrenica – A "Safe" Area: Reconstruction, Background, Consequences and Analyses of the Fall of a Safe Area*, Amsterdam, April 2002:

http://www.srebrenica.nl

Office of the High Representative in Bosnia-Herzegovina (OHR):

http://www.ohr.int

Parlementaire Enquêtecommissie Srebrenica, *Missie zonder vrede* [Mission Without Peace], The Hague, 27 January 2003:

https://zoek.officielebekendmakingen.nl/kst-28506-3.pdf

Republika Srpska Government – The Commission for Investigation of the Events in and around Srebrenica between 10th and 19th July 1995, *The Events in and around Srebrenica between 10th and 19th July 1995*, Banja Luka, 11 June 2004:

http://www.domovina.net/srebrenica/page_006/rs_final_srebrenica_report.doc

Republika Srpska Government – The Commission for Investigation of the Events in and around Srebrenica between 10th and 19th July 1995,

Addendum to the Report of the 11th June 2004 on the Events in and around Srebrenica between 10th and 19th July 1995, Banja Luka, 15 October 2004:

http://www.domovina.net/srebrenica/page_006/rs_final_srebrenica_report_add.pdf

United Nations, General Assembly, *Report of the Secretary-General Pursuant to General Assembly Resolution 53/35: The Fall of Srebrenica,* New York, 15 November 1999:

http://www.un.org/peace/srebrenica.pdf

Chronology

April–December 1990 – Free elections are held in the six constituent republics of Yugoslavia. Nationalist parties are victorious in all republics but Macedonia. Slobodan Milošević is elected president of Serbia, Franjo Tuđman president of Croatia, and Alija Izetbegović president of the collegial presidency of Bosnia-Herzegovina.

25 June 1991 – Independence is declared by Slovenia and Croatia.

August–December 1991 – War is waged in Croatia between the Yugoslav People's Army and Serb militias, on the one hand, and the nascent Croatian army, on the other. The "Republic of Serb Krajina" is created on territories controlled by the Yugoslav People's Army.

September–November 1991 – "Serb Autonomous Regions" are created by the Serb Democratic Party (SDS) in Bosnia-Herzegovina on territory they claim as Serb.

14 October 1991 – The sovereignty of the Republic of Bosnia-Herzegovina is reaffirmed by the Bosnian Parliament, despite the opposition of the SDS MPs.

3 January 1992 – A cease-fire is proclaimed in Croatia. The UN Security Council decides to deploy the United Nations Protection Force (UNPROFOR) along the front lines.

9 January 1992 – The SDS merges the "Serb Autonomous Regions" into a "Serb Republic of Bosnia-Herzegovina" presided over by Radovan Karadžić.

29 February / 1 March 1992 – The referendum on the independence of Bosnia-Herzegovina is boycotted by the SDS. The turnout is 63.7 percent, with 99 percent voting in favor of independence.

6 April 1992 – The war begins, with the Yugoslav People's Army laying siege to Sarajevo. The European Community recognizes the independence of Bosnia-Herzegovina.

7 April 1992 – The SDS proclaims the secession of the "Serb Republic" (Republika Srpska) from Bosnia-Herzegovina. The United States recognizes the independence of Bosnia-Herzegovina.

April–May 1992 – The Yugoslav People's Army launches a vast offensive in eastern and western Bosnia. The first massive wave of "ethnic cleansing" is carried out against the Bosniak and Croat populations of these regions.

9 May 1992 – Bosniak combatants united under Naser Orić recapture control over Srebrenica, in eastern Bosnia.

12 May 1992 – The Yugoslav People's Army units stationed in Bosnia-Herzegovina are transformed into the Army of the Republika Srpska (VRS), under the command of General Ratko Mladić.

29 June 1992 – The UN Security Council decides to deploy the UNPROFOR in Bosnia-Herzegovina to ensure the functioning of Sarajevo airport and the delivery of humanitarian aid.

September–December 1992 – Bosniak combatants from the Srebrenica enclave increase the territory under their control.

2 January 1993 – The Vance-Owen peace plan is presented, in which it is proposed that Bosnia-Herzegovina be divided into ten ethnic provinces.

22 February 1993 – The UN Security Council creates the International Criminal Tribunal for the former Yugoslavia (ICTY).

March 1993 – The VRS launches an offensive against the enclave of Srebrenica and threatens to capture the town.

11–12 March 1993 – General Philippe Morillon, commander of the UNPROFOR in Bosnia-Herzegovina, travels to Srebrenica and declares the town a zone under the protection of the United Nations.

16 April 1993 – The UN Security Council transforms the Srebrenica enclave into a "UN safe area."

6 May 1993 – The UN Security Council creates five new safe areas in Sarajevo, Tuzla, and the Bosniak enclaves of Bihać, Goražde, and Žepa.

May 1993–March 1994 – Fighting breaks out in Herzegovina and in central Bosnia between the Army of the Republic of Bosnia-Herzegovina (ARBiH) and the Croat Defence Council (HVO).

20 August 1993 – The Owen-Stoltenberg peace plan is presented, in which it is proposed that Bosnia-Herzegovina be divided into three ethnic republics.

18 March 1994 – An agreement is signed in Washington, DC, to end the fighting between Croats and Bosniaks and create the Federation of Bosnia-Herzegovina, consisting of eight ethnic, Bosniak and Croat cantons.

April 1994 – The VRS launches an offensive against the enclave of Goražde, which is stopped by a NATO ultimatum.

5 July 1994 – The Contact Group's peace plan is presented, in which it is proposed that Bosnia-Herzegovina be divided between the Federation (51 percent of the territory) and the Republika Srpska (49 percent of the territory).

October–November 1994 – The ARBiH carries out an offensive from the Bihać enclave, followed by a counter-offensive by the VRS.

January–April 1995 – A cease-fire is maintained in Bosnia-Herzegovina for four months.

25 May 1995 – Seventy-one people are killed by a Serb shell in the safe area of Tuzla.

26 May 1995 – NATO launches air strikes against Serb positions. The VRS retaliates by taking four hundred UNPROFOR blue helmets hostage.

June 1995 – The ARBiH offensive to end the siege of Sarajevo fails. France and Great Britain create the Rapid Reaction Force (RRF)

18 June 1995 – The last of the blue helmets being held hostage are released.

6 July 1995 – The VRS begins its offensive against the enclave of Srebrenica.

11 July 1995 – The VRS captures Srebrenica.

13–18 July 1995 – The VRS carries out the evacuation of women and children to territories under Bosnian control and the mass execution of men.

14 July 1995 – The VRS begins its offensive against the enclave of Žepa.

25 July 1995 – The VRS captures Žepa.

4–9 August 1995 – The Croatian army launches its offensive against the "Republic of Serb Krajina." In five days, the Croatian army takes back most of the territories lost in 1991.

29 August 1995 – NATO launches massive air strikes against Serb positions following the deadly shelling of a Sarajevo marketplace.

9–19 September 1995 – A joint offensive is launched by the ARBiH and the Croatian army. In ten days, Bosnian and Croatian forces capture a significant amount of territory in western Bosnia.

20 September 1995 – NATO ends air strikes against Serb positions.

1 November 1995 – Peace negotiations begin on the American air base in Dayton, Ohio.

16 November 1995 – The ICTY charges Radovan Karadžić and Ratko Mladić with genocide.

21 November 1995 – Peace agreements provide for the division of Bosnia-Herzegovina into the Federation of Bosnia-Herzegovina (51 percent of the territory) and Republika Srpska (49 percent of the territory). Srebrenica and Žepa remain in Republika Srpska.

14 December 1995 – Dayton peace agreements officially signed in Paris, France.

1 August 1996 – A debate concerning the circumstances of the fall of Srebrenica is held in the Parliament of Bosnia-Herzegovina.

15 November 1999 – The UN report on the fall of Srebrenica is presented by Kofi Annan.

5 October 2000 – The regime of Slobodan Milošević is overturned in Serbia.

28 June 2001 – Slobodan Milošević is transferred to the Netherlands for trial at the ICTY.

2 August 2001 – The ICTY finds General Radislav Krstić, former commander of the VRS Drina Corps, guilty of genocide.

22 November 2001 – The French Parliamentary Fact-Finding Mission publishes its report.

10 April 2002 – The Netherlands Institute for War Documentation (NIOD) publishes its report.

27 January 2003 – The Dutch Parliamentary Inquiry Commission publishes its report.

11 June 2004 – The Government of the Republika Srpska adopts a report recognizing the Srebrenica massacre.

June 2005 – The United States Senate and House of Representatives adopt a resolution qualifying the Srebrenica massacre as genocide.

11 March 2006 – Slobodan Milošević dies before the end of his trial.

26 February 2007 – The International Court of Justice renders a decision finding Serbia in violation of its obligation to prevent and punish genocide in Srebrenica.

22 July 2008 – Radovan Karadžić is arrested in Belgrade and transferred eight days later to the Netherlands for trial at the ICTY.

15 January 2009 – The European Parliament passes a resolution qualifying the Srebrenica massacre as genocide.

26 October 2009 – The trial of Radovan Karadžić begins at the ICTY.

9 January 2010 – The Serbian president, Boris Tadić, asks the Parliament of Serbia to adopt a resolution on the massacre of Srebrenica.

31 March 2010 – The Parliament of Serbia votes a resolution condemning the Srebrenica massacre of July 1995, accepting the decision of the International Court of Justice and requiring the arrest of General Ratko Mladić.

26 May 2011 – Ratko Mladić is arrested in Serbia and transferred five days later to the Netherlands for trial at the ICTY.

MAP 1. The former Yugoslavia

MAP 2. Bosnia-Herzegovina

Introduction

THE JUDGE, THE HISTORIAN, THE LEGISLATOR

Isabelle Delpla, Xavier Bougarel, and Jean-Louis Fournel

On 11 July 1995, the enclave and town of Srebrenica in eastern Bosnia fell into the hands of General Mladić's Serb nationalist forces. They organized the forced transfer of women and children, massacred about eight thousand Bosniaks,[1] and, in the months that followed, unearthed and transported the corpses to secondary graves in order to conceal evidence of their crimes.[2] Yet the enclave had officially been declared a "safe area" by the United Nations in 1993 and its inhabitants—including thousands of refugees from across eastern Bosnia—had been put under the protection of the international community, which was represented in this case by a battalion of Dutch blue helmets (*Dutchbat*). The Srebrenica massacre quickly came to be seen as the symbol of the contradictions, errors, faults, and even crimes that had marked the policy of "peace keeping" advocated in the former Yugoslavia by the great powers and the UN. The horror of this last great massacre of the war in Bosnia (1992–1995) no doubt played an important role in NATO's decision to intervene against the Bosnian Serbs in late summer 1995, which in turn led to the conclusion of the Dayton agreements several months later. The Srebrenica massacre was thus a sad milestone for post–Cold War Europe and, more particularly, for the development of a European security and defense policy. At a more global level, the tragic result of the "safe areas" policy in eastern Bosnia contributed to redefining the rules of engagement and establishing national and international responsibility in operations of a military-humanitarian nature.

The fall of Srebrenica and the massacre that followed have been the object of a large number of investigations and reports conducted by the institutions and countries that were party to the events, most notably

---

Notes for this chapter begin on page 19.

the UN, the Netherlands, and France. In this respect, too, the case of Srebrenica is exceptional: few events in contemporary history have given rise to so many reports from such different perspectives, institutions, and places. Srebrenica became a universal object of investigation even before the massacre was acknowledged by the Serb side. Through critical examination of these investigations and reports, this book seeks to analyze a threefold process: (1) writing the history of the events in Srebrenica in 1995; (2) determining criminal, political, and moral responsibility; and (3) constructing a public debate about foreign policy. In regards to the writing of history, the focus here is on the inquiry, as such (rather than the judgment process, for example), and the means for establishing knowledge about and patterns of intelligibility for the events. These investigations and reports also raise the question of the manner in which the countries and institutions involved confronted their own responsibility. In so doing, these international or state institutions contributed to the creation of a debate and to official awareness and recognition of the scale of the massacre. It is thus necessary to understand how these diverse institutions conceive of the publicity of debates, make their sources accessible and see themselves (or not) as sources of documentation contributing to "history." In examining these texts, the present work thus devotes particular attention to the overlapping issues of justice and the writing of history. Before presenting these reports and setting out this book's framework of analysis in more detail, however, we should first set the fate of Srebrenica in the broader context of the war in Bosnia.[3]

The Place of Srebrenica in the War in Bosnia

How did Srebrenica, a small town in eastern Bosnia, become the theater of the largest massacre in Europe since the end of the Second World War and the symbol of the failure of the international community in former Yugoslavia? In order to understand this, the war in Bosnia must first be put in the broader context of the violent breakup of Yugoslavia.[4] Against the backdrop of the collapse of communist regimes in Central and Eastern Europe, free elections were organized in 1990 in all republics of the Yugoslav Federation. However, these elections were won by nationalist parties, including in Bosnia, a republic populated by Bosniaks (43.7 percent of the population), Serbs (31.4 percent), and Croats (17.3 percent)[5] where the three nationalist parties—Bosniak, Serb, and Croat—together received 71.1 percent of the vote.[6] From that point on, Bosnia faced a double threat. On the one hand, it became the object of territorial claims on the part of the neighboring republics of Serbia and Croatia. This external threat increased with Croatian independence in June 1991, when a war pitted the Yugoslav People's Army (JNA) against the newly created Croatian army, leading to the formation of a "Republic of Serb Krajina" covering a third of Croatia's territory (see map 3).[7] On the other hand, the three nationalist parties, although sharing power, found themselves in ever more severe conflict over the future of Bosnia.[8] The Party of Democratic Action (SDA, Bosniak), the Croat Democratic Community (HDZ), and the non-nationalist parties reaffirmed the sovereignty of Bosnia on 14 October 1991. The Serb Democratic Party (SDS), for its part, opposed this step toward independence and proclaimed on 9 January 1992 a "Serb Republic of Bosnia-Herzegovina" covering the territories that it considered as Serb. On 1 March 1992, 63.7 percent of Bosnian voters turned out for the self-determination referendum boycotted by the SDS, with 99 percent voting for independence. The referendum was immediately followed by the erection of Serb barricades around the capital Sarajevo. One month later, on 6 April 1992, the European Community recognized the independence of Bosnia. The next day, the SDS proclaimed the secession of the "Serb Republic" (Republika Srpska, RS) in the territories that it controlled. Sarajevo thus found itself encircled by Serb forces and, in the weeks that followed, the entire country spilled over into war.[9]

Initially, the war in Bosnia pitted the Army of the Republika Srpska (VRS), which was drawn from the Yugoslav People's Army,[10] against the Army of the Republic of Bosnia-Herzegovina (ARBiH), which was drawn from the Bosnian Territorial Defense[11] and mainly consisted of Bosniaks, and the Croat Defense Council (HVO). With the support of neighboring Serbia, the VRS endeavored to link up Serb population areas and in a few months seized 70 percent of the territory of Bosnia (see map 3).

This Serb offensive was accompanied by a first wave of "ethnic cleansing," the violent expulsion of populations on the basis of ethno-national criteria. This "ethnic cleansing" took particularly violent forms in certain strategic municipalities mainly populated by non-Serbs, such as Prijedor and Sanski Most in western Bosnia, Brčko in the valley of the Sava, and Foča, Višegrad, and Zvornik in the valley of the Drina in eastern Bosnia.[12] It was then accompanied by massive or selective (i.e., above all targeting men) executions, sexual violence (mainly against women), and the opening of camps, including the infamous camps of Omarska and Keraterm in the municipality of Prijedor. Beginning at this time, Srebrenica occupied a particular place in the war. Indeed, in April 1992, it was among the towns of eastern Bosnia that had been conquered by Serb forces in their effort to gain control over this region bordering with Serbia. The Bosniak population of Srebrenica was thus also victim of "ethnic cleansing." But, one month later, Bosniak combatants led by Naser Orić succeeded in retak-

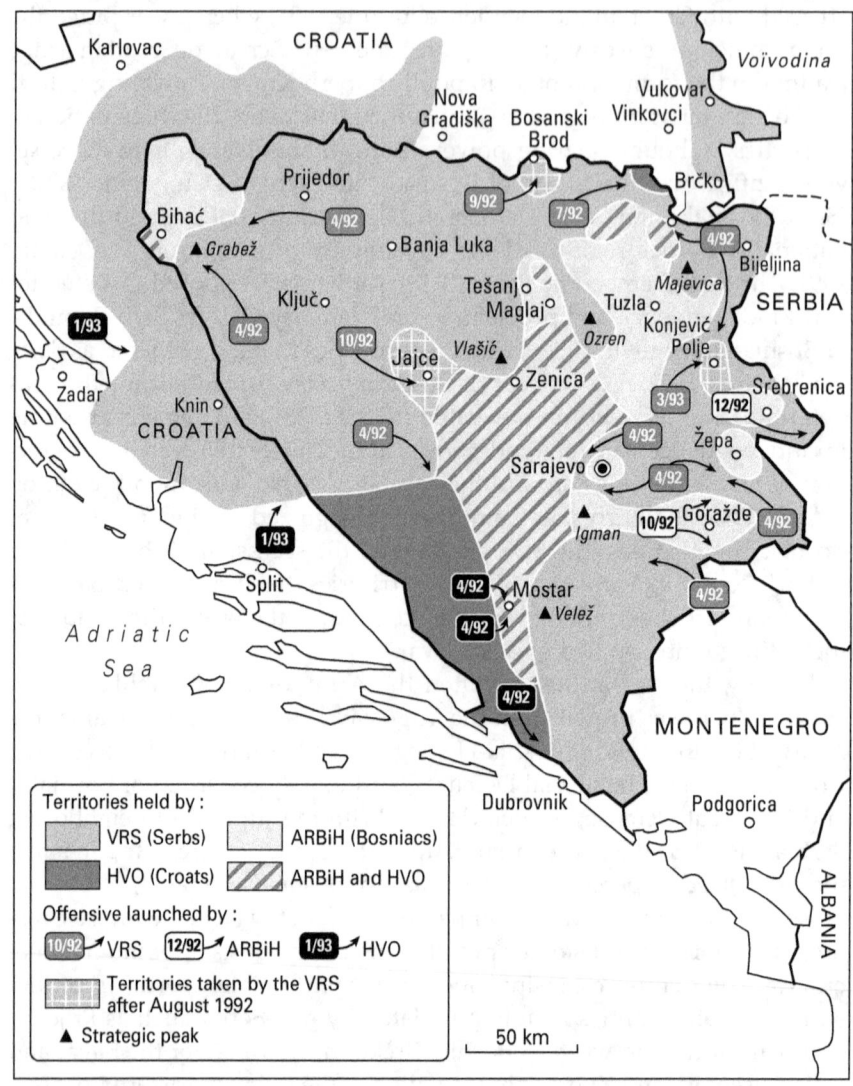

MAP 3. The frontlines in Bosnia-Herzegovina (April 1992–March 1993)

ing control of the town. From that point on, Srebrenica became a refuge for the Bosniak populations of eastern Bosnia who had been driven out by "ethnic cleansing," with the number of its inhabitants growing from around thirty thousand to around sixty thousand people. Given the lack of housing, provisions, and medicine and the difficulty of moving in humanitarian aid, living conditions in the enclave rapidly became dire. In order to obtain supplies, the enclave's inhabitants carried out raids against neighboring Serb villages that sometimes resulted in several dozen deaths among the local Serb population. At the same time, the Bosniak combatants succeeded in enlarging the territory under their control, joined up with other, smaller Bosniak enclaves, and even threatened to cut the Serbs laying siege to Sarajevo off from their supply lines (see map 3). In March 1993, the VRS launched an offensive against the Srebrenica enclave, considerably reducing its size and threatening to take the town (see map 4).

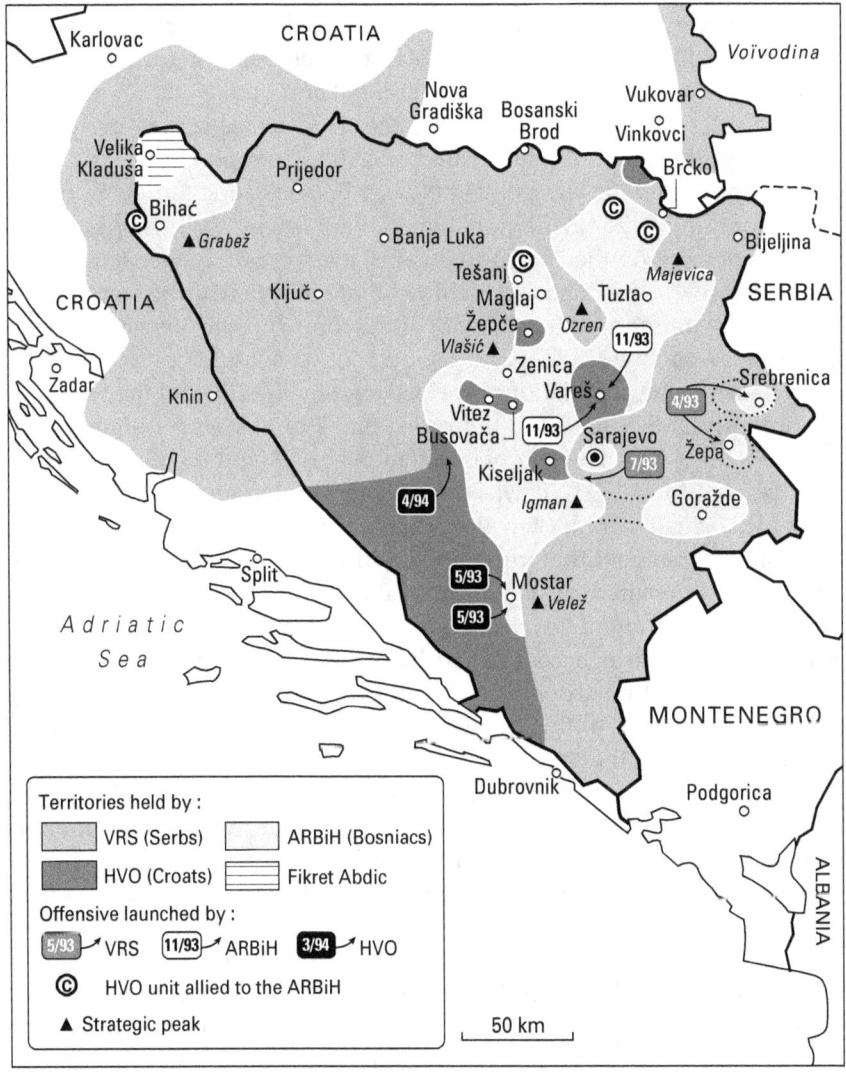

MAP 4. The frontlines in Bosnia-Herzegovina (April 1993–March 1994)

But the intervention on 16 April 1993 of General Philippe Morillon, commander of the United Nations Protection Force (UNPROFOR) deployed in Bosnia to ensure that humanitarian aid reached its destination, led to the Srebrenica enclave being transformed into a "safe area." Placed under UN protection, the latter was supposed to be protected by a contingent of blue helmets and, if needed, by NATO aircraft. One month later, five other "safe areas" were created for Sarajevo, Tuzla, and the Bosniak enclaves of Bihać in western Bosnia and Goražde and Žepa in eastern Bosnia. Srebrenica was thus at the origin of a profound redefinition of the UNPROFOR mandate in Bosnia.[13] But, straightaway, the "safe areas" appeared as highly vulnerable: of the 34,000 blue helmets requested by the UN to protect these zones, only 7,600 were granted and deployed.

From March 1993 to March 1994, the war in Bosnia was marked by intense fighting between the ARBiH and the Croat HVO and by violent campaigns of "ethnic cleansing" between Bosniaks and Croats in central Bosnia and in Herzegovina (see map 4). Serb forces, for their part, made do with preserving their territorial gains, even if a Serb offensive against the "safe area" of Goražde in April 1994 was stopped at the last moment by a NATO ultimatum. But the fate of the three Bosniak enclaves of eastern Bosnia—Srebrenica, Žepa, and Goražde—constituted one of the principal issues in the negotiations presided over by the UN and the European Community and helped foil the peace plans presented by international mediators (the Vance-Owen plan of January 1993 and the Owen-Stoltenberg plan of May 1993). It was the unilateral intervention of the United States that finally unblocked the situation with the signature in March 1994 of an agreement that put an end to the fighting between Croats and Bosniaks and created a Federation of Bosnia-Herzegovina composed of several Bosniak and Croat cantons. The reestablishment of the Croat-Bosniak alliance was accompanied by a discreet lifting of the UN arms embargo. With the hardening of economic sanctions against Serbia and the Republika Srpska, this allowed for a gradual shift in the balance of military power on the ground.

Yet it was not until 1995 that broader and more rapid political and military changes were set in motion. In May, a deadly bombardment of the town of Tuzla by Serb artillery provoked NATO to retaliate with air strikes. The VRS then took more than four hundred blue helmets hostage, thereby demonstrating UNPROFOR's vulnerability. The air strikes ceased and UNPROFOR decided to focus on its own security to the detriment of the safety of civilian populations. In June 1995, the French and British governments sent a heavily armed Rapid Reaction Force (RRF) to Bosnia. The ARBiH, for its part, launched an offensive against the Serb positions around Sarajevo but failed to break the siege. Several weeks later, on 6 July

1995, the VRS attacked the Srebrenica enclave. Despite its status as a "safe area," Serb forces advanced on the enclave without being confronted by a determined response on the part of the *Dutchbat* or NATO aviation. On 11 July, General Ratko Mladić's soldiers entered the town, which had by then been abandoned by its inhabitants. In the days that followed, about eight thousand Bosniak men were massacred by the Serb forces and the rest of the population of the enclave was expelled toward central Bosnia. Finally, on 14 July, the VRS attacked the enclave of Žepa, which fell in its turn on 25 July (see map 5).

The capture of the Srebrenica and Žepa "safe areas" and the massacre that followed in Srebrenica marked the definitive failure of UNPROFOR and led the major western powers to opt for a policy that privileged the use of air strikes. Thus, they threatened to bombard Serb forces if they attacked the Goražde "safe area." At the same time, the Croatian army launched a vast offensive against the "Republic of Serb Krajina" on 4 August and in a few days recaptured most of the territory that had been lost in 1991, thereby opening up the region of Bihać (see map 5). At the end of the same month, following a deadly shelling of Sarajevo, NATO and the RRF bombarded Serb military installations for several weeks. The Croatian and Bosnian armies took advantage of the bombardments to recapture large areas of western Bosnia. In three months, the map of the frontlines that had emerged in 1992 was significantly changed (see map 3 and map 5). The United States then exploited the new situation on the ground to launch new peace negotiations and, starting in September 1995, two framework agreements were signed on the future institutional architecture of Bosnia. The peace negotiations continued in November at the American air base in Dayton, Ohio, and on 21 November 1995 a territorial compromise was found, providing for the partition of Bosnia between two constitutive entities: the Federation of Bosnia-Herzegovina (51 percent of Bosnian territory) and the Republika Srpska (49 percent) (see map 2). The Dayton agreements, signed on 14 December 1995 in Paris, officially put an end to the war in Bosnia-Herzegovina. Goražde was brought under the jurisdiction of the Federation of Bosnia-Herzegovina but Srebrenica and Žepa remained in the RS.

It thus appears that Srebrenica played an important role in the main phases of the war in Bosnia. Obstacles to the conquest of eastern Bosnia by the VRS, the enclaves of Srebrenica, Žepa, and Goražde were the object of violent fightings and fierce negotiation throughout the war. In April 1993, Srebrenica became the first "safe area" protected by UNPROFOR, before this model was extended to other towns. Two years later, the capture of the Srebrenica "safe area" by Serb forces and the massacre that followed revealed the complexity of decision-making procedures within UNPRO-

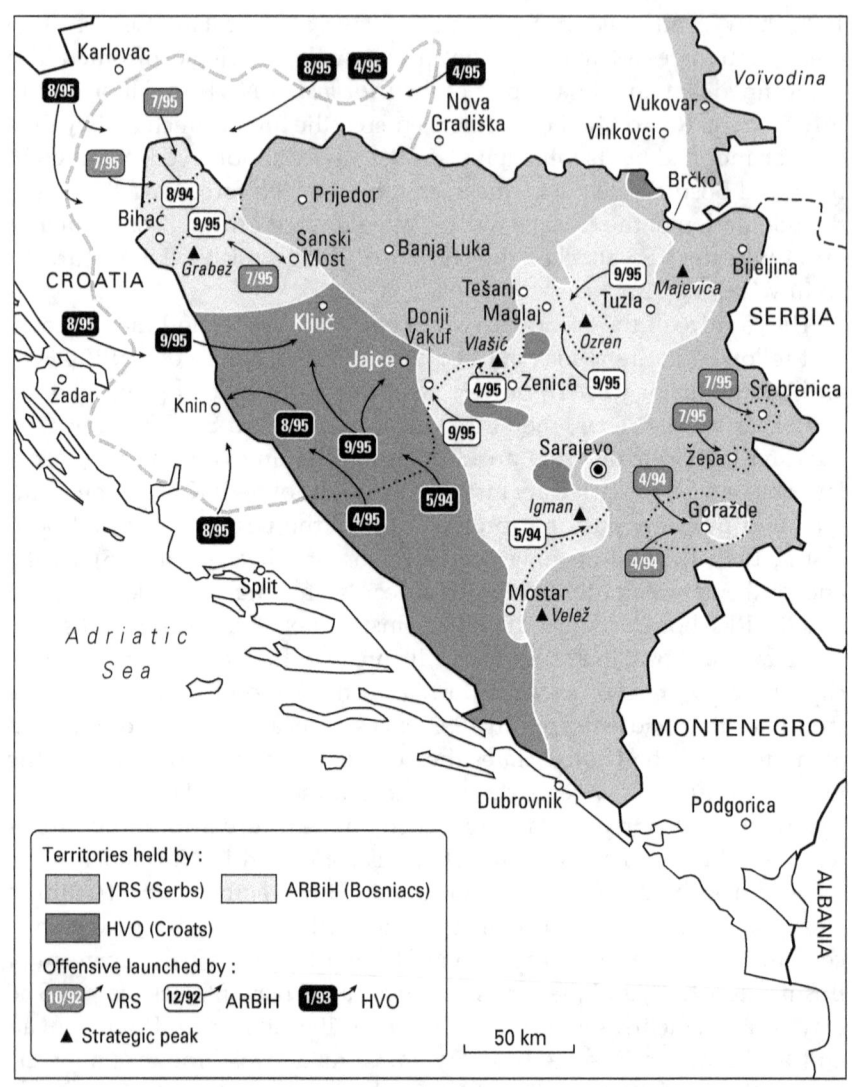

MAP 5. The frontlines in Bosnia-Herzegovina (April 1994–October 1995)

FOR, represented its definitive failure in Bosnia, and precipitated the massive intervention of NATO aviation. Beyond the single case of Bosnia, the painful experience of Srebrenica influenced the attitude that the major western powers adopted toward the Kosovo crisis several years later and led the UN to revise its conception of its peace-keeping operations. The unparalleled extent of the Srebrenica massacre also explains why it became the symbol of the "ethnic cleansing" that had been massively practiced by Serb forces over the course of the 1990s. The trials relating to the Srebrenica massacre are among the most significant conducted by the International Criminal Tribunal for the Former Yugoslavia (ICTY).

Investigations, Reports, and Public Debates about Srebrenica

Indeed, starting in July 1995, the ICTY opened investigations into the Srebrenica massacre, which in 2001 led to the conviction for genocide of Radislav Krstić, former commander of the VRS' Drina Corps.[14] General Ratko Mladić and the President of the Republika Srpska, Radovan Karadžić, the principal organizers of the massacre, were also charged with genocide—in particular, for Srebrenica. After years on the run, Radovan Karadžić was arrested in Serbia in July 2008 and his trial at the ICTY started in October 2009. Ratko Mladić was also arrested in Serbia in May 2011. Even if the testimony of thousands of victims and the rare survivors of the executions, as well as the writings of certain journalists, had already informed the public about the scale of the crimes, it was only through the ICTY's investigative work that the various phases of this vast operation of forcible transport, massacre, and moving of corpses were successfully reconstructed (especially as the latter phase of dissimulation could not be established on the basis of victims' testimony). Without the ICTY investigations, which allowed most of the primary and secondary graves to be found, it is very likely that the fate of the men of Srebrenica as well as the number who died in the massacre would remain a matter of speculation, rumor, and denial.

However important the investigations and judgments of the ICTY, this tribunal nevertheless only judges criminal responsibility in the massacre. It is not within its mandate to judge moral or political responsibility for the enclave's fall, whether on the part of the blue helmets or on that of the international leaders in charge of protecting the "safe area." Under pressure from survivors of Srebrenica, the Sarajevo authorities, public opinion, and various NGOs, several investigative reports were carried out in the months and years that followed by international or state institutions involved in various ways in the course of events (the UN, France, the Netherlands, Republika Srpska). By contrast, certain states that might also have been called into question—Great Britain and the United States, for example—did not produce investigations or reports.[15]

The main investigations and reports were produced by the ICTY beginning in 1996, the UN in 1999, the French National Assembly's Fact-Finding Mission in 2001, the Netherlands Institute for War Documentation

(NIOD), an independent historical research institute, at the request of the Government of the Netherlands in 2002, and the Dutch Parliament in 2003. In Bosnia itself, major controversies within the Bosniak community led to a parliamentary debate being organized as early as 1996 and the Government of the Republika Srpska submitted several reports, including that which finally came to terms with the massacre in 2004. The latter was in response to firm orders on the part of the Office of the High Representative (OHR) of the international community in Bosnia, which drew on decisions by that country's Human Rights Chamber demanding that the RS inform families concerning the fate of their missing loved ones.

Until now, these reports have never been the object of comparative analysis.[16] Yet the reader may wonder what is to be gained through devoting considerable attention to these often tedious investigations and reports. A first answer may be found by adopting a broader perspective, in terms of both the historical and the analytical scope. On the one hand, the work of historians has shown the importance of investigative commissions concerning crimes and atrocities in the construction of accounts of war.[17] On the other hand, it should be recalled that these international tribunals and investigative commissions, though they often bring to mind American, French, and British investigators, also have a history in the Balkans. The Balkan wars of the late nineteenth and early twentieth centuries were the object of international investigations.[18] During the First World War, the Serbian Government asked Rodolphe Reiss, a Swiss criminologist and one of the founders of forensic science, to write reports on the crimes committed by the Austrian, German, and Bulgarian armies of occupation.[19] Likewise, at the end of the Second World War, communist Yugoslavia created a State Commission for the Investigation of the Crimes of the Occupants and Their Collaborators that brought together documentation on crimes committed on Yugoslav territory, transmitting a part of it to the Nuremberg Tribunal.[20]

The present work also contributes to critical reflection on such investigations. More than fifteen years after the facts, it is not simply a matter of denouncing or commemorating them. It is a matter of analyzing the manner in which the history of an event of this gravity is written as well as the manner in which the question of responsibility in the area of foreign and international policy is addressed by the countries and institutions concerned. Indeed, the institutions that carried out these investigations and reports benefited from significant powers: a considerable mass of otherwise inaccessible information and documents was assembled on this occasion and decisively contributed to the history of the enclave's fall and the subsequent massacre. What is more, the *comparison* of these investigations and reports helps us to assess their results as well as the particular conditions and rationales that preceded their production. In this respect, it is necessary to understand the powers of investigation and their limits and the working methods that permitted and determined the collection of information. This is why the chapters of this book emphasize the importance of the investigative component, the reports' preparation, and the production of knowledge.[21]

Faced with the difficulty of finding words to name and describe, these investigations and reports offer frameworks for narration and intelligibility that shape public discussions on Srebrenica. They thus amount to an effort to instill rationality into a process of clarification which, from the outset, left too much room to rumor, disinformation, invective, and various conspiracy theories. They remain the principal source of knowledge concerning the enclave's fall and the massacre, the organized character of which they have solidly established. And, even if significant grey areas remain, the investigations and reports have broadly contributed both to minimizing the extent of rumors and denials concerning the number of deaths and the men's fate and to rationally examining suspicions of secret bargains or the deliberate abandonment of the enclave. Moreover, it is significant that certain attempts to deny the massacre or its scale, which one finds circulating on Serb nationalist websites, also take the form of reports, as a would-be gauge of truth and authenticity.[22]

These international or state institutions have thus contributed to the construction of a rational public debate and knowledge about the events.[23] It is therefore necessary to clarify their relationship to publicity and the constitution of archives (do they make their results, their sources, their procedures, and even their internal disagreements available?), especially given that their striving for transparency also aims to counter rumors and denials. Indeed, it is quite remarkable that, ten years later, a relative public consensus among international and state institutions, including the Republika Srpska, has been achieved on certain of the most contentious points, such as the number of the dead and the criminal nature of their elimination. By contrast, it is often forgotten that no consensus of this type or acknowledgment by the RS exists concerning "ethnic cleansing" in Prijedor, Zvornik, Foča, or Višegrad, or even in Srebrenica in 1992. In this respect, the shift from the 2002 RS report denying the massacre[24] to that of 2004 acknowledging it constitutes a decisive step. Even if its annexes remain classified, the forty public pages of the report, which are remarkable for their dullness, constitute first and foremost a public speech act.

Despite their limits, these investigations and reports thus circumscribe a (public) space of reasonable discussion concerning Srebrenica. It could be said that the Bosnian, French, and Dutch debates and reports fall short in analyzing the respective responsibility of these countries; there remains room for discussion about the predictability of the massacre, the motives of those who organized and carried it out, the models of intelligibility that allow one to understand it, and the more general place of Srebrenica in the war in Bosnia and in the international politics that preceded and accompanied it. In fact, the chapters offered in this volume may express divergent views on the validity of the historiographical models applied to the massacre and the analysis of national and international responsibility in the enclave's fall. But there can be no debate about the murder of thousands of Bosniaks in Srebrenica, on the pretext that this is a myth aiming to discredit the Serbs. Such negationist efforts, even when—indeed, above all when—they are expressed in an academic context are as humanly appalling as they are intellectually grotesque.

The comparison that we offer does not claim to be exhaustive.[25] It does not extend to the various commemorative parliamentary resolutions on Srebrenica, such as the one adopted by the Serbian Parliament in March 2010 (see below).[26] It does not extend to the numerous NGO reports,[27] in particular because these organizations had no decision-making power in the events. Nor does it extend to the history of testimony—in particular, that of the victims—for that would entail another type of study with its own methodology and objectives. The editors and authors of this volume do not consider the personal experience of the victims of Srebrenica or individual testimony in general to be of lesser importance as a source; after all, these often constitute the principal basis upon which the investigations and reports are based. The aim of this comparison, however, is to clarify the construction of a public debate and the manner in which international and national institutions face up to their own responsibility in the events. What is more, certain phases of the events—in particular, the vast corpse-moving operation—are not known to us through testimony. Accordingly, without the ICTY's exhumation efforts and the work of identification carried out by the International Commission for Missing Persons (ICMP), it would have been impossible to establish the fate of the men of Srebrenica and their mortal remains.

Moreover, the various attempts by victims of Srebrenica to pursue legal proceedings against international organizations have been unsuccessful. During the past few years, victims from Srebrenica and Dutch human rights organizations and lawyers have been attempting to work through the legal system to wrest formal apologies and reparations from the Dutch state and from individual Dutch politicians and soldiers. Till today, they have met with very little success. In a number of court cases, judges have consistently dismissed claims from Srebrenica victims. These claims were initiated above all by surviving family members of Bosniaks who had worked at the UN-compounds in the Srebrenica "safe area."

Dutchbat handed over a number of these employees and their relatives to the Bosnian Serbs, which in fact amounted to a death sentence. According to the Dutch courts, victims would have to address UN headquarters in New York: *Dutchbat* had after all been part of the UN chain of command. However, judges admitted, the UN itself was necessarily immune from judicial claims, implying that the victims had nowhere to go. This point of view—shared by the Dutch state—caused intense debate among legal and political experts. Some felt the opinion of the courts was too "cold," "technical," and biased in favor of the Dutch authorities. After all, human rights lawyers stressed, just how serious would any intrusion on basic human rights have to be, before *ius cogens* (general and enforceable rule of law) could be invoked to replace the immunity enjoyed by the UN?²⁸

The ICJ Decision and the Serbian Parliamentary Debate

The present work focuses on the investigations and the construction of knowledge concerning Srebrenica. Hence, it does not include a specific chapter addressing the decision by the International Court of Justice (ICJ) in The Hague concerning the complaint for genocide filed by Bosnia-Herzegovina against the Federal Republic of Yugoslavia (Serbia-Montenegro) in 1993, a decision that was made public on 26 February 2007.²⁹ The ICJ ruled on the responsibility of Serbia as a state, not the criminal responsibility of individuals (the object of the ICTY) or the political responsibility of countries or institutions in the enclave's fall (the object of the UN, French, and Dutch reports). In the February 2007 ruling, the ICJ held that genocide had been committed in Srebrenica but not in the rest of Bosnia and that Serbia was responsible neither for genocide nor for complicity in genocide but that it had violated its obligation to prevent and punish this crime.³⁰ This decision both directly and indirectly exemplifies the rationale that permeates the investigations and reports presented here. Directly, for it pushes the rationale of inter-report reference and citation to its limit. The ICJ ruling, which also refers to the NIOD report, is nearly entirely based on UN reports about the war in Bosnia (in particular, the report on the fall of Srebrenica) and on the judgments of the ICTY. The ICJ ruling thus contributes no new element or document vis-à-vis the judgments of the ICTY and the other reports cited and seems guided more by a desire to conform to these judgments and documents than by any desire to produce truth or clarify the nature of the events. Indeed, this decision follows those of the ICTY in declaring that a genocide has been committed in Srebrenica but not elsewhere in Bosnia, modeling the principle of determination of state responsibility on that of individual penal responsibility. This approach is all the more surprising given that the ICJ's decision relies on ICTY judgments that are temporary, contingent, and revisable, thereby weakening the authority of its decision. The logic of this decision suggests that it could have turned out differently had the trial of Slobodan Milošević reached a conclusion or if one of those charged by the ICTY had later been condemned for genocide elsewhere than in Srebrenica.[31] This division of labor—or deference in regards to the ICTY—is doubly problematic.

Indeed, by adopting the term *genocide* for Srebrenica, the ICJ uncritically and without justification endorsed a term that is an object of debate among legal scholars and, in so doing, also weakened its significance in marking the specific nature of the violence of Srebrenica, which consisted in the differential treatment of men and women and the systematic elimination of the former.[32] By rejecting Serbia's responsibility for participation or complicity in genocide, moreover, the ICJ decision made no effort to more thoroughly explore the role of Serbia in the Srebrenica massacre or publish the relevant documents concerning it. If the decision gave rise to a heated public discussion, it was in large measure due to its refusal to contribute to the work of investigation.[33] Indeed, the Court refused Bosnia's request to order Serbia to furnish the ICJ with the minutes of the Supreme Defense Council, the body in charge of the Yugoslav army. These minutes had been delivered to the ICTY in the framework of the Milošević trial on condition of confidentiality[34] and were available to the judges when they decided to refuse to acquit Milošević of charges of genocide in several municipalities of Bosnia.[35] Although the verdict that would have been issued in the Milošević trial had it reached its conclusion cannot be presumed, it is puzzling that the ICJ chose to focus on the ICTY judgments rather than that tribunal's investigative work, archives, and evidence. Even as it refused to order Serbia to produce these documents—something it was legally entitled to do—the ICJ based its exoneration of Serbia for responsibility or complicity in the commission of genocide precisely on the absence of such evidence. The stir to which this decision gave rise was thus inversely proportional to its contribution to establishing the facts.

As for the judgment's contribution to public discussion about Srebrenica, such an effect is clearly observable in Serbia. Attempts have long been made in Serbia to obtain acknowledgment of the Srebrenica massacre. In June 2005, on the eve of the tenth anniversary of the Srebrenica massacre, eight human-rights NGOs called for the adoption of a resolution condemning the genocide committed in Srebrenica. This initiative was supported by two MPs but the main parties opposed it, advocating instead that a resolution condemning all war crimes be adopted. The matter was then buried.

Over the following years, small opposition parties continued to demand that such a resolution be adopted, but without success. In an official communiqué following the ICJ decision, President Boris Tadić called on Serbia to recognize and condemn the Srebrenica massacre, though he did not use the term *genocide*. On 15 January 2009, the European Parliament proclaimed 11 July Srebrenica Genocide Commemoration Day; other parliaments in Europe did likewise. The same small opposition parties then asked the Parliament of Serbia to follow suit. In the meantime, Serbia filed a complaint with the ICJ against Croatia for genocide and another protesting the independence of Kosovo. It also signed on 29 April 2008 a Stabilization and Association Agreement with the European Union. The positions taken by President Tadić concerning Srebrenica were thus also interpreted as an effort to facilitate Serbian accession to the EU and strengthen its position in the ICJ against Croatia and Kosovo.

Appearing on Republika Srpska television on 9 January 2010, Boris Tadić stated that Serbia had the duty of condemning the Srebrenica massacre, provoking sharp reactions in the RS and Serbia. In concrete terms, Tadić proposed the adoption of two resolutions, one concerning Srebrenica in particular, the other concerning all of the crimes committed in the former Yugoslavia in the 1990s. In doing so, he benefited from the support of the small parties mentioned above as well as his own party (the Democratic Party—DS) and the G-17 party, both of which were in the Government. But he came up against opposition from Vojislav Koštunica's Democratic Party of Serbia (DSS), the Socialist Party of Serbia (SPS), and other parties that did not want a specific resolution addressing Srebrenica. The debates also concerned the possible inclusion of the term *genocide* in the Srebrenica resolution following the precedent of the ICJ and the European Parliament. After three months of negotiations, the ruling parties presented to the Parliament of Serbia a compromise resolution on Srebrenica at the end of March 2000. This resolution was adopted on 31 March 2010 with 127 votes for, 21 against, and 15 abstentions. It condemned the crime perpetrated in Srebrenica against Bosniaks "in the way established by the decision of the International Court of Justice," regretted and apologized that not everything had been done to prevent this crime, and required full cooperation with the ICTY, including the arrest of general Ratko Mladić. But the resolution carefully abstained from using the term *genocide* and did not require any parliamentary investigation into the role of Serbia in the Srebrenica events.[36]

A Dialogue between Actors and Researchers

The ICJ decision and the resolution of the Serbian Parliament thus underscore—indirectly and as counter examples—the specificity of the texts studied here, which all examine the issue of criminal or political responsibility and seek to establish the facts or at least improve knowledge of them, by giving access to confidential documents, for example. Given the role played by the ICTY investigations in establishing the facts about what happened after 11 July 1995, it is clear that our knowledge of Srebrenica is in large measure indebted to the legal narrative of the Tribunal. In this respect, clarifying the ICTY's rationale and investigative limits contributes to discussions of the relationship between the judge and the historian. As the police commissioner who directed the ICTY investigation into the 1995 massacre, Jean-René Ruez, explains in the interview with which this volume opens, the ICTY investigation is concerned neither with the issue of international responsibility for the enclave's fall nor with combat operations nor even with the responsibility of secondary actors such as police forces. Historians will certainly devote themselves to tying together the various dimensions of the events separated by the ICTY and distancing themselves from the purely legal reconstruction and categorization of these events, as historians of the Second World War have endeavored to do vis-à-vis the Nuremberg trials.[37] But the interest of comparing these investigations and reports is also to be found in going beyond and displacing the terms of the debate concerning the nature of the relationship between the judge and the historian. According to the predominant model, a judge is simply responsible for criminal justice proceedings—including investigations, in contexts where there is an examining magistrate—while it is the historian who holds the position of independent, external critic relative to the official documents from these proceedings and their production. In the present case, by contrast, police inspectors and legal scholars, just as much as historians, have engaged in critical reflection concerning the legal narrative of the events and its limits. What is more, the legal procedures of the ICTY and the Human Rights Chamber of Bosnia-Herzegovina provide an enlightening contrast with the European model centered around the examining magistrate, which has shaped reflections on the relationship between the judge and the historian. According to the accusatory procedures that prevail in the ICTY, the judges who draft the rulings and "write history" do not investigate, a duty that instead falls to police officers and prosecutors. And the decision of the Human Rights Chamber that led to the Republika Srpska report fell under the jurisdiction of civil, not criminal, procedures and bodies. Moreover, in the case of the NIOD report and that of the RS, it is historians who found themselves in the position of investigators producing official documents capable of being used or contested in the ICTY trials. Finally, parliamentarians and high-ranking officials contributed as much as historians to the production of these reports.

A complex relationship is thus established among police commissioners, judges, historians, parliamentarians, and high-ranking officials via this very self-referential body of investigations and reports. The process by which they were produced thus does not allow one to establish a clear separation, much less an opposition, between the role of judges and professional investigators and that of historians and academics, since both can be seen as bringing a critical perspective to bear on these investigations. It is thus neither history "from below," keeping as close as possible to the accounts of witnesses, nor history "from above." This fact is reflected in the very structure of the present work, which is based on a dialogue between various participants, some of whom more or less actively participated in elaborating these investigations and reports while others tried to understand their logic from outside by means of comparison.

It seemed essential for the present book to include perspectives from individuals who have, to one degree or another, participated in the realization of these investigations and reports on Srebrenica, both because of the institutions for which they have worked and because of their competence and personal involvement in promoting understanding and acknowledgment of the massacre. As a police commissioner, from 1996 to 2001 Jean-René Ruez led the ICTY investigation into the massacre. He has testified in all of the trials of those indicted by the ICTY in this affair and continues to do so. Michèle Picard was President of the Human Rights Chamber of Bosnia-Herzegovina from 1997 to 2003 and actively participated in the "Selimović" decision, which led to acknowledgment of the massacre by the RS. Asta Zinbo, former director of the ICMP's Department of Civil Society Initiatives, here intervenes on behalf of that institution, which participated in the preparation and work of the RS commission, and on account of her patient and precious work with the victims' associations of Srebrenica during her years within the ICMP. Pierre Brana, a former MP, participated in the French Parliamentary Fact-Finding Mission on Srebrenica and was the rapporteur for its counterpart on Rwanda. Although he did not serve as spokesman for the Srebrenica mission, a reading of the report and the hearing of the Parliamentary Fact-Finding Mission more than adequately show that his stances were among the freest and most constructive in the Commission's work. The career of Christ Klep, a historian and author of a dissertation on international interventions and, in the present volume, a chapter on the Dutch parliamentary report, also illustrates how porous the barrier is that separates the role of actor from that of researcher. As part of a team of historians within the Dutch Ministry of Defense, he interviewed *Dutchbat*-soldiers in Zagreb on their return from Srebrenica in late July 1995. These interviews were later used as source material by several Dutch Srebrenica commissions. He subsequently served as both witness and advisor during the Interim Parliamentary Commission (the first Bakker Commission) and as a commentator in the media on all Srebrenica commissions.[38]

The UN report is not the object of a separate chapter and the retrospective remarks on this report by David Harland, who was its principal author, are presented in the final and conclusive chapter by Isabelle Delpla. The chapters by Pieter Lagrou and Xavier Bougarel, both of whom are historians, bring an external perspective to bear on the rationales that cut across the preparation of the NIOD report (in the case of Pieter Lagrou) and the course of the debate in the Bosnian Parliament (in the case of Xavier Bougarel), each underscoring how these inquiries reflect specific political styles and practices. Those written by Jean-Louis Fournel, a historian of political thought, and Isabelle Delpla, a philosopher, present complementary analyses of the principles guiding comparison between these investigations and reports. Jean-Louis Fournel's chapter analyzes the "report-form" and the conflicts among temporalities that cut across the drafting of the reports. Isabelle Delpla's chapter compares how these texts establish facts, assign responsibility, and produce intelligibility, in particular by their choice of descriptive and interpretive levels (local, regional, national).

In the programmatic preface to his masterwork on the Mediterranean and the Mediterranean world in the age of Phillip II, Fernand Braudel called upon his readers to distrust "the burning passions" of the time of men: it is about precisely this sort of history that the present work tries to speak—about it and about the various ways in which one can and must try to put it into words. By bringing together institutional and academic contributors, detailed monographs, and comparative approaches, this book contributes to a reflection on the manner in which the history of an event of this gravity is written. More generally, it seeks to displace and overcome the usual historiographical frameworks of contemporary history and mass violence. On the one hand, the various chapters open up perspectives on national and international styles of action, political debate, and academic research without leading to a relativistic perspectivism. On the other hand, they contribute original information and reflection concerning the interactions between international organizations, national institutions and individuals during the events of July 1995 and the subsequent investigations and public debates. By various means, they insist as much on the role of state structures as on individual responsibility in the massacre itself. Similarly, they show the relationship between various degrees of institutional and personal responsibility, between institutional rationales and the active role of individuals, both in the attitude of the international community in July 1995 and in the conduct of international and national investigations.

In this respect, the present work aims to contribute to an informed and critical discussion of the Srebrenica massacre and its aftermath. Further, it seeks to underscore the importance of this massacre, not only for understanding the wars in the former Yugoslavia and the spiral of exactions and crimes that accompanied them, but also in order to contribute to broader reflections on violence, the prevention of conflicts, and relations between citizens, states, and international organizations in extreme crises and their effects at the dawn of the twenty-first century.

Translated from French by Ethan Rundell

Notes

1. In this volume, the term *Bosnians* (*Bosanci*) refers to all inhabitants of Bosnia while the term *Bosniaks* (*Bošnjaci*) only refers to members of the nation that has been called Muslim until 1993 and is distinct from the two other constituent nations of Bosnia (Serbs and Croats).
2. For a detailed description of the methods for assessing the number of victims and identifying bodies, see Asta Zinbo's contribution on behalf of the ICMP and Isabelle Delpla's chapter.
3. A first version of this work appeared in French under the title *Srebrenica 1995. Analyses croisées des enquêtes et des rapports* in the journal *Cultures & conflicts*, no. 65 (Spring 2007). This first edition was updated and supplemented, in particular by the addition of a chapter by Christ Klep concerning the Dutch parliamentary debate.
4. On the breakup of Yugoslavia, see Susan L. Woodward, *Balkan Tragedy: Chaos and Dissolution after the Cold War* (Washington, DC, 1995); Lenard Cohen, *Serpent in the Bosom: The Rise and Fall of Slobodan Milosevic* (Boulder, CO, 2001); Valère P. Gagnon, *The Myth of Ethnic War: Serbia and Croatia in the 1990s* (Ithaca, NY, 2004).
5. On the history of Bosnia, see Noel Malcolm, *Bosnia: A Short History* (London, 1994); Robert J. Donia and John V. Fine, *Bosnia and Herzegovina: A Tradition Betrayed* (London, 1994).
6. In Srebrenica, populated by Bosniaks (72.9 percent) and Serbs (25.2 percent), the Party of Democratic Action (SDA, Bosniak) and the Serb Democratic Party (SDS) respectively won 42 and 14 of the 66 seats on the city council.
7. In January 1992, a ceasefire in Croatia led to the creation of four "United Nations protected areas" (UNPA) covering the regions populated by Serbs and to the deployment of a United Nations protection force (UNPROFOR) that was to have its mandate extended to Bosnia in May 1992.
8. On Bosnia before the war, see Neven Andjelic, *Bosnia-Herzegovina: The End of a Legacy* (London, 2003).
9. On the war in Bosnia, see Steven L. Burg and Paul S. Shoup, *The War in Bosnia-Herzegovina: Ethnic Conflict and International Intervention* (New York, 1999); Xavier Bougarel, *Bosnie, anatomie d'un conflit* (Paris, 1996).
10. On the Yugoslav People's Army, see Miroslav Hadžić, *The Yugoslav People's Agony: The Role of the Yugoslav People's Army* (Aldershot, 2002).

11. In the framework of the Yugoslav "general people's defense" system, each republic possessed its own Territorial Defense equipped with small arms, the Yugoslav People's Army keeping a monopoly over heavy weapons. On the origins of the ARBiH, see Marko Hoare, *How Bosnia Armed: The Birth and Rise of the Bosnian Army* (London, 2004).
12. On "ethnic cleansing," see Norman M. Naimark, *Fires of Hatred: Ethnic Cleansing in Twentieth-Century Europe* (Cambridge, MA, 2001); Cathie Carmichael, *Ethnic Cleansing in the Balkans: Nationalism and the Destruction of a Community* (London/New York, 2002); *Final Report of the United Nations Commission of Experts Established Pursuant to Security Council Resolution 780 (1992)—document S/1994/674*, available at http://www.ess.uwe.ac.uk/comexpert/REPORT_TOC.HTM.
13. On the international dimensions of the war in Bosnia, see James Gow, *Triumph of the Lack of Will: International Diplomacy and the Yugoslav War* (New York, 1997); Thierry Tardy, *La France et la gestion des conflits yougoslaves (1991–1995)* (Paris, 1999).
14. The conviction upheld after appeal was that of aiding and abetting genocide.
15. The case of Greece is particular to the degree that the parliamentary report requested by certain NGOs did not concern the role of the Greek authorities but rather the participation of Greek volunteers in the attack against Srebrenica.
16. At least not in an academic framework. For analyses of several of these reports containing elements of comparison between them in an activist framework, see Mient Jan Faber, *Srebrenica. De genocide die net werd voorkommen* [Srebrenica. The Genocide That Was not Prevented] (Utrecht, 2002) and the website *Domovina*, which in particular brings together texts written by victims of Srebrenica, such as Hasan Nuhanović, concerning these various reports: http://www.domovina.net/srebrenica/page_006.php, last accessed on 8 December 2011.
17. See, in particular, John Horne and Alan Kramer, *German Atrocities, 1914: A History of Denial* (New Haven, CT, 2001) and the dossier "Enquêter sur la guerre" in *Le mouvement social*, no. 222 (January–March 2008). The present work is the result of work carried out in the framework of the GDR 2651 "Crises extrêmes." In this connection, see Marc Le Pape, Johanna Siméant, and Claudine Vidal, eds., *Crises extrêmes. Face aux massacres, aux guerres civiles et aux génocides* (Paris, 2006) and more particularly the comparison between the investigative reports on the genocide in Rwanda offered in this work by Marc Le Pape, "Vérité et controverses sur le génocide des Rwandais Tutsis. Les rapports (Belgique, France, UN)," 103–118.
18. See in particular Dzovinar Kévonian, "L'enquête, le délit, la preuve: les 'atrocités' balkaniques de 1912–1913 à l'épreuve du droit de la guerre," *Le mouvement social*, no. 222 (January–March 2008): 13–40.
19. Zdenko Levental, *Rodolphe Archibald Reiss, criminaliste et moraliste de la Grande Guerre* (Genève, 1992) ; Nicolas Quinche, "Reiss et la Serbie: des scènes de crime aux champs de bataille, l'enquête continue," in *Le théâtre du crime: Rodolphe A. Reiss (1875–1929)*, eds. Christophe Campod et al. (Lausanne, 2009), 289–306.
20. Albert Vajs, "Rad komisije za utvrđivanje zločina okupatora i njihovih pomagača" [The Activity of the Commission for the Investigation of the Crimes of the Occupants and their Collaborators], *Anali pravnog fakulteta* 9, no. 4 (October 1961): 387–400. On the use of the notion of genocide in communist Yugoslavia, see Xavier Bougarel, "Du code pénal au mémorandum: les usages du terme 'génocide' dans la Yougoslavie communiste," in *Peines de guerre. La justice pénale internationale et l'ex-Yougoslavie*, eds. Isabelle Delpla and Magali Bessone (Paris, 2010), 67–84.
21. The approach here is complimentary to that adopted in Isabelle Delpla and Magali Bessonne, eds., *Peines de guerre. La justice pénale internationale et l'ex-Yougoslavie* (Paris,

2010), which is more concerned with the history and use of legal categories such as genocide.
22. A striking example of a website using the report form in a fallacious manner is one calling itself the "Srebrenica-report." It presents itself as an official report by researchers and former UN officials and borrows from the form of the report both its style and its material presentation, imitating the websites of international organizations, in particular in order to claim that the number of eight thousand Bosniaks killed has no foundation in fact and is essentially a political fabrication.
23. In this respect, our discussions are indebted to the cosmopolitan reflections of Kant and Habermas concerning how public norms can be used to exert republican control over foreign policy (Immanuel Kant, *Perpetual Peace and Other Essays* [Indianapolis, IN, 1988]; Jürgen Habermas, *Perpetual Peace: Essays on Kant's Cosmopilitan Ideal* [Cambridge, MA, 1997]). In a reflection on transitional justice, Mark Osiel also very rightly underscores that trials and judgments for mass crimes matter as much for the judgments of the crimes themselves as for their contribution to public debate (Mark Osiel, *Mass Atrocity: Collective Memory and the Law* [New Brunswig, NJ, 1997]).
24. See the chapter by Michèle Picard and Asta Zinbo in this volume.
25. This comparison does not present the content of the reports, which in most cases may easily be consulted on the Internet. Nor does it seek to be exhaustive or systematic in the approaches and analytical methods it employs, which can vary from one chapter to another. In particular, it does not carry out a sociology of the institutions and persons who produced these reports.
26. The House and Senate of the US Congress passed resolutions on the Srebrenica genocide in June 2005, including all the atrocities that occurred in Bosnia as well. The European Parliament passed a resolution on 15 January 2009, marking 11 July for the Srebrenica Genocide Commemoration Day. In July 2009, the former Yugoslav countries of Croatia and Montenegro adopted declarations condemning the genocide and designated 11 July as a day of commemoration. Macedonia did likewise in February 2010, and Canada in October 2010.
27. Among the NGOs that were the most active in favor of investigations concerning international responsibility in the fall of Srebrenica, the local associations of families of the missing "Mothers of the Srebrenica and Žepa Enclaves" and "Women of Srebrenica" should be mentioned in particular (http://www.srebrenica.ba) as well as Médecins sans frontières in France (http://www.paris.msf), the Ecumenical Council for Peace in the Netherlands (http://www.ikvpaxchristi.nl), and the Greek Helsinki Monitor (http://www.greekhelsinki.gr) in Greece.
28. We thank Christ Klep for this paragraph.
29. International Court of Justice, *Application of the Convention on the Prevention and Punishment of the Crime of Genocide (Bosnia and Herzegovina v. Serbia and Montenegro)*, http://www.icj-cij.org/docket/files/91/13685.pdf, last accessed on 8 December 2011.
30. Another reason not to linger over this question is that a number of journals have devoted special issues to this decision. See, in particular, *Annuaire Français de Droit International* 53 (2007); *Journal of International Criminal Justice* 5, no. 4 (September 2007); *Leiden Journal of International Law* 21, no. 1 (March 2008); *European Journal of International Law* 18, no. 4 (September 2007); *Rutgers Law Review* 61, no. 1 (Fall 2008). In the context of the present work, we refer in particular to the article by Vojin Dimitrijević and Marko Milanović, "The Strange Story of the Bosnian Genocide Case," *Leiden Journal of International Law* 21, no.1 (March 2008): 65–94. This article describes the evolution of the legal and political strategies of the various protagonists, whose legal status and political aims changed over the course of the proceedings.

31. See in particular Richard J. Goldstone and Rebecca J. Hamilton, "Bosnia v. Serbia: Lessons from the Encounter of the International Court of Justice with the International Criminal Tribunal for the Former Yugoslavia," *Leiden Journal of International Law* 21, no. 1 (March 2008): 95–112.
32. For the meager contributions of this decision to the definition of genocide, see Claus Kreß, "The International Court of Justice and the Elements of the Crime of Genocide," *The European Journal of International Law* 18, no. 4 (September 2007): 619–629.
33. See in this regard Edina Bećirević, "ICJ Judgment Significant Despite Flaws," *IWPR's Tribunal Update*, no. 491 (4 March 2007), http://iwpr.net/fr/node/12606.
34. ICTY, *First Decision on Admissibility of Supreme Defence Council Materials*, 23 September 2004, http://www.icty.org/x/cases/slobodan_milosevic/tdec/en/040923-2.htm, last accessed on 8 December 2011.
35. ICTY, *Decision on Motion for Judgment of Acquittal*, 16 June 2004, http://www.icty.org/x/cases/slobodan_milosevic/tdec/en/040616.htm, paragraph 289, last accessed on 8 December 2011.
36. *Deklaracija skupštine Republike Srbije o osudi zločina u Srebrenici*, 31 March 20110, http://www.parlament.gov.rs/akti/ostala-akta/doneta-akta/doneta-akta.1039.html, last accessed on 8 December 2011.
37. On the relationship between the judge and the historian—to borrow the title of Carlo Ginzburg's book—or on the writing of contemporary history, we are in particular indebted to the work of Henri Rousso, Annette Vieworka, and Carlo Ginzburg as well as to the more general reflections of Paul Veyne and Pierre Vidal Naquet on writing history. On the distance taken by historians toward the historiography inherited from the Nuremberg trials, see in particular Donald Bloxham, *Genocide on Trial: War Crimes Trials and the Formation of Holocaust History and Memory* (New York, 2001).
38. The career of Ger Duijzings is also exemplary of this shift from the position of actor to that of researcher. A Dutch anthropologist who participated in the NIOD report, Ger Duijzings was one of the report's only contributors who had real expertise on the former Yugoslavia. He expressed his reservations over the final results of the NIOD's work in an article entitled, "The Road to Hell Is Paved with Good Intentions: The Srebrenica Report of the Netherlands Institute for War Documentation (NIOD)," *South-East Europe Newsletter*, London, no. 54 (June 2003): 1–7. He afterward worked as an investigator for the ICTY. For a reflexive examination of his own contribution to the NIOD report, see also his chapter, "Commemorating Srebrenica: Histories of Violence and Politics of Memory in Eastern Bosnia," in *The New Bosnian Mosaic: Identities, Memories and Moral Claims in a Post-War Society*, eds. Xavier Bougarel, Ger Duijzings, and Elissa Helms (Aldershot, 2007), 141–166.

Chapter 1

THE ICTY INVESTIGATIONS
Interview with Jean-René Ruez

Isabelle Delpla (I.D.): Between 1995 and 2001, you led the inquiry into the July 1995 Srebrenica massacre. You have on several occasions presented the results of your investigation before the ICTY, in particular during the trial of General Krstić, commander of the Drina Corps of the Army of the Republika Srpska,[1] where your testimony lasted three days.[2] Could you provide a general idea of the scope, objectives, and principal findings of your investigation into these events? In particular, can you explain how the distinction between combatants and non-combatants — the foundation of international humanitarian law — was applied?

Jean-René Ruez (J.-R.R.): The inquiry began in Tuzla on 20 July 1995; in judicial terms, it was thus a *flagrante delicto* investigation. The ICTY investigation concerned the criminal events that followed the fall of the enclave on 11 July 1995. These introductory remarks set the limits of the criminal inquiry. The investigation therefore did not relate to the causes of the enclave's fall and no one was charged with the "crime of seizing a UN safe area." Nor did the investigation address air strikes or the reasons why they were not carried out.

"Krivaja 95" is the codename that was given by the Army of the Republika Srpska to the operation that aimed not to occupy the Srebrenica enclave, but rather to reduce it to the size of the town in order to make residents' living conditions so intolerable that the UN would be forced to evacuate the area.

Against the advice of his staff officers, Ratko Mladić nevertheless decided on 10 July to capture the town. This had not been part of the initial plan. When the Army of the Republika Srpska took Srebrenica on 11 July, the population fled in two directions: women, children, the elderly,

---

Notes for this chapter begin on page 39.

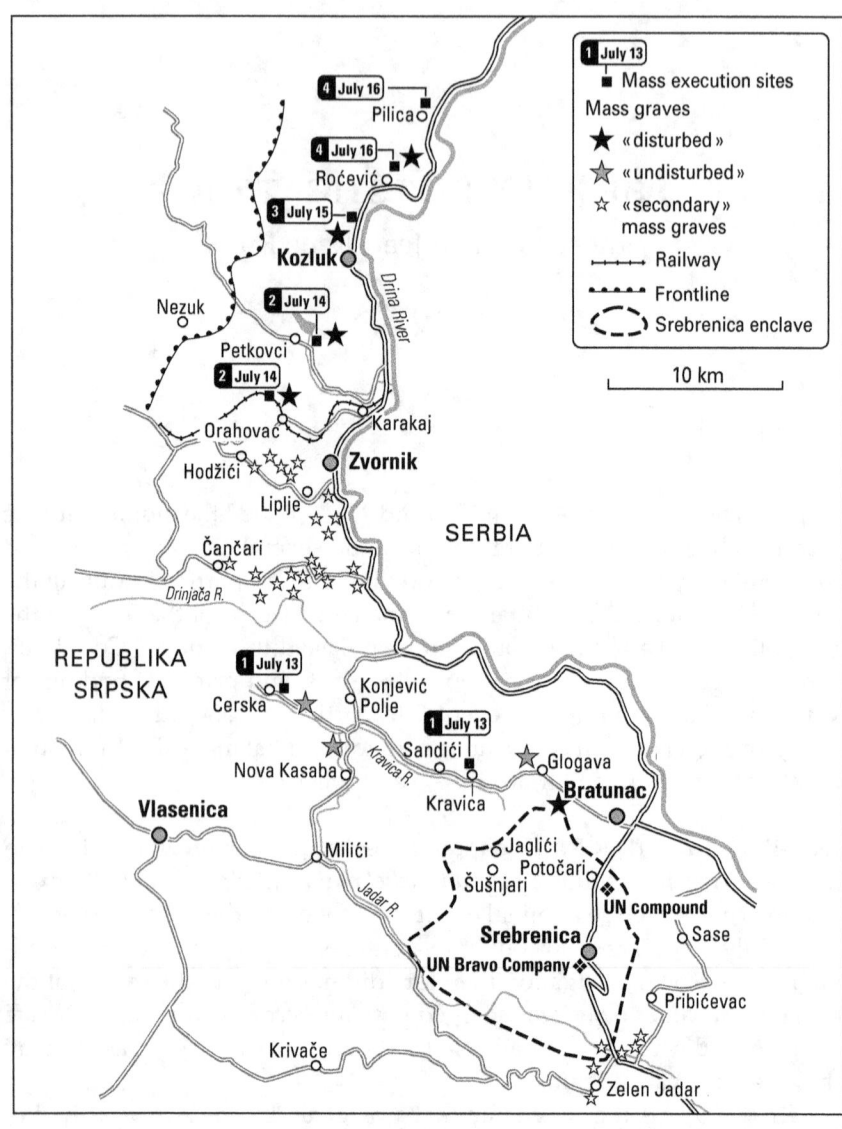

MAP 6. Srebrenica: Execution sites and mass graves

and men who did not want to abandon their families or thought they had nothing to fear from General Mladić's forces set off toward a small industrial zone called Potočari, where the main UN base was housed in an abandoned factory. Around 25,000 refugees assembled in this area.

Most of the men gathered at a place called Šušnjari, in the northwest corner of the enclave, where they later decided to cross the lines, traversing minefields in single-file formation. They included the soldiers of the twenty-eighth division of the Army of the Republic of Bosnia-Herzegovina as well as all able-bodied men who had not left for Potočari. It was not until the following day at noon that the tail end of the column finally left Šušnjari. The column was comprised of a mix of armed men and unarmed civilians. At this point, it was possible to consider every man as a "potential combatant though in civilian dress"—the previous day a general mobilization order had been issued to the entire male population of the enclave—or in any case as legitimate military targets to the degree that men were still carrying arms or were marching among soldiers.

This column reached the road intersection located at Konjević Polje. With the soldiers leading, around eight thousand crossed this sector in the evening of the 12th. I will say nothing further of the fate of this military column because it is not part of the inquiry: six thousand of them joined the Bosnian forces after breaking through the lines near Zvornik on 16 July, an episode that belongs to military history, not to the criminal record. Since we are unable to prove that they were murdered, those killed while seeking to flee the enclave must be considered as combat deaths and so are not counted among the victims who were executed while being held by the Army of the Republika Srpska.

Indeed, the ICTY inquiry, in conformity with international humanitarian law, does not judge military combat or the fate of combatants. It does, however, apply to the fate of non-combatants, whether originally soldiers or civilians; it applies, in other words, to all those who are not, or are no longer, in a position to fight.

After the head of the column passed through Konjević Polje, Serb forces closed the area, trapping the other refugees and runaways in the hills between Konjević Polje and Srebrenica (see map 6). On 13 July, this group decided to surrender to the Serb forces, enticed to do so by the fact that some Serb soldiers were wearing stolen blue helmets and claimed through megaphones that the UN and the International Red Cross were present.

At the same time, a process of forced transfer of the population that had sought refuge in Potočari began on 12 July using buses and trucks. In Potočari itself, troops created an atmosphere of terror, committing numerous murders while proceeding to separate men from women and children. Chaos reigned among the refugees. The evacuation was completed in the late afternoon of the 13th.

Widely known to the media, these events represent only the "tip of the iceberg." Next, the men were assembled in several places. This was Phase One of the extermination operation. Among others, these assembly points included Bratunac, Sandići, the soccer stadium of Nova Kasaba, and the Kravica hangar. At Bratunac, the executions began on the 12th with clubs, axes, and throat-cutting. This was not a mass execution but rather a matter of sporadic murders. Summary executions also took place along the road between Konjević Polje and Sandići. At the road intersection of Konjević Polje, there were two assembly sites at which sporadic murders also took place. Correlations between several survivor accounts and our research shows that some men were even killed in mass graves previously dug for them, where they were subsequently buried, since we found bullets under the bodies. At Nova Kasaba, there were also sporadic executions, as well as some that were more systematic. At this stage, it is clear that, regardless of the men's initial status, they could no longer be considered combatants. Notwithstanding Mladić's claims that, in this area, only soldiers and runaways were killed in combat operations, many of the cadavers had their hands or arms tied behind their backs. The type of restraint used, especially in this southern zone, is a flexible metal band that is highly practical for tying someone up from behind and impossible to slip out of once attached. A group of at least five hundred individuals were taken into the Kravica hangar and executed using automatic weapons and offensive grenades. The crime scene technicians who minutely examined the site found blood, skin, and other human tissue as well as explosive residue on the walls. One hundred and fifty prisoners, their hands tied behind their backs and some with bound feet, were transported in three buses to the Cerska valley. All of them were shot along the roadside and their bodies covered by an excavator. Still other prisoners were transported to the Jadar River, where they were executed by being shot from behind.

Thus, by 13 July, numerous executions had begun taking place, but the process was still disorganized, even anarchical. In reality, you could sum things up by saying that anyone who wanted to pull a trigger that day had license to kill. The same day, Serb army leaders, realizing that not all of the prisoners could be executed in this way, decided to begin by assembling the prisoners in Bratunac. While this was being done, officers of the security branch of the Drina Corps moved more than thirty kilometers northward to the Zvornik zone to scout out detention and burial sites, which were in fact to serve as execution sites. The transfer of the prisoners was thus planned to begin on the night of the 13th to the 14th. No provision for food or drink was made for the prisoners. Records of security officer movements were found during searches of the headquarters of the Bratunac and Zvornik brigades, their drivers having failed to destroy these records. It is the drivers' log-books that enabled us to confirm that we had in fact found all of the crime scenes, since these sites matched those listed in the drivers's handwritten records. For lack of transportation, those who could not be relocated on the day of the 13th were executed on the spot.

Phase Two of the extermination operation began during the night of the 13th to the 14th July, when a first convoy headed north from Bratunac to Zvornik. The prisoners were informed that they were being transferred as part of an exchange and taken to schools in Grbavci and Petkovci. Those held at the Grbavci school were blindfolded and executed in nearby Orahovac. After a number of them were tortured, those held at the Petkovci school were executed at the bottom of a nearby dam. In Orahovac, the wounded and dead were gradually buried, some while still alive, by excavators and backhoes. At the Grbavci school, we found a large number of blindfolds at the surface. In the trenches, numerous cadavers also had blindfolds that, when compared to those found at the surface, enabled us to link the execution site with the burial site. At the dam, near Petkovci, we found spent cartridge cases and a very large number of cranial fragments, evidence that the killers often shot their victims in the head.

The evacuation of Bratunac continued into the night of the 14th to the 15th. Approximately 500 prisoners were transferred to the Roćević school, north of Zvornik. On the 15th, they were all executed not far away, near Kozluk. The same day, the prisoners remaining in Bratunac were taken to two public buildings in Pilica, the school and the cultural center. The approximately 1,200 prisoners held at the school were executed on the 16th at the Branjevo military farm and 500 more from the Pilica cultural center were executed that same afternoon. We later found the same type of residue in the cultural center as that found in the Kravica hangar.

The chronology of the "clean-up" operation on the ground—i.e., the burial of bodies—proceeded from the south northward. If you consider all of the crime scenes, they fall into a northern zone and a southern zone, where the executions were less organized, if equally systematic. In both cases, all of crime scenes were within the area assigned to the Drina Corps.

Next came Phase Three of the operation. During the Dayton negotiations in the Fall of 1995, it became clear to the Republika Srpska authorities that there would be inquiries into these events. The Drina Corps then launched an effort to camouflage evidence of their crimes that was logistically as great as the extermination operation itself. They cleverly—and even maliciously—left a small number of cadavers in the primary mass graves so that, if we found them, we would conclude that there had indeed been murders and that witnesses had thus probably told us the truth even if, instead of numbering in the hundreds or thousands, the victims numbered in the tens and twenties.

Nearly all of the primary mass graves were dug up in 1996 thanks to the efforts of Professor Bill Haglund who, as chief of the ICTY exhumation team, spearheaded this critical operation.[3] A fair number of the cadavers were found with their hands tied behind their backs, and one victim had an artificial leg and vertebrae that were so fused together that he would not have been able to stand erect. The very fact that these individuals were executed obviously contradicts claims that the victims were combatants. At this point, we faced a serious problem, however: How could we be sure whether the bodies that we had located represented 10 percent or 90 percent of the total number of victims, since at each site eye-witnesses referred to hundreds of victims killed?

During this third phase of the Drina Corps's operation, primary mass graves were reopened with excavating equipment and the cadavers were transported in trucks toward more remote locations and dumped into twenty-six secondary gravesites spread throughout the zone controlled by the Drina Corps. All of these trenches were dug along similar lines, and they were obviously excavated by engineering units, since each is of the precise depth of a combat tank buried so that only its turret protrudes. Anywhere between one and four truckloads of bodies were dumped into each trench. Analysis of the objects found at these locations, such as cartridge cases, blindfolds, ligatures, and fragments of broken glass, along with examination of the soils and pollens, offer a cluster of clues that allow us to link the mass graves that we called *primary* to those that we termed *secondary*.

The teams of experts we sent to carry out the exhumations were multinational and made up of highly qualified archeologists. Their responsibilities ranged from preserving each body part and object that they uncovered to examining the excavator tracks in the trench bottoms, which allowed us to identify anomalies in the treads of individual machines.

With the exception of a handful of sites, the southern zone was also part of this effort to conceal evidence. One such exception was a site in the Cerska valley that went untouched. There are three possible reasons for this. The first is that the site contained only 150 bodies and that the officers deemed this too insignificant a number to be worth the trouble of reopening the trench. The second hypothesis is that because of a lack of organization during the day of 13 July, the security officers may well have been unaware of this particular execution site. The third hypothesis is that the site is so remote that they thought it would not be found. Indeed, we did not locate it using aerial imagery[4] but by cross-referencing witnesses' testimony.

Simply presenting these facts before the Tribunal, documented by maps and photographs, took up three days. For each visual document, one could present a large number of additional photographs to better explain all of the details of these crime scenes. In addition, there were reports from expert witnesses, including crime scene technicians and exhumation reports.

The military analysis constitutes a whole separate body of evidence concerning the situation. I should add to that the analyses of all of the transcribed radio interceptions at our disposal. It is the whole array of these nested "Russian dolls," one fitting into the other, that gives an overall picture of the situation. As the indictments show, there were many crime scenes, especially when one considers that, during the investigation, we only examined situations in which a "large number" of victims had been assassinated. Let us just say that there was a period of several years where we would not have even traveled to a site with fewer than a hundred bodies, due to a lack of time and resources.

I.D.: The difficulty that an outsider may have in understanding the nature of such investigation, which is essentially a criminal one, is due to the distance separating it from more familiar models in such contexts—that of historical investigations drawing on the archives of the Nuremberg trials, for example, or NGO investigations. Your presentation clarifies this difference, if only through the investigative powers conferred upon you. The inquiry reveals a state crime that used the apparatus of the state (the army) and public tools and buildings (schools and so forth). It seems that, for investigating into this state crime, your inquiry also draws upon the resources of the state. Here, I am referring to your use of aerial photographs and the transcripts of intercepted radio communications prepared by the Army of the Republic of Bosnia-Herzegovina. This might lead one to revise one's vision of international criminal justice as an expression of an international civil society that is independent of states.

In order to clarify the nature of this inquiry and the kinds of evidence it yielded, could you be more specific about what place you occupied as a police chief relative to the teams of specialists and experts who participated?

J.-R.R.: I need to make it clear that I cannot take a personal position on this matter because it relates to an ongoing judicial process.

Given the sheer scale of the drama, the situation was new. Nobody before us had had to soil their hands with this kind of work. The role of a police chief is that of coordinator. He is not supposed to be a one-man band who plays all of the instruments himself. He has to use what he knows in order to surround himself with people who can bring their own expertise to bear and thereby cover the many facets of such a situation. We are engaged in a judicial inquiry whose goal is to produce trials before an international court. Some trials have already taken place, and others are in progress or will be in the future. The role of the leader of the investigating team is therefore to try to understand what happened, to give a direction to the inquiry, and subsequently to assemble experts who will contribute to efforts to find out the truth. And finally, once we think we have reached a reasonable stage in that search and thus are in a position to bring charges, we have to supply technical evidence in support of them.

I.D.: What kinds of organization and skills does such an investigation require?

J.-R.R.: Whether the head of a group leads two people or ten people, his role does not change. However, if he lacks sufficient resources or manpower, he will end up having to act as a one-man band instead of a conductor. In the beginning of this inquiry, I must confess, we had two rather than ten people. It was not until 1998 that the international court assembled what might reasonably be called an "investigative team" as defined by the ICTY—that is, a team that includes a coordinator, a judicial counselor, several investigators, analysts, a full-time interpreter and a secretary.

As far as skills are concerned, they depend on the situation that is facing you.

First of all, we needed people to conduct interviews, which comprise the initial mass of information. During the summer of 1995, there were 25,000 refugees scattered among I do not know how many refugee centers in Tuzla alone. There were 6,000 of them at the air base and the others were scattered among the refugee centers in the city and surrounding villages.

A second massive source of information was the database of the War Crimes Commission directed by Mirsad Tokača, which contained an inventory of 600 accounts.

Furthermore, a huge effort to compile witnesses' accounts had been undertaken by the Tuzla police and AID, the Agency for Information and Documentation—that is, the Bosnian secret service. So we had to analyze this pre-existing data to select high-priority witnesses.

When we arrived in the area at the end of July, we had thus identified a population of 1,200 potential witnesses, with half-page to one-page interview summaries available for each of them.

To reconstruct the facts, you have to approach them from several directions at once, beginning with what happened at Potočari on 12 and 13 July. Potočari is crime scene number one. Next, we need to know what was happening during the forced transfer. In reality, there are hundreds of situations, hundreds of eye-witnesses and events. Next, there are those who survived in the woods and crossed the lines on their own before winter 1995. Finally, there is the very small number who survived the mass executions.

One further source of information came from the witnesses located by the press. I have always said that the press constituted a small army of extra investigators who compensated for the insufficient personnel available for the inquiry. I want to take this opportunity to praise all of the journalists who worked on this subject. It is shocking to compare certain journalists in Nice who, when I was a police chief there, larded their articles with information that could only be of use to the bad guys, with journalists in Bosnia, who first briefed ICTY investigators about the information they had gathered before calling their editorial offices.

The sheer mass of the data is colossal. If a single one of the crime scenes we are discussing had been in Paris, London, or New York, it would obviously have become an affair of state. In 1995, for example, there were three hundred Belgian investigators assigned to the Dutroux inquiry alone. At the same time, there were only ninety people in the prosecutor's office, just thirty of them with police experience, to cover all criminal aspects of a conflict that had begun in 1992 and was ongoing at the time, since the war was not over then and nobody knew when it would end.

But let me return to your question. Once crime scenes are located, you must surround yourself with experts; nobody in the world can single-handedly deal with the mass of information that comes out of this kind of investigation. Three kinds of expertise are required to manage a project of this type.

First are the medico-legal experts, who manage all aspects of exhumation, which is unfortunately a fundamental dimension of this case. In addition to what is called the "scientific police" analysis of the execution sites, each crime scene is a gigantic mass grave. Without a body, you have no crime, and this inquiry began as a crime without any bodies. At the end of 1996, once Bill Haglund's team had exhumed all of the primary mass graves, *Newsweek* magazine ran a story with the well-chosen headline, "Genocide Without Corpses."[5] Only around five hundred bodies had been located and autopsied by the end of 1996, whereas 80 percent of the major crime scenes had been dealt with. This first phase of the exhumations had nevertheless demonstrated that the mass grave sites had been reopened as part of a cover-up effort and that most of the bodies they had contained had been concealed and very probably removed to another location (see map 6).

So we had to launch a search in 1997 for the secondary mass graves.

All of this was done in stages, just as when you are building a house. First you have to dig the foundations, which is the reconstruction of the events, then build the walls—that's the crime-scene analysis—and it's only once the basic facts have been fully established that you can build the roof, which is to say begin to assign responsibility and develop charges. We only launched the "hunt for the perpetrators" in early 1998. That's where the process of seeking documentation and material evidence comes in.

What tools do we use? Well, we use the classics: basically, search and seizure. We searched the headquarters of the Bratunac and Zvornik brigades. We also undertook a massive weapons seizure operation that kept us busy throughout the fall of 1997 and part of the winter of 1998. Thirty-five hundred weapons were seized and all of them tested ballistically using comparative firing tests. So we went into micro-details, because finding what the Americans call the "smoking gun" can be very useful in implicating a brigade and indicting particular individuals. In short, it shows the necessity of exploring every avenue. But there are leads in an inquiry that get dropped because they are dead ends. This arms seizure, which produced no useful findings, concerned two brigades, a special forces unit known as the "Drina Wolves" and other brigades located elsewhere. Unfortunately, the analyses of the weapons that we seized led nowhere because of weapons transfers within the Army of the Republika Srpska between 1995 and 1998. Time works against investigations and the collection of incriminating evidence. All time lost to an inquiry is time gained for the perpetrators. Time alters material objects, bodies, testimonies, and memories.

Dealing properly with the mountain of documents recovered through searches requires military analysis aiming to determine which units were involved and what was the chain of command. The investigator in charge of this was Richard Butler, an American, and he was therefore the chief witness for the prosecution concerning military aspects of the extermination operation.

A series of different analysts also worked on criminal analysis, which involves reconstructing the crimes. Criminal analysis is essential in this type of case. The chronology of the events has to be gleaned from what is at first a morass of information, sifting through piles of testimonials that all point in a single direction: horrible things happened. Next, things have to be organized along a timeline. For that, you must try to separate the wheat from the chaff since, unfortunately, there is some chaff among the witnesses' accounts, no matter how honest they are. This is understandable given the working of human psychology.

The next step was to analyze transcripts of the radio communications intercepted by the Army of the Republic of Bosnia-Herzegovina. These transcripts are helpful in reconstructing the facts and in identifying which units were involved, allowing us to trace who played what role in the chain of command and thereby identify perpetrators.

The multinational character of the investigating team was important in allowing us to avoid being accused of bias for or against one warring party or another. The team included, at various times, a Pakistani, a Swede, a Norwegian, Americans, Australians, Britons, a South African, and a Canadian. Unfortunately, however, there was a rapid turnover rate, and we had few permanent staff members.

Another important element of our fieldwork was the work of many teams of crime scene technicians. It was important that they be able to remain on the sites for extended periods, but for security reasons, the teams had to arrive on the sites in the morning and leave before nightfall. Returning the next day to an unguarded site carried the risk that it had been booby-trapped during the night, meaning we had to completely start over in terms of security measures. This created considerable slow-downs. What is more, the investigation was directed from the Netherlands but concerned crime scenes were in the Republika Srpska, with all that that implies—flying to and from, purchasing airline tickets, keeping up with paperwork—and all that overseen by the investigators themselves.

So, there you have a catalogue of all of the skills that have to be coordinated in order to produce a credible overall report.

I.D.: And what about the American satellite imagery? In August 1995, Madeleine Albright showed some photographs that could have given the impression that there was knowledge of the massacre even as it was occurring.

J.-R.R.: That's a good point. But we have to completely stop using the term "satellite image." The official term is "imagery taken by aerial reconnaissance platforms." In other words, these were U2 images. On this subject, we need to shatter a few illusions. In what concerns imagery, things are at once complicated and simple. The U2 spy planes are a 1960s technology. Inside of the image, which covers a thirty-by-thirty kilometers zone, everything can potentially be seen. You can zoom in up to a certain point. So theoretically, anybody in possession of a particular image knows what happens in that zone. In practice, though, it is impossible to read an image if you do not already know what you are looking for and if you do not cross-reference it with field observations.

The imagery was above all an enormous help in narrowing our search for the sites because the witnesses we were dealing with were not from the area. They were victims of the ethnic cleansing of 1992 in northeastern Bosnia. They had been displaced to Srebrenica and often knew nothing about their new surroundings. It was impossible with these witnesses to establish distances between the various crime sites. They often did not even know where they were, not to mention the fact that they were blindfolded and in a state of panic, wondering whether they were going to be exchanged or killed. In such cases, aerial imagery is a critical asset because it enables you to develop an understanding of numerous features. After all, it's the "story" unfolding through the investigation that allows you to make sense of the image, not the other way around. The image in itself often makes no real sense and can even become a source of interpretative errors. This was true in Srebrenica, was confirmed in Kosovo, probably held for Iraq, and will continue to be the case elsewhere. In fact, what is intelligence? It is the analysis of all of the available information. Anybody who claims to come up with any sort of truth based on a single source of information, whether that be a witness or a technical source, will inevitably have three out of four chances of being wrong.

Here is a typical example. When Madeleine Albright showed pictures of the mass grave trenches at Nova Kasaba to the UN General Assembly, she associated them in complete good faith with the preceding picture, that of the Nova Kasaba soccer stadium. On the photo dating from 13 July, you see large groups of prisoners in a soccer stadium in Nova Kasaba. Then on the photographs taken from nearby that were shown to the UN General Assembly, you see the mass graves. The logical conclusion for anybody seeing these pictures is that you have people in the stadium then you have mass graves so the people are in the mass graves. In fact, that is not the case at all; although the exhumations were not done in Nova Kasaba until the end of 1998, we have known since August 1995 that it was not an execution site but rather an assembly site. According to the accounts we obtained, there were only individual killings, and the prisoners held there were transferred to Bratunac. The bodies found in the mass graves shown in those pictures were connected with other executions that took place in the area.

This is proof that intelligence, no matter how technologically advanced, cannot be disconnected from human reality—that is, testimony followed by verification in the field, in situ, in order to fit the pieces together. If the pieces are not put together, believing that a single piece of the puzzle gives an overall picture is the best way to make an error sooner or later.

For a variety of reasons, no images of a number of other aspects of these events were available. One of the reasons that imagery was available in 1995 is that there were around thirty UN soldiers being held hostage by General Mladić, either voluntarily or against their will. You could therefore logically assume that a huge intelligence effort would be concentrated on the area. Why indeed was there a transfer of prisoners from Bratunac to Zvornik? It's because General Mladić and his aides were not fools: they had to suspect that, given the situation, intelligence assets would be highly focused on the area. It is also worth noting that a U2 flight is like a space shuttle flight and demands a fair amount of time to prepare. And, of course, U2s are not continuously in the air. So there are days, particular dates, when there are holes in the image data and then these images are after all just snapshots. Furthermore, a country only provides what it wants to provide, within the limits of what it deems necessary. It is understandable that they do not unveil their full intelligence capacities just to satisfy the wider public.

I.D.: My next question concerns the relationship between judicial truth and historical truth. In the end, the investigation, with its various levels of expertise and, in particular, its military analysis, primarily resulted in charges being brought against military personnel—this despite the fact that, in the judgments handed down by the ICTY, the role played by civilians in some executions appears in the background. This pattern of indictment contrasts with that found in other regions of Bosnia where significant massacres took place—in Prijedor, for example. There, charges were filed against both civilians and police officers. In this regard, it should be noted that no civilian leader from the Srebrenica region was charged in connection with the 1995 massacre. Some ICTY judges, among them Judge Schomburg, publicly expressed their surprise that Miroslav Deronjić, political leader of Bratunac, was not among those charged in the 1995 massacre. What does this pattern of indictment reflect? The nature of the operation itself? Or is there a gap between the findings of the inquiry and the charges that resulted from it in point of the determination of responsibility, civilian or military?

J.-R.R.: In order for such an operation to proceed, you have to have at least a minimal level of collusion between military, police, and civilian authorities. We should have pursued them all, but it did not happen, first of all because an investigation does not necessarily produce a completely successful outcome. If Miroslav Deronjić was not charged with the massacre of 1995, it is because the evidence was not sufficient for us to prove his awareness and participation, i.e., to bring together enough evidence to establish his individual responsibility within the operation. A large meeting—what is known as an indictment review meeting—is held in the prosecutor's office to determine which indictments should be brought before the court. There, the least charges against individuals are relentlessly debated. It stands to reason that the prosecutor has no intention of embarking on trials that are lost before they begin.

It is inaccurate to say that no civilians were indicted, since President Radovan Karadžić was. However, no police officers were charged, although we know that the police played a role, albeit a secondary one. In reality, it was a military operation, and it was masterminded by the security branch of the army. Prudence is called for here as some of those indicted are currently being tried in The Hague. Of course, with so much information on this subject having been revealed during the Krstić trial, and more recently in the joint trial of Popović, Beara, Nikolić, Borovčanin, Miletić, Gvero, and Pandurević, it is now clear that security officers supplied the backbone of this operation, including the security branch of the general staff directed by Colonel Beara and, above him, General Tolimir, who was in charge of both intelligence and security. Ratko Mladić obviously sat at the top of this pyramid.[6]

Let us quickly go over the list of those who were indicted, keeping in mind that many of them were charged after my departure in 2001.

I cannot go into detail about individuals whose trials are presently underway. Dražen Erdemović is a simple case because he pled guilty to participating in the 16 July 1995 execution of 1,200 prisoners at the Branjevo military farm as a member of the tenth sabotage detachment. His cooperation with the prosecutor's office was taken into consideration and he was sentenced to five years in prison. He supplied critical information, even if it mostly related to the participation of his own unit. In fact, this unit was the principal armed force of the security branch in charge of carrying out sabotage and assassination behind the lines and it was linked to the army's intelligence services. Furthermore, he enabled us to discover a crime scene that we previously knew nothing about, the massacre of 500 prisoners at the cultural center in Pilica. Despite General Krstić's denial, the prosecutor was able to prove that he was commander of the Drina Corps as of 13 July and not starting from the 20th as he had claimed as part of his defense. He was sentenced on appeal to thirty-seven years for aiding and abetting genocide and for crimes against humanity. Dragan Obrenović, who had been deputy commander of the Zvornik brigade, pleaded guilty and was sentenced to seventeen years in prison, a sentence which he did not appeal. Dragan Jokić, commander of the engineering unit of the Zvornik brigade, did not plead guilty even though his immediate superior had done so and was sentenced to nine years in prison, confirmed in appeal. Momir Nikolić, the intelligence and security officer of the Bratunac brigade, also "pled guilty." He appealed his sentence, which was reduced to twenty years. Vidoje Blagojević, commandant of the Bratunac brigade, did not plead guilty and received a sentence of eighteen years' imprisonment, reduced to fifteen years in appeal.

The case of Milorad Trbić, deputy commander of a battalion but above all assistant to Drago Nikolić for the Zvornik brigade, was referred to the authorities of Bosnia-Herzegovina. On 16 October 2009, the Court of Bosnia-Herzegovina sentenced Milorad Trbić to thirty years' imprisonment, verdict upheld in appeal.

The following individuals were sentenced in 2010 and their case is on appeal: Colonel Ljubiša Beara, the key character in the entire operation, present at every phase of the process and chief of the security branch of the general staff headquarters of the Army of the Republika Srpska, was sentenced to life imprisonment. Lieutenant Colonel Vujadin Popović, likewise a key figure because he was responsible for the security branch of the Drina Corps, was also sentenced to life imprisonment. Drago Nikolić, chief of security of the Zvornik brigade, also charged with personal participation in executions, was sentenced to thirty-five years' imprisonment; Vinko Pandurević, commander of the Zvornik brigade who, on 15 July 1995, sent a highly significant memorandum to his headquarters. This is the sole written document that mentions the existence of prisoners, otherwise referred to as "packages" in other radio communications. He was sentenced to thirteen years' imprisonment. And Colonel Ljubomir Borovčanin, commander of a special police brigade of the Republika Srpska, a military unit not to be confused with the special police companies that belonged to the police and as such were under the authority of the Ministry of Interior. Borovčanin in particular had to answer for the massacre in the Kravica hangar and was sentenced to seventeen years' imprisonment.

Then there are General Radivoje Miletić, chief of operations and training administration in the general staff of the Army of the Republika Srpska, sentenced to nineteen years' imprisonment and General Milan Gvero, Mladić's assistant for morale, legal, and religious affairs in the general staff of the Army of the Republika Srpska who was sentenced to five years' imprisonment.

The trial of the following individuals is ongoing: General Zdravko Tolimir, head of the security and intelligence branches at the general staff of the Army of Republika Srpska; President Radovan Karadžić, who was arrested in July 2008.

General Ratko Mladić, chief of the Army of Republika Srpska, who was arrested in May 2011, is awaiting trial in the ICTY.[7]

So that is where ICTY indictments stand today. In principle, they should not change with respect to this institution, although there is obviously a whole host of other individuals who have been or may yet be identified as having participated in the operation. They are basically the executors, the "trigger-men." Fourteen of them, members of the special police battalion, have been prosecuted by the Court of Bosnia-Herzegovina in Sarajevo for their involvement in the Kravica warehouse massacre.[8] Seven of them have been convicted and received sentences reaching as high as forty-two years' imprisonment.

As for the police authorities, the answer is that the inquiry did not bring evidence before the prosecutor that they participated in organizing the massacre or that they conducted executions themselves. No evidence was forthcoming, then, that allowed police officials to be charged and provided the prosecutor a reasonable chance of winning at trial. It is as simple as that. In fact, the police authorities did everything they could to stay on the sidelines. That said, they could have been scrutinized more closely by the inquiry but they were not, given their secondary role in what was essentially a military setting.[9]

As for politicians, the future will decide. In the case of Deronjić—apart from his contacts with Beara and Karadžić, apart from his knowledge of the situation—the prosecutor's office was unable to show that he had participated in planning or carrying out the operations. It was a military operation. Clearly, from a historical perspective, the ties between the army, the police and the political personalities are certainly more interwoven but for our purposes we need to have enough evidence to prove the individual criminal responsibility of the accused.

Regarding the question "who did what?" I will not answer it because the inquiry is still ongoing and other trials are either scheduled or may later be brought before the courts in Bosnia-Herzegovina. In 2001, the units that had participated were identified (the Bratunac and Zvornik brigades as well as the special police brigade of Borovčanin, the role of which has been addressed during his trial). As for determining which units were involved, things have continued to move forward and the structure and specific role of the different units has been more fully presented in the trial of Popović, Beara, Nikolić, Borovčanin, Miletić, Gvero, and Pandurević. In 2001, there were things we were confident about but that we did not use during the trials. It is all still fairly delicate: we can only assert what we can substantiate. That is the problem with an investigation, a prosecutor, a court: even when you have the most intimate certainty, it makes no difference to anybody else. It cannot be presented as a fact in a trial. Let us take an example: the "Scorpions." This unit was apparently under the direct command of Belgrade and was present in the region, participating in the murder of six teenagers. We learned this in 2005 through channels that I will not discuss here. Other discoveries may be made in the future. I am not going to discuss other possible leads in detail but there are many.

It is not really my place to say how all of this background sorts itself out regarding the pieces of evidence that will allow the prosecutor to use his arguments to lead to a conviction. Unfortunately, everyone who was in the zone in question—not just the soldiers but also the paramilitaries—in principle had the opportunity of participating in the execution of prisoners. There must have also been volunteers for the job. Some things are clear from the intercepted radio communications. It takes a lot of people to commit mass executions but there was fighting going on at the same time. There was the Žepa offensive mounted by the Army of the Republika Srpska as well as the column of runaways, some of whom split off to lead a diversionary attack on Zvornik. From a military point of view, it was a confusing time. So the inquiry will always be "in progress" in terms of identifying all those who participated in murdering the prisoners.

Given that some archives have been destroyed, however, the only way to make progress now is through the outcomes of the indictments and possible guilty pleas, not further investigation. In this area, there is nothing worse than someone who refuses to plead guilty because his attitude does not help the truth to come out. If an individual pleads guilty, on the other hand, it enables us to confirm the veracity of the facts and, if he is really in good faith, he can in this way contribute new evidence to the proceedings. This will of course need to be verified and corroborated. One cannot simply settle for "yes, it is true, I am the one who did it."

Translated from French by Ethan Rundell

Notes

1. Editors' note: see the initial and appeal indictments and judgments of Krstić at the ICTY website under the heading "The Cases": http://www.icty.org/action/cases/4, last accessed on 8 December 2011.
2. Editors's note: http://www.icty.org/x/cases/krstic/trans/en/000313it.htm; http://www.icty.org/x/cases/krstic/trans/en/000314ed.htm; and http://www.icty.org/x/cases/krstic/trans/en/000315it.htm, last accessed on 8 December 2011.
3. Editors's note: On the excavations conducted by the ICTY investigation, see the testimony of Dean Manning at the Krstić trial, 26 May 2000: http://www.icty.org/x/cases/krstic/trans/en/000526it.htm, last accessed on 8 December 2011.
4. Editors's note: on the role of aerial imagery, see below.
5. Editors's note: Stacy Sullivan, "Genocide Without Corpses," *Newsweek*, 4 November 1996.
6. Editors's note: see the text of the judgment in the trial of Popović, Beara, Nikolić, Borovčanin, Miletić, Gvero, Pandurević, dated 10 June 2010. This judgment contains a synthetic presentation of the military and civilian structures involved, available at http://www.icty.org/x/cases/popovic/tjug/en/100610judgement.pdf, last accessed on 8 December 2011.
7. Editors's note: it should be noted that the cases of Milošević, Perišić, Stanišić, and Simatović at the ICTY have also included charges for the Srebrenica crimes in 1995.
8. Editors's note: see the decision of this court in the cases of Miloš Stupar et al. (http://www.sudbih.gov.ba/files/docs/presude/2009/Stupar_Milos_Second_Instance_Verdict.pdf) and Petar Mitrović (http://www.sudbih.gov.ba/files/docs/presude/2009/Petar_Mitrovic_Second_Instance_Verdict.pdf) (Kravica cases). See also Vaso Todorović's case (http://www.sudbih.gov.ba/files/docs/presude/2008/Vaso_Todorovic_-_Prvostepena_presuda.pdf). Last accessed on 8 December 2011.
9. Editor's note: for a presentation of the role of the civilian police (MUP), see the judgment of Popović et al., p. 55 and sq., available at http://www.icty.org/x/cases/popovic/tjug/en/100610judgement.pdf, last accessed on 8 December 2011.

Chapter 2

INTRODUCTION TO THE "REPORT-FORM"
Characteristics and Temporalities of a Production of Public Truth

Jean-Louis Fournel

For Fahrudin Kreho, from Bratunac and Sarajevo

The Report-Form: Preliminary Considerations

Between 1999 and 2004,[1] various reports on the "Srebrenica event" were made public. They had been prepared by parliamentary commissions (in France and the Netherlands, at least), international agencies (the UN), and governments (the Dutch Government's report, which was entrusted to an independent research institute, the NIOD, and the Republika Srpska (RS) Government's report that was firmly requested by the Office of the High Representative of the international community in Bosnia-Herzegovina, the OHR, and prepared by a mixed commission of experts, including legal experts, historians, and the head of the International commission on missing persons).[2] In each of these cases, we will thus be considering a "public" discourse produced by a representative authority.

For this reason, all reports entail a collection of formal procedural characteristics and constraints that are imposed on all participants.[3] This system of constraints is obviously not without consequence for the construction of the event's meaning and the manner in which it is interpreted. In order to consider what will be schematically referred to here as the "report-form," we should begin with two remarks. On the one hand, comparing and contrasting the various reports helps measure the relative reliability of each of them and, at the same time, helps establish (however partially or hypothetically) the facts of the case, which is the principal objective set

Notes for this chapter begin on page 53.

forth in all the reports. On the other hand, though the texts in question tell us as much about who wrote them as they do about the matter under discussion, there are at least two reasons why this must not lead us to disregard their impact. First, the institutions that commissioned these reports were, in various ways, involved in the event, and their responsibility therein has to be determined (UN, national contingents and leaders of the UNPROFOR, the warring parties, etc.). The judgment of their action—and this includes cases in which the judgment is rendered in an "internal" fashion by an institution with which an involved party is connected—constitutes a necessary component of the analysis of the event. The second and more important reason has to do with the very form of the report and its particular temporality—that is, the time needed to gather the necessary data as well as the time separating the report from the original event. This temporality can introduce a gap between the reasons that led to commissioning the report and those leading it to be completed and made public. It is as if the institution did not totally control what it set into motion, as if the institutional yoke were unable to completely frame the history of the recent past, especially when one is dealing with such a grave and historically weighty event.

From this perspective, examining the formal data common to all of the inquiries and reports concerning Srebrenica does not represent a merely formalistic exercise—something that would be particularly inappropriate in the discussion of a large-scale massacre. Indeed, these official texts are part of a common approach for producing a public discourse of truth. Moreover, the reports of both the French Parliamentary Fact-Finding Mission and the NIOD cite and claim to use other completed and ongoing reports, and all of the reports refer to ICTY publications and investigations.[4] By the same token, this type of text corresponds to a relatively determined "reading contract," which implies a predefined framework. Its main specificity is the fact that such reports are by definition the product of a collective effort in which the contribution of particular authors is eclipsed: the UN report is the only case in which the personal pronoun *I* is to be found and, even here, it is used artificially inasmuch as it is obviously not the secretary general of the UN himself who drafted the report but actually, in this case too, an anonymous author.

It is easy, and necessary, to study the implementation of this particular reading contract, by attending to its departures from the expected norm, especially in terms of the objectivity and neutrality of the discourse. Thus, for example, the occupation, intellectual background, and even national origin of the various people responsible for elaborating reports as well as the historical moment in which they made their contributions can condition their respective conclusions. By the same token, questions that fall under the purview of classic discourse analysis are particularly useful here. Who gathers the data and writes the report (MPs, historians, police officers, high-ranking international civil servants, legal experts)? How does the diverse and changing nature of potential readers (all or part of a national community, the international community, legal professionals, etc.) affect the writers? What is the nature of the elements taken into consideration in the epistemic approach (what types of evidence, traces and proof are drawn upon in the work)?

As a final premise, one might be predisposed to believe that the report-as-object involves a certain "neutrality," that it assumes an "objective" stance guaranteed by its detachment from the event and by the functional separation between participants in the event and the role of drafting a comprehensive survey of that event. However, even if some defend this claim to objectivity—in particular, the authors of the NIOD report—things turn out to be more complicated. On the one hand, the writers or investigators, too, can sometimes practically be considered as "participants," as when they are marked by a personal on-site experience or carry out their activity in the context of a legal procedure. This was the case of David Harland, a UN official and the principal author of the report on the various "safe areas" (and not just Srebrenica) that the international organization requested be rapidly prepared. Harland spent the war in Sarajevo and had been present at the negotiations accompanying the fall of Žepa. Indeed, the passage of the NIOD report devoted to Žepa is based on David Harland's report. Much the same might be said of Jean-René Ruez who, arriving on the scene of the crime a few weeks after the massacre took place, thereby became a "participant" in the event.[5] On the other hand, nearly all of the reports show awareness of the limits of their work and of the negative effects produced by the various temporal constraints inherent to such processes, constraints to which I will return below. The "report-form" thus reveals itself to be a hybrid and complex object that we will attempt to circumscribe by identifying the modalities and procedures at work, the logics deriving from different institutions and individuals, and the problems of temporality.

Modalities and Procedure (Hearings and Inquiries)

The Double Injunction

Whatever their claims to being comprehensive (UN), "methodical" (the French parliamentary report), "systematic" (NIOD), cathartic (Dutch parliamentary report), or "detailed" and "scientific" (RS), all of the reports assign themselves two objectives: to contribute to establishing the "truth" (the term explicitly recurs in all of the texts) and to evaluate possible moral, political, and criminal "responsibility" for the massacre. The French Parliamentary Fact-Finding Mission thus sought to develop a "methodical inquiry" with a twofold aim: to understand how the fall of Srebrenica came about despite its status as a "safe area," and to study the "role of France in this tragedy." Indeed, concerning the latter, the parliamentary report presents accusations of the French for responsibility in the massacre as "paradoxical." Even if Harland believed that his work consisted less in assigning responsibility than in chronologically reconstructing the totality of UNPROFOR's activity,[6] the UN report ultimately contributes to understanding the UN's share of responsibility for the fall of two of the "safe areas." The short Dutch parliamentary inquiry sought to enable Parliament to pass a final political judgment on its own role and that of the Dutch administration, soldiers, and bureaucrats in the fate of Srebrenica so as to close definitively the Srebrenica case for politics in the Netherlands. Although the RS report confines most of its discussion of specific responsibility to the confidential sections, it must tell the families of missing persons what has become of their loved ones and this leads it to adopt a tally of the number of victims that is telling in and of itself.[7] Finally, the NIOD report, as well as the Dutch and French parliamentary reports, seeks to analyze the attitude of the Dutch battalion of blue helmets (*Dutchbat*) in Srebrenica and that of the French command of the UNPROFOR, as well as their respective degrees of responsibility for the fall of the enclave.

These two objectives, appearing in various guises in all of the reports, express an ambivalence that is as manifest as it is problematic: indeed, the reports address two different audiences (one more universal and "external," the other more national and "internal"), mixing different kinds of approaches (historical, legal, moral, administrative, investigative) that do not necessarily overlap and can even prove contradictory. Moreover, one may come away with the impression that the national or particular objective was parasitical on the other, more "universal" one (this is patent in the case of the NIOD report and that of the Dutch Parliament and is not without consequence for those of the UN, the RS, and the French Parliament). In one of the most extreme versions of this conflict of interest, the epilogue of the NIOD report seems to accord more importance to the harm done to the image of the Netherlands abroad than to the history of the massacre itself (though this lengthy report has other, more positive qualities).

The Mechanics of the Hearings

All of the reports draw on a limited number of hearings but rely on different procedures for implementing the work. As Pierre Brana underscores in his chapter, the report must be analyzed as an essential and autonomous object, but also as just one of the elements in a more complex system based on the relationship between the "report" itself (less than two hundred pages in the French case) and the transcripts of the hearings (six hundred pages in the same case). This explains why things may differ both quantitatively and qualitatively from one report to the next, something due as much to their varying lengths as to the issue of whether they are based on public or confidential hearings. Thus, while the UN, the French, and the Dutch parliamentary reports are of about the same modest length, the NIOD report is surprisingly lengthy (nearly seven thousand pages with annexes!). Conversely, the version of the RS report made public is very short (around forty pages), though this report also includes confidential annexes (more legal in nature than the main body of the report).

The synthetic nature of the report thus contrasts with the hearings, which are potentially infinite in number and unlimited in the directions they can take. The hearings feed the synthesis carried out in the reports but also keep raising legitimate questions concerning the necessarily selective choice of those who speak before the hearings and the equally indispensable work of rewriting the transcripts (providing that it is even possible to gain access to the hearings). Indeed, in the case of the reports of the UN, the NIOD, and the RS, the hearings are mentioned and the list of those who spoke is even supplied but the content of the auditions is not made public.[8]

The cases of the French Parliamentary Fact-Finding Mission and the Dutch parliamentary report are the only ones in which the hearings have nearly all been made public (and put online). They are also the only ones in which the hearings were not held in close sessions or in private, at least not when held in Paris or in The Hague rather than in the field: except in the event of an explicit and legitimate request on the part of the individual addressing the hearings, speakers were received in public by the MPs and the discussion partly took place live and without mediation or oversight. The French Parliamentary Fact-Finding Mission thus clearly manifested its desire for transparency. In this one case, then, the hearings play more than a subordinate role; easy access to the transcripts of the hearings furthermore makes it possible to compare and contrast them to the report and to raise questions about the relationship between what is made public and what is kept secret. Once again, the logic at work in each of these apparently similar reports can prove radically divergent, a fact that is not without bearing on their respective conclusions.

The Composition and Work of the Commissions

One of the factors contributing to such differences concerns the composition of the commissions. In the French case, the MPs, as representatives of the people, are at once (and rightly so) activists, elected officials, "ordinary people," and political leaders. The plurality of identities among the members of the French Parliamentary Fact-Finding Mission contrasts with the more circumscribed character of the UN, RS and NIOD commissions. The effects of this contrast were particularly noticeable in both the choice of those to be heard and the nature of the questions they were asked. The choice of speakers in most of the reports, especially that of the French, is often predictable and hardly subject to critical examination: those called upon or heard were individuals who occupied posts of official responsibility (ambassadors, generals, special correspondents of the international press, directors of NGOs, etc.), represented victims (the women of Srebrenica), or were considered prominent figures in public discussions about the war in Bosnia (opinion makers and key witnesses). Researchers on the Balkans or the war were, with one exception,[9] utterly absent from the list of people heard (unlike in the case of the French Parliamentary Fact-Finding Mission on the Rwandan genocide).[10]

The NIOD report represents a case apart, inasmuch as it is based on nearly systematic interviews with members of the *Dutchbat*, a large number of interviews with victims, as well as expert opinions. For the other reports, by contrast, the overwhelming tendency still seems to be to favor interviews with those who had positions of responsibility in the history of this particular moment at the expense of expert analysis or, indeed, even testimony from victims and ordinary soldiers.[11] The collective construction of a public truth (an "official" truth, without any pejorative nuance), combined with a search for historic responsibility that goes beyond merely legal questions, leads the report's authors to emphasize—in a nearly "spontaneous" way, though no doubt also for reasons of time and simplicity—the role played by the main actors in this story.

As concerns the nature of the questions posed, the French and Dutch parliamentary reports are the only ones for which transcripts of the hearings are available, enabling us to express a judgment in this regard. While in the French report, the questions are sometimes very precise and specific, they are often rather general or based on an immediate moral foundation that has little to do with any attempt at analysis. Therefore, it is difficult to see in the remarks of the MPs any attempt to settle on a causal hierarchy. A sometimes surprising dialectic results from this: the succession of questions and question-askers is sometimes so ingenuous as to suggest (false?) naivety and yet is not devoid of ellipses and leaps of reasoning. Thus, in the French parliamentary report, the opinions concerning the attitude of General Janvier and the responsibilities of the UN chain of command remain ill defined even though, at various moments in the hearings and even in the report itself, certain conclusions seem to be on the point of emerging. Some of the hearings, moreover, offer no more information than what a careful reader might glean from a serious daily paper. Worse, the Dutch Parlamientary report manifests self-centeredness and a tendency *not* to take foreign or UN reports as a starting point for debate: the ICTY judgments and the NIOD report are the sole basis of a report that is not written to increase understanding, but to defend the Netherlands and prove that the country is not responsible for what happened.

Yet here, too, things are equivocal: this procedure is sometimes astonishing but it doubtless contributes to establishing a certain liberty of tone, allowing certain "errors" (including in regard to actors who are almost considered public "icons," like General Morillon)[12] to be identified and highlighting essential questions that have sometimes been left aside by more sophisticated examinations, such as the violence perpetrated against civilians. The tone of the French report is of course very polished (since a consensus has to be reached in the Commission, even at the price of compromise), but that does not exclude sharply defined opinions and the recognition of disagreements when essential issues are at stake. Pierre Brana reminds us that this was in the last analysis the case—for Marie-Hélène Aubert and for himself—concerning the question of a possible agreement between General Janvier, commander in chief of the UNPROFOR, and General Mladić, commander of the Army of the Republika Srpska. Similarly, only Pierre Brana distinguishes himself from his colleagues concerning the question of the term *genocide*, which he demands be used since it appears in the Krstić judgment in 2001 (as the Commission could have known).[13] The absence of genuine final "recommendations" in the French report is also a product of these divergent positions. The Mission is able to globally agree on the description of the facts in order to better inform national representatives, yet it is unable to reach agreement concerning the manner in which this information should affect policy. This can be seen either as a sign of the inadequacy of the process or as the necessary expression of democratic disagreements that tend to favor the later emergence of the truth in other places and before other bodies. The expression of such disagreements is not, however, inherent to parliamentary reports, since the Dutch report favored a more uniform consensus based on the a posteriori construction of a self-serving defense of the Dutch Government.

Institutional Logics, Individual Logics

The status of this type of report should also be considered in relation to the highly regulated institutions that request them (parliaments, governments, international organizations, OHR, courts) and the representatives chosen by these institutions (ad hoc commissions, academic research centers, specialized civil servants). Thus, in the French case, the technical rules of parliamentary logic (e.g., the distinction between a commission of inquiry and a fact-finding mission, discussed at length by Pierre Brana in his chapter here) have their importance, of course, but they have no bearing on the question of the traditional equilibrium (or disequilibrium) in the relations between the executive and legislative powers. One thus understands why Brana so insists on the weakness of the culture of investigation concerning international affairs within the French Parliament.[14] The various fact-finding missions and other commissions of inquiry could, however, play an important role in developing a culture of investigation in a domain that has for too long been considered—and especially in France—a prerogative of the head of state or the executive branch. In this way, elected officials could genuinely play their role as "representatives" of the people, by stepping into the space between public opinion and the executive power, between absolute publicity and state secrecy. These elected officials thereby take on the responsibility of constructing a culture of investigation capable of engendering a form of truth that, though official, is not entirely removed from the beliefs that are autonomously developed in the sphere of public opinion. The individuals who are members of the commission thus become an important variable.

In the Dutch NIOD report, the researchers (historians, sociologists, anthropologists, etc.) demonstrate a more abstract expertise based on an approach to history writing characteristic of "specialists" in the domain, systematically seeking out all of the details according to an academic methodology and only constrained in carrying out their work by the demands of confidentiality. In the UN report, a small number of high-ranking international civil servants, conflict and conflict-resolution specialists, all put their experience and knowledge of this kind of conflict into the service of producing a synthesis that would subsequently be adopted by the organization's secretary general. In the case of the RS, the members of the commission are chosen by the RS and Federation authorities and accepted by the OHR.[15] They were to act according to precise and very explicit instructions, which sometimes took the form of OHR press releases and resulted in the dismissal of certain high-ranking RS officials. By comparison, the specificity of the French Parliamentary Fact-Finding Mission stems from the fact that its members are elected officials. The publicity of the discussions, as mentioned above, is not the sole consequence of this fact. The MPs' work is furthermore marked by an explicit desire to act without the aid of specialized training and knowledge about the subject under consideration and, as far as possible, proceed according to a sort of methodological and historical "virginity." This, too, is a function of the MPs' multiple identities (and individual autonomy).[16]

Moreover, the manner in which these reports were drafted cannot be understood without saying a word about their relations with the international institutions (UN, NATO, ICTY, NGOs present in Bosnia) and other governments (United Kingdom, Netherlands, Bosnia-Herzegovina) that are potential stakeholders in the process, particularly in the collection of information. In practice, the delicate intersection of these various spheres (parliaments, states and governments, international institutions, courts) often leads to data being collected in an incomplete and non-systematic manner[17] and sets in motion what are often significantly divergent temporalities.

Temporalities

Friction between the various temporalities that are entailed in the "report-form" is one of the constants of this system for gathering together data, explanations and pieces of evidence (the form-report furthermore maintains an ambiguous relationship with judicial processes). We speak of "friction" because what is involved here is not an obvious linkage, voluntary juncture, or organized stratification. For the purposes of clarity, we will limit ourselves to three noticeable temporalities: the time during which events took place, the time frame referred to in the report (i.e., the temporal scope of the inquiry), and, finally, the time of the investigation.

The first of these temporalities—the massacre that took place over a few days in July 1995—is obvious, even if the construction of the event is always complex.[18] For similar (if not identical) reasons, the inquiries of the ICTY and the RS both have to limit themselves to this temporality. In fact, they are explicitly tied to these chronological limits because they seek to establish criminal responsibilities. Both of these inquiries are indeed conducted under pressure from legal requirements, all the more intense in the case of the RS due to OHR's oversight. The other reports, by contrast, do not seek to limit themselves to this temporality, since the questions they wish to raise have more to do with moral and political responsibility than with criminal responsibility. From this perspective, the topic of the report and the choice of temporality are interrelated and they depend on which actors the analysis focuses. They also depend on whether priority is given to criminal or to political responsibility.

The second temporality is of great importance, above all in this part of the Balkans where, probably more than elsewhere, history is an inexhaustible source of more or less adulterated disputes: choosing to consider only the war in former Yugoslavia and the country's collapse has a precise meaning. This is the dominant choice made within these reports, which follow the lead of the UN report in this respect. In the same way, it may be said that the factuality of the executions follows the logic established by the ICTY. The UN report seems more or less to serve as a chronological model for all the others because it comes first, and also because it imposes an "international" perspective tied both to the question of the "safe areas" and to the commitments by which the various states involved in the UN mission in Bosnia may feel bound. The temporality of the explanation duplicates that of the intervention of the UN as a participant of the war in Bosnia. Another scope might just as well have been adopted: one placing greater emphasis on the legacy of Tito, that of the Second World War, and even that of the wars of the nineteenth and early twentieth centuries. The choice one makes here is obviously not without consequence for the manner in which one establishes a causal hierarchy. In this respect, the fact that the OHR explicitly asks the commission preparing the RS report not to delve further back than 10 July 1995 is no accident (the OHR request is likely motivated by the memory of an earlier RS report carried out for the ICTY in 2002, which lingered on the Second World War in order to justify denial of the Srebrenica massacre). The French MPs limit themselves to a short period of reference (around two years, from the establishment of "safe areas" in March 1993 to July 1995). The NIOD historians, for their part, adopt a very similar chronology (beginning with the intervention of the *Dutchbat* rather than the establishment of the "safe areas") but occasionally refer to the history of the nineteenth century (in Appendix IV written by Ger Duizjings) in an "interplay" of chronological scales, wherein the aim is to clarify the event in part by placing it in the context of the long term.

But it is the temporality of the inquiry that no doubt has the most to teach us here and it is to this that I will devote the final part of this chapter. All of the reports are subject to temporal constraints. The most obvious case is the RS report, a sort of "constrained" report par excellence. Here, temporal requirements are explicitly enumerated (the commission was to submit its conclusions at the end of six months and provide monthly progress reports). But the same holds true even for the NIOD report, which initially seemed to dispose of an unlimited time frame in which to work. Indeed, at the end of the process, the final draft of this report suffered from being rushed. In order to satisfy the Dutch governmental calendar, the summary "epilogue" written by the head of the commission was thus not submitted to the other members of the commission, nor has it been endorsed by them.[19] The time of publication—in the sense of the procedure that renders the completed study public—can thus hasten the time of the inquiry and its formalization. A similar haste marks the UN, French Parliament and RS reports as well as the ICTY inquiries. In each of these cases, those who commissioned the report pressed for the report to be finished within a reasonable time limit. It is as if the reports and investigations needed to be carried out as rapidly as possible, in keeping with a very tightly defined temporality more characteristic of the media or administrative services than of the academic world. From this perspective, the two main variables are as follows: how much time elapsed between the event and the preparation of the report and how much between the preparation and the drafting of the report?

The first of these variables seems to revive the old question of the effects of the detachment proper to the historian.[20] This detachment can, for example, be contrasted with the urgency of police work, in which immediate, rapid action is necessary to ensure that the evidence does not disappear, in a sort of never-ending race against time with the "authors" of the crime (well illustrated in the interview with Jean-René Ruez in this volume). What is a virtue for the historian is a handicap for the police officer. Yet, only the NIOD report lays claim to such a detachment as a methodological requirement.[21] Indeed, independently of ongoing investigations, the events that took place between 1995 and 2005 tend to preclude bringing closure to the time of the event.[22] The Kosovo war, the fall of Milošević, the trials launched by the ICTY (and used, among others, in part IV, chapter 2 of the NIOD report), the internal political conflicts in post-Dayton Bosnia, the changes of president and secretary of state in the United States, and the emergence of hyper-terrorism and the "war against terrorism"—to cite only a few obvious variables—all significantly modify the perception of the event as well as (and above all) the meaning assigned to it and the conditions of acceptability affecting discourse about it.[23] It is no accident that the formalization of the first major report, that of the UN, was contemporaneous with the violent resolution of the war in Kosovo via the military intervention of NATO, a move in part approved by the UN itself.[24] Nor should it be forgotten that the fall of Milošević allowed for the partial opening of Serbian archives, something that is mentioned in the NIOD report. In this respect, it is difficult to believe any claim to "detachment."

The second variable (the time between the preparation and the drafting of the report) poses a problem typical to historians, to wit, the relationship between the gathering of sources and the narrative. As is the case with the NIOD report, a sort of mystique of the detail can draw out this time indefinitely. The researchers for that report get caught up in a logic of accumulation, having the liberty to spend several years in their pursuit. One sometimes has the impression that they are above all occupied with constructing the archives of their own discourse. There is a great risk in such cases that all strong causal claims be rejected, save only those referring to the simplistic realpolitik / generic moralism dichotomy.²⁵ The members of each commission thus attempt to invent and construct for themselves a relation to the various temporalities that does not consist in detachment or immediacy or gathering evidence but has recourse simultaneously to all these various modalities. For example, one might say that, for the NIOD, this relation amounts at least in part to academic and social self-legitimization (affirming the unique, exclusive nature and social utility of one's expertise) while, for the UN, it amounts to a form of public repentance (which may, moreover, represent an element in a process of institutional re-legitimization). In the case of the French Parliament, one is witness to the hesitant construction of a space of democratic debate and investigation concerning the functions traditionally reserved for the head of state. In the Dutch parliamentary report, the conclusion is even more disappointing for the construction of public debate: the aim seems only to ensure protection of national institutions. Finally, in the case of the RS report, what is at stake is the articulation between, on the one hand, the challenge to the symmetry of "warring parties" (defended in Serbia and elsewhere throughout the war and the years following the Dayton agreements) and, on the other, the search for a way of admitting that a mass crime did indeed take place without undermining the legitimacy of the RS (in particular, by assigning all blame to particular individuals).²⁶

Comparing the effects of this specific temporality of commission work with the various knots that remain in the reports highlights the constant oscillation between the information to be gathered (despite a lack of resources, time, training, and sometimes even competence) and the implicit or explicit judgment that is to be rendered (in the absence of the necessary prerogatives and sometimes also a desire to do so).

Moreover, the attitude of the commissions in regard to the question of "judgment" varies from one report to the next: while the NIOD and RS reports do not seek to offer a judgment, the UN report and that of the French Parliament (not to speak, of course, of the ICTY investigations) expressly claim the function of working toward judgment (including criminal judgment) and do not limit themselves to the Hegelian judgment of history. "The United Nations' global commitment to ending conflicts does not preclude moral judgments, but makes them necessary," proclaims the secretary general's report in its penultimate sentence.²⁷ The French parliamentary report, for its part, seeks to "reestablish the facts," on the grounds that the victims "deserve the truth, not polemics, demagogy or black-and-white reasoning,"²⁸ and concluded by "demanding" that "the French, the British and the Americans, in particular, devote the necessary resources to capturing these criminals against humanity."²⁹ In contrast, the NIOD report claims to be only an "analytical monograph" that takes no stance in "the political arena" or "the public debate"[30] and refuses to render any "political judgments."

A great many ambiguities therefore remain, whether they be epistemological (methods for collecting and selecting data, then drafting the report; construction of the legitimacy of the collective author), institutional (degrees of autonomy and censorship/self-censorship), legal (status of the published data and public use of the results), historical (credibility of the reconstitution of causalities), or political (effects produced by the report in the given public opinions and/or among policy-makers). That which is constructed in the reports is a radically hybrid and unstable object, at once historical, investigative, legal, political, and pedagogical.

The complexity of the temporalities at work in the construction of a report is an essential factor in explaining this hybridization and, above all, the nearly natural weakness of the information report (as well as its radically incomplete status). The reports encourage a defense and illustration of complexity. Paradoxically, this both benefits the search for truth and, occasionally, undermines the historical meaning. With regard to the uncovering of truth, the reports are simultaneously and indissolubly essential and problematic; their structural flaws, in the form of specific gaps and omissions, are closely tied to the constraints that determine their nature, as we have tried to show above. The constraints imposed on the report-as-object—in particular, constraints requiring collegiality in composition and investigative and publishing deadlines—have obvious consequences, independently of the stance of those who draft it and whatever their political identity or sociological profile.

In the course of collective work and due to the search for a minimal consensus among participants, all commissions have a tendency to "smooth out" their analyses to such an extent that their deeper meaning and historical relevance end up getting watered down.[31] But it is precisely the necessary consciousness of this weakness that can make these reports indispensable. We should not see this as paradoxical. Indeed, it is only by accepting and analyzing this weakness, with all the conclusions it involves, that we are able to distinguish between what needs to be kept and what must be discarded in each of these reports. In this way, we may throw light on the lessons of a terrible event, lessons that, taken together, are at once particular and universal: particular in what concerns the fact under consideration, universal in what concerns the ethical and analytical values set in motion by it.

Translated from French by Ethan Rundell

Notes

1. The various reports that we will discuss are those of the UN secretary general (15 November 1999), the French Parliament (November 2001), the NIOD (April 2002), the Dutch Parliament (January 2003), and the RS Government (June 2004). See the list of abbreviations and acronyms at the beginning of this volume.
2. By contrast, we will not discuss NGO reports, which do not enter into the definition of our object—that is, the construction by an official body of public truth about a dramatic event.
3. Those constraints are imposed on them whatever their intellectual or political backgrounds. We will thus not be carrying out a sociological examination of the actors here, much less a systematic prosopographic study. Though both of these approaches are interesting in their own right, they do not fall within the scope of this chapter.
4. In fact, it was possible to reconstruct most of the dynamic of the events thanks to the fact that ICTY investigations began so shortly after the massacre (see the introduction to this volume as well as Jean-René Ruez's chapter). By contrast, the reports do not adopt a purely legal approach nor undertake an exclusively descriptive, chronological account of the events, but advance reflection on their larger context. They even offer epistemological considerations concerning the difficulties experienced in elaborating a given form of public truth.
5. On the distinction between these two forms of "participation" in the event, see the other chapters in this volume and, in particular, those of Isabelle Delpla and Jean-René Ruez.
6. For that matter, David Harland would have preferred that his report not be entitled *The Fall of Srebrenica*.
7. See Michèle Picard's and Asta Zinbo's chapter in this volume as well as that of Isabelle Delpla.
8. The three reports offer different justifications for their choice to hold closed hearings and these differences stem from the respective natures of these reports. In no case was it a question of protecting witnesses, contrary to the ICTY trials. In addition to its imposing length, which would only have been increased by adding the transcripts of the hearings, the NIOD report presents—without precisely laying claim to—the classic distinction between the historian's text (the historical account) and the archives (in this particular case, largely assembled for the occasion by those involved in the project). Since the UN report is called upon to take stock, offer solutions and be first circulated at the leadership level (that is to say, among the leaders of the international organization and the governments concerned), its main objective is not to have an impact on international public opinion or, for that matter, a potential academic community. Finally, the RS report has a legal origin (see Michèle Picard's and Asta Zinbo's chapter in this volume) but its political function takes priority: the Office of the High Representative of the international community in Bosnia-Herzegovina, the OHR, puts all of its weight behind having the report produced as rapidly as possible in order to obtain recognition of the crime by the successors of the authorities under whom the massacre had been perpetrated.
9. Thierry Tardy, who had just defended a dissertation on the UNPROFOR, was the sole researcher auditioned.
10. It can be supposed that this was due to the presence in France of a strong tradition of African studies that has no equivalent in the area of Balkan studies.
11. It is possible to see a distinction here with the work of the ICTY, given the Tribunal's tendency to hear multiple expert-witnesses and the prosecutors' eagerness to draw upon

as many victim-witnesses as possible in building each case (even when that means using the anonymous testimony of protected witnesses).
12. The French general Philippe Morillon, commander of the UNPROFOR in Bosnia-Herzegovina, became famous following his expedition to Srebrenica in March 1993. Despite the fact that all access routes to the enclave had been mined by the Serbs, Morillon succeeded in clearing a path with a small convoy and reach the city via an unlikely mountain road. Just before setting off again, he voluntarily let himself to be taken hostage by the population of the enclave. It was on this occasion that he committed to putting the refugees of Srebrenica "under the protection of the United Nations" and to "never abandon them," something that contributed greatly to the birth of the six UN "safe areas" Sarajevo, Bihać, Tuzla, Srebrenica, Žepa, Goražde (according to Security Council Resolution 824 adopted on 6 May 1993). What the French report in its subtitle termed "General Morillon's coup de force" was in the last analysis described by the MPs as a "brilliant intuition" that nevertheless led to a "political error" (*Evénements de Srebrenica. Rapport d'information déposé par la Mission d'information commune sur les évé-nements de Srebrenica*, Paris, 22 November 2001, 13–14). Nicknamed "General Courage" by the Bosniaks and long adulated by the residents of Sarajevo, the French general does not seem to have been congratulated by his hierarchy for this initiative.
13. He did it explicitly both in the report—see *Evénements de Srebrenica*, 152—and in his chapter in the present volume.
14. See also, on the Dutch case, Pieter Lagrou's chapter on the NIOD report and, in particular, his remarks concerning how the traditional "culture of compromise" characteristic of Dutch political life affected the manner in which the report was drafted.
15. On the composition of the commission called upon to prepare the RS report, see Michèle Picard's and Asta Zinbo's chapter in this volume.
16. To be clear, the aim here is not to contrast the writing of history, as the exclusive domain of licensed "specialists" and "experts," with an "amateur" practice, that of the elected officials. Indeed, the reports devoted to the Srebrenica massacre show that the search for truth can suffer from the specific competencies of the historian when these are not properly mobilized and that, conversely, it can profit from the relative technical "incompetence" of members of a parliamentary commission or a high-ranking civil servant when political will compensates for their lack of expertise.
17. While it is useful to think about the inevitable lacunae brought about by this situation, one must do so without a priori assumptions. Indeed, these structural lacunae do not prevent committee members from occasionally identifying essential elements in the dynamic of events. Thus, for example, the question of the violence perpetrated against civilians may or may not be an essential parameter depending on the logic of the report: it is in the French case, it is much less so in that of the UN and NIOD reports. Thus, the precise chronology of the facts (nearly hour by hour) becomes a central element for understanding the dynamic of the enclave's fall and represents a major achievement of the UN report (subsequently adopted by all the other reports), just as the comparison between the fall of Srebrenica and that of Žepa (where the NIOD report explicitly relies on the testimony of Harland, that is, on his dispatches as a UN official—see NIOD, *Srebrenica—A "Safe" Area: Reconstruction, Background, Consequences and Analyses of the Fall of a Safe Area*, Amsterdam, 2002, part IV, chapter 9, section 2).
18. For the debate concerning the event's construction, see the studies cited below in note 23.
19. For more on these questions, see Pieter Lagrou's chapter in this volume.
20. On this question, already raised by Aristotle, see Carlo Ginzburg's collection of studies entitled *Wooden Eyes: Nine Reflections on Distance* (New York, 2001).

21. Even if the commission that prepared the RS report also included historians and even if all of the reports claim to set up an historical account of the event.
22. It is useful to recall the dates of "publication" of the various reports: UN secretary general (November 1999), French Parliament (November 2001), NIOD (April 2002), Dutch Parliament (January 2003), RS Government (June 2004).
23. Concerning the event as a concept, many of the key articles were published in the 1970s. In particular, see Pierre Nora, "Le retour de l'événement," in *Faire de l'histoire. Nouveaux problèmes*, eds. Jacques Le Goff and Pierre Nora (Paris, 1974), 210–228 as well as those that were to mark the debate over contemporary history twenty years later (Institut d'histoire du temps présent, *Ecrire l'histoire du temps présent* [Paris, 1993]; Jacques Revel, ed., *Jeux d'échelles. La microanalyse à l'expérience* [Paris, 1996]; Alban Bensa and Eric Fassin, eds., Dossier "Qu'est-ce qu'un événement," *Terrain*, no. 38 [March 2002]).
24. The UN report on Srebrenica has been prepared in the course of the year 1999. It should be recalled, moreover, that the interpretation of Security Council Resolution 1199, which was adopted on 23 August 1998, on the basis of which the NATO military intervention in Kosovo took place in Spring 1999, is still being debated, in particular in what concerns the application of chapter VII of the Charter of the United Nations concerning the use of force (but this is not the question that concerns us here).
25. Isabelle Delpla's chapter in this volume addresses this point.
26. Due to the temporal limits that are fixed for it and its very factual character, the RS report does not address (at least not explicitly) the question of the degree of responsibility of the warring parties but affirms the reality, scale, and systematicity of the Srebrenica massacre as well as the involvement in this mass crime of the armed forces of the RS and their military hierarchy. Indeed, beginning in the early part of the 2000s, one of the leading concerns of the RS is to find a way of admitting the reality of the Srebrenica massacre without for all that delegitimizing the RS as such. It thus searches to assign responsibility for the massacre to individuals—including Mladić if necessary but without doing anything to bring about his arrest. By contrast, the government of the RS searches to protect the institutions that have been borne of the war and, above all, avoid establishing a connection between the ethnic cleansing and the political origins of the RS. From this point of view, the temporal limits fixed for the RS report are not necessarily harmful to this objective.
27. *The Fall of Srebrenica*, 111.
28. *Evénements de Srebrenica*, 151.
29. Ibid., 151–152.
30. NIOD, *Srebrenica—A "Safe" Area*, introduction, 10.
31. On this point, see Jean Baubérot's interesting paper concerning his participation in the French Stasi Commission, entitled "Le dernier des Curiace. Un sociologue dans la Commission Stasi," in *La nouvelle question religieuse. Régulation ou ingérence de l'Etat? / The New Religious Question: State Regulation or State Interference?*, eds. Pauline Côté and Jeremy T. Gunn (Frankfurt am Main, 2006), 247–272. Constituted by the President in 2003, the commission was named after the former MP who presided over it, Bernard Stasi. Its goal was to propose national measures for applying the principle of secularism.

Chapter 3

REASSESSING THE FRENCH PARLIAMENTARY FACT-FINDING MISSION ON SREBRENICA (2001)

Pierre Brana

This chapter examines the work carried out by the Fact-Finding Mission on Srebrenica in the light of the logic and specificities inherent to this kind of parliamentary procedure. The issue under consideration here is the way public institutions—in this case, the French Parliament—can contribute to a better understanding of the truth concerning an event of the utmost importance and gravity. It also involves the forms such parliamentary oversight of executive power can take, especially in the areas of foreign affairs and national defense—two highly sensitive domains in the traditional balance between executive and legislative power.

To understand what follows, it is essential to begin with a brief presentation of what is meant by the terms "commission of inquiry" (*commission d'enquête*) and "fact-finding mission" (*mission d'information*). Article 140 of the National Assembly's Rules of Procedure states that the proposals to create a commission of inquiry "must specify in detail either the events requiring investigation or the government services or state-owned companies whose management demands investigation by the committee" (art. 137) and that the creation of such a commission by the Assembly requires the vote of a proposed resolution that has been duly registered and referred to the appropriate permanent committee, and examined and debated according to the conditions established under these rules (art. 140 and 141).[1] Article 145 also states: "Permanent committees provide the Assembly with the information it needs to exert its oversight over the Government's policy. To this end, they can confer upon one or several of their members responsibility over a temporary fact-finding mission on, most notably, the

---

Notes for this chapter begin on page 66.

conditions surrounding the implementation of a given law. These fact-finding missions can be jointly established by several committees."[2]

The Rules of Procedure then indicate that the permanent committee that requests the creation of a Fact-Finding Mission "must specify in detail the purpose of the mission for which the prerogatives allocated to commissions of inquiry are requested."

In the case of both commissions of inquiry and fact-finding missions, if the minister of justice (*Garde des sceaux*) informs the Assembly that legal proceedings are currently underway on the facts that motivated the request to establish a commission or a mission, such a request cannot be further debated. If the discussion has already begun, it must be immediately halted. Likewise, if a preliminary judicial investigation is opened after the creation of a commission or a mission, the entity in question must immediately cease its work.

The differences between a commission of inquiry and a fact-finding mission may seem minimal as spelled out by the rules, but in practice they can be quite significant. A commission of inquiry implies presumption or at least suspicion of wrongdoing, while a fact-finding mission only indicates that the deputies wish to be better informed on a matter. As is the case in common parlance, *inquiry* and *fact-finding* have different meanings within the National Assembly, as well, and the choice between one or the other is never neutral. This is all the more so given that people receiving a subpoena to appear before a commission of inquiry must comply and take an oath, which is not the case for those appearing before a fact-finding mission. The difference between the two is thus important, even if only on a symbolic level.

That said, I would like to draw particular attention to the fact that, until 1997, major commissions of inquiry and fact-finding missions had been created in every major policy area except those of foreign affairs and national defense, both of which had been considered the *"domaine réservé"* of the president of the Republic. Upon my return to the National Assembly in June 1997, following a four-year hiatus, I reclaimed my seat on the Foreign Affairs Committee, where I was in charge of reporting on cooperation funding, in addition to being the president of the France-Bosnia-Herzegovina Parliamentary Friendship Group. From that position, I attempted to take stock of what had really happened in Rwanda and the former Yugoslavia. I established preliminary contacts within my group—the Socialist parliamentary group—and asked for the creation of commissions of inquiry. I was first told that this was not done in matters of foreign affairs and national defense. After searching (in vain, of course) for the legal document declaring this interdiction, I informed my colleagues of my findings and opened up the discussion again. Finally, on 3 March 1998, the Committee on National Defense and the Armed Forces, presided over by Paul Quilès, ordered the creation of a fact-finding mission on the military operations carried out in Rwanda from 1990 to 1994 by France, other countries, and the UN.

For the reasons mentioned above, I would have preferred the creation of a commission of inquiry. Since the Defense Committee had decided otherwise, however, the Foreign Affairs Committee was forced to abide by this decision. On 11 March 1998, it officially decided to participate in the Fact-Finding Mission constituted by the two Committees, each of which designated twenty of its members (ten sitting members and ten deputy members) representing every parliamentary group in the National Assembly. Two rapporteurs were elected: Bernard Cazeneuve for the Defense Committee and myself for the Foreign Affairs Committee. The Mission was officially entitled: "Inquiry into the Rwandan tragedy (1990–1994)."

That I have thus far devoted so much attention to the circumstances surrounding the creation of this parliamentary Fact-Finding Mission is due to the fact that it represented a historically unprecedented event. Never before, since the founding of the Fifth Republic, had the deputies decided to exercise oversight authority over the executive branch in the sensitive areas of national defense and foreign affairs. Never before, since 1958, had they dared to intervene in the so-called *"domaine réservé"* of the president of the Republic. Considering the heavy burden of customs and rites weighing on parliamentary life, this decision was of enormous significance. It was said afterward that the creation of this Mission was the consequence of the publication of a series of articles on the Rwandan tragedy in a major newspaper. Since 1958, however, there have been many such press campaigns on matters related to defense and foreign affairs and none have resulted in the creation of a parliamentary mission. It was also said that the whole affair had ended with a whimper rather than a bang, that the results did not live up to expectations and that the deputies had not gone nearly far enough. All this may be true, but once again, this situation nonetheless represented a historic first; a taboo had been broken and other major fact-finding missions would follow, including the one on Srebrenica. Events whose gravity mobilized many citizens and directly compromised the image of France abroad were finally, at least in part, pushed out of the shadows of state secrecy so that legitimate representatives of the nation could seize them and study them. The executive branch was forced to defend its actions, "top secret" documents were declassified and a considerable amount of documentation was made public, constituting a boon for researchers. Of course, such an exercise has its limits. A fact-finding mission, just like a commission of inquiry for that matter, operates according to its own rules and under specific constraints. One must remember that its powers of inquiry are greatly inferior to those of an investigating magistrate (*juge d'instruction*). For example, such a mission does not have the power to conduct house searches and therefore cannot verify that the documents that have been obtained are the most relevant ones.

The creation of the French Parliamentary Fact-Finding Mission on Srebrenica was decided in December 2000 by the National Assembly. A joint mission of the Committees of National Defense and Foreign Affairs, it only included ten deputies (five from each committee), with at least one from every parliamentary group of the National Assembly. Once again, I would have preferred the creation of a commission of inquiry for the reasons I previously indicated. I continue to believe to this day that, due to the solemn feeling it imparts, taking an oath can cause some people to try to stick more closely to the truth. Hence, during the hearings on the Rwandan tragedy and on Srebrenica, a great deal was not revealed to the deputies and several depositions took great liberties with the truth. In practice, then, the lack of an oath can produce somewhat different testimonies, as some people tend to confer a different status to their words when not under oath and thus feel less compelled to reveal everything they know. It may even be possible that some answers that seemed strangely compatible and similar were the products of prior agreements between some of the people providing testimony. Those arguing for the creation of a simple fact-finding mission claim that, since foreigners are not legally obligated to testify before a French commission of inquiry, they may be put off by the prospect of having to take an oath and thus refuse to appear—a situation that can result in the loss of valuable testimony. While this is an argument that has some relevance and in this case majority support, I nonetheless remain skeptical: despite our decision to proceed with a fact-finding mission, numerous foreigners still refused to testify, including some key actors. This is one of the main reasons why I continue to favor the creation of a commission of inquiry on tragedies such as Rwanda or Srebrenica.

Let us now turn to the Mission on Srebrenica. I am not going to present the report of the Mission—which would be both long and tedious—as it is readily available on the Internet.[3] Rather, I will limit my discussion to a few key points. The first involves the Mission itself. We were ten deputies in all, half the number who were involved in the Rwanda Mission. This in itself constituted a step in the right direction. Indeed, during any hearing, an excessively large number of participants can often prevent the person who is asking questions from being able to fully pursue his aims and arguments. A discussion that is broken up by too many interruptions, moreover, prevents the effective interrogation of an actor or a witness who is reluctant to speak. The composition of the Mission, which faithfully reflects that of the National Assembly, explains both its large number of members and its lack of consensus on the questions to be posed, with different members responding to the case in keeping with their respective political sensibilities. While this diversity makes the work of the Mission more complex, it also prevents any risk of connivance or submission to the *"raison d'Etat."*

The second point concerns the manner in which those who were to testify were selected. This was decided at a meeting of the Mission during which various members proposed names to be discussed and voted upon. It is important to emphasize that a typical mission only lasts for a few months—nine months in the case of Srebrenica—and that during this period the deputies still have their other regular obligations to fulfill: committee work, plenary sessions, and responsibilities in their districts. It was thus necessary to limit the number of hearings, which, in turn, led to selecting actors and direct witnesses rather than experts of the former Yugoslavia and the Balkans. The selection was also made rather empirically by compiling the names proposed by Mission members rather than as the result of a collective examination or specific procedure. For my part, I established a list of proposed names based on the contacts I had made while heading the France-Bosnia-Herzegovina Parliamentary Friendship Group, but I do not know how my colleagues came up with their own proposals. This is why the choice of those heard by the Mission may appear questionable and may give the reader the impression that some hearings were of limited use, redundant or privileged facts and even anecdote over analysis. Regardless, the publication of almost every hearing in the appendix of the report provides a clear view of the selection process that ultimately enabled the Mission to draw its conclusions from the minutes of the hearings. It thus highlights the weaknesses of our procedure in terms of the Mission's composition, internal balances, and the management of its schedule.

We were not able to hear testimony from all of the prominent actors we had identified. General Rupert Smith, who was at the time commander of the UNPROFOR in Bosnia-Herzegovina, and Mrs. Sadako Ogata, the high commissioner for refugees, both refused to testify. In such cases, the Mission is powerless, since it does not possess any means of compulsion. Their refusal is all the more regrettable in that we are still uncertain about the reasons for the absence of General Rupert Smith at a key moment of the tragedy as well as that of the NATO liaison officer assigned to General Janvier, the commander of the UNPROFOR in former Yugoslavia. While it is understandable that General Rupert Smith went on leave on 1 July 1995, it is more surprising that the commander of the UNPROFOR in Bosnia-Herzegovina did not make an appearance at any time during the entire crisis. We would have liked to pose this question directly to him, and to have asked him about the nature of his conversations with General Mladić, whom he met on two occasions—on 15 and 19 July 1995. We also would have liked to ask Mrs. Sadako Ogata about the astonishing inertia of the high officials of the UNHCR.

A delegation of the Mission went to Srebrenica to conduct additional hearings. There were only five of us and we were thus able to further inquire into several issues. We were also able to meet some people who would have been difficult to bring to France, such as representatives of the organization "Women of Srebrenica" and some average citizens who witnessed the situation in Srebrenica and who, during informal conversations, brought new light to the general state of mind and atmosphere prevailing on the ground. I must say that I attach great importance to these on-site visits and meetings. They are often essential to understanding the sequence of events. When we went to Srebrenica to discover the topography of the place, taking the same southern route that the Serb troops had, it became clear that given the narrowness of the road, which is located inside a steep-sided gorge, a group of fifty well-trained, well-armed, and determined men with the assistance of two or three tanks could have blocked the progression of the Serb soldiers. This observation had a key impact on the report, most notably in assessing the failings of the Dutch battalion, as well as the enormous responsibility that was taken when Bosniaks were refused the right to fight and their already weak defensive capacities were dismantled (with heavy weaponry—tanks, artillery, etc.—being handed over to the UNPROFOR).

In addition to conducting hearings and on-site visits, the Mission also sought out documents. As was the case for Rwanda, all the documents that came into our possession were appended to the published report: notes from the ministries of Defense and Foreign Affairs, UN reports, as well as official statements and communiqués issued around the time of the events. While this collection of documentation represents a useful resource for researchers, it is nonetheless incomplete. Obviously, not everything was handed over to us. While we were not technically refused any specific document, we can reasonably conclude that among the documents furnished to us, some of rather limited use for our work replaced others that would have been much more critical. This is what is being referred to when the report, employing the kind of measured tone that is so common in this type of work, expresses its regret that the Ministry of Defense had "followed a rather blurry line in its policy on the disclosure of documents," adding: "While the Fact-Finding Mission is pleased to have obtained part of the Ministry's internal notes, which it had requested, it is rather surprised to have received some documents that are no doubt important but which are of rather limited use for its work. Fortunately, in some cases, these gaps were filled thanks to the collaboration of certain non-governmental organizations."[4]

Besides, the UN did not provide us with all of the information we had requested and NATO simply refused to respond to our queries. These few examples offer insight into the difficulties a parliamentary fact-finding mission faces in conducting its work, despite the fact that it is an official institution supported, in theory, by the authorities.

Within the Mission itself, most discussions went smoothly. The prospect of working together for nine months, with one work session per week, discouraged the development of enduring conflicts. Changes occurred, some involving compromise and others differences of opinion. When the moment arrived to write the final report, votes were sometimes held to decide between two analyses or even between two sentences or two words. Most often, an editorial compromise was struck. This process of negotiation is constantly underway in such missions. Members are always looking for the right balance, which is all the more necessary since the report of the fact-finding mission has to be approved by a vote before being disclosed to the National Assembly and to the Government. As the project as a whole is collective, the practices that characterize it are no less so and, thus, the report that develops within this framework bears the imprint of these collective dynamics.

The examination of the case of the commander of the UNPROFOR in former Yugoslavia led to persisting differences of analysis. The text of the report is unambiguous:

> There is no doubt that the stalling of the commander of the UNPROFOR, his obvious error in judgment about his interlocutor, General Mladić, played a role in the drama, as did General Nicolaï's refusal to grant requests for air support prior to 9 July, requests that never reached Zagreb. More specifically, on the night of 10 July, General Janvier should have ordered close support air strikes, since all the legal conditions for the command of such an action, though very restrictive, had been met. Blue helmets had been directly attacked, an ultimatum had been given to the Serbs and they had violated it.[5]

But this conclusion did not receive the agreement of two key members of the Mission—Mr. François Léotard, who served as rapporteur of the Mission in its early stages before being appointed European Union representative to Macedonia, and his successor, Mr. René André. Both men expressed in writing the view that the criticisms voiced against General Janvier did not take into account a complex reality that is "always hard to measure when judging an operational decision in hindsight and far from the context within which it was made," as René André said.

Mrs. Marie-Hélène Aubert and I both stated that no element justified dismissing the possibility that General Mladić had secured an agreement from General Janvier to refrain from ordering air strikes during their meeting in Zvornik on 4 June 1995. We then declared that we could not share the opinion expressed by the rapporteurs and supported by the majority of the Mission, which dismissed the idea that General Janvier and General Mladić had entered into an agreement that involved the exchange of a promise to refrain from carrying out air strikes for the liberation of the French hostages held by the Serbs. We were merely asking that the Mission take the same stance on this issue as it had on the hypothesis that the Bosnian Government would have abandoned Srebrenica in exchange for the Serb-held neighborhoods around Sarajevo. Indeed, the Mission wisely indicated in its report that, for lack of evidence, it could not settle this issue with any certainty. In our view, and for the sake of fairness and uniformity, it should have taken the same position concerning the possibility that the absence of air strikes was compensation for the liberation of French hostages one month before.

Moreover, I regretted at the time and, personally, still do that the word *genocide* was not explicitly used in the report on Mladić and Karadžić. I think that the use of the word *genocide* would have enabled us to clearly characterize what happened in Srebrenica. Was this not an attempt, following a deliberate plan (setting up the means of transportation required elaborate logistics), to totally eliminate the men of the enclave because they were Bosniak, ultimately killing between seven thousand and eight thousand of them? Besides, since our Mission, the ICTY has stated that genocide was committed in Srebrenica, most of the accused for the Srebrenica events have been charged with genocide, and General Krstić was convicted of aiding and abetting genocide—on appeal on 19 April 2004.

But I would like to return to an issue we encountered throughout the meetings of the Mission, as well as in the discussions on the Rwandan tragedy: that of the responsibilities of France and of the French army. Does admitting mistakes and even misdeeds weaken our country and blacken the image of our armed forces? This is an old debate dating back to the Dreyfus Affair, but it remains very topical, as I can assure you after serving on both the Mission on Rwanda and the Mission on Srebrenica. Generally, the opinions of the deputies on this issue fall into two opposing camps. In one camp are to be found the proponents of great moderation when France's responsibilities and that of its army are at stake. These deputies systematically minimize the errors or misdeeds committed, as they believe that making them public would tarnish the image of France in the eyes of the world. And when they cannot avoid the revelation of some specific facts, they demand—insistently and often in strong terms—that we highlight as a counterweight the importance of our country's involvement in terms of humanitarian action and the number of soldiers mobilized, as well as the ultimately pacifying actions of the French army.

The other camp—which I am happy to say is the one I belong to—believes, on the contrary, not only that publicly acknowledging the dysfunctions, mistakes, misdeeds and even crimes that have been committed does not diminish the country's image, but indeed that doing so tends to improve it. It was not by chance that the president of the United States and the secretary general of the UN presented their regrets and apologies in the form of a mea culpa—the former about Rwanda, the latter about Srebrenica. However, the will to recognize that we have made a mistake or, worse, committed a misdeed, does not yet seem to be a part of French culture. Of course, the point here is not to fall into permanent repentance or self-flagellation but to clearly state what happened without minimizing or exaggerating the facts.

This is why, to conclude, I would like to anticipate a question that I am often asked: with hindsight, what should we make of these major fact-finding missions? I will not return again to the reasons for my preference for commissions of inquiry, which are more solemn and therefore better suited, in my opinion, to serious matters, such as military interventions, in which France's responsibility is directly or indirectly at issue. I will also not go over the constraints on fact-finding missions: their limited powers of investigation, their limited duration (although they can last longer—and this is one of their few advantages—than the six-month limit imposed on commissions of inquiry), the more or less active collaboration of national ministries and international institutions, and the lack of follow-up by the executive branch on recommendations or lessons to be learned.

Despite all these reservations, my overall opinion remains positive. First, as deputies serving on the Mission discover the ins and outs of events they formerly knew no better than any other French citizen and then start discussing their findings, especially within their own parliamentary groups, they thereby contribute to increasing the awareness of other deputies and politicians more generally. Second, the final report is made public. Even if this report may be questionable or incomplete, thanks to the media it can nonetheless be brought before the general public, provoking reactions, discussions, and controversies, which can only advance the quest for truth. Considering the fact that it always includes long appendices with declassified or hard-to-get documents, this report also constitutes a vital source of information for researchers, investigative journalists, and even the judicial system. Finally, the work of a mission is followed very closely by the executive branch, the president of the Republic and the Government, as well as by diplomats, the military, high officials, and everyone who held or holds responsibilities in the fields under scrutiny. I can tell you that many people worry about—it is never pleasant to "get caught"—and reflect on the situation and, indeed, draw lessons for the present and the future.

I believe that if there were more parliamentary fact-finding missions and, more importantly, more commissions of inquiry, if the Parliament exercised its oversight power—as recognized by the Constitution—over the domains of national defense, the armed forces, and foreign affairs, the executive branch would be more attentive to the responses of the nation's representatives and would sometimes change its behavior on the ground. I am convinced that the lack of constant pressure explains why the executive branch did not follow the recommendations made in the report on the Rwandan genocide. I deeply regret this fact, as their implementation would have constituted both a decisive step toward greater democracy as well as significant protection against the risk of such a tragedy happening again. In particular, I am here referring to the proposal to improve the transparency of the decision-making process for military operations conducted outside of France and of the proposal to improve Parliament's oversight through more effective use of its current powers and through the creation of new means of action.

Today, the French Constitution assigns a very limited role to Parliament regarding the use of military force. A vote is only required for an official declaration of war, a form of oversight that has become, in view of the circumstances of today's conflicts, totally obsolete. We should thus modify the Constitution and establish new procedures for the authorization of external military operations by Parliament, including situations when French troops participate in a UN force. The report on Srebrenica does not put forward concrete recommendations to the French executive branch and the UN in such an explicit way. Colleagues of mine who were members of the Mission have told me that these recommendations implicitly appear throughout the report. This is partly true but to state them again and to bring them together in a single chapter, although it may seem redundant, would give them more power and would allow an explicit and vigorous message to be sent to the president of the Republic, the Government, and the UN.

There has been constant talk about reforming the UN since the genocides in Rwanda and Srebrenica. These reforms should seek to increase the efficiency of the UN, streamline its procedures, and give greater autonomy to its representatives in the field. We must hope that under a truly unified command, blue helmets will no longer be torn between national and UN chains of command. Thus, alongside legitimate concerns to protect committed soldiers from harm, the engagement of UN forces would also involve another priority: the no less legitimate concern of protecting civilians. As concerns France, I believe we will need many more fact-finding missions and commissions of inquiry before real change can occur. To tell the truth, I even worry that the process initiated in 1997 will be halted. We would need more deputies to become actively interested in foreign affairs. But issues of foreign affairs do not rally members of the French parliament to action, nor for that matter do they garner much interest among the general public. Parliament, after all, tends to reflect its constituents.

We should strive for the development of a culture of investigation, which is somewhat foreign to our parliamentary traditions: such a culture would likely encourage parliamentarians to participate in the education of public opinion, and would thereby reinforce their ties with the citizenry. But a culture of investigation—one effect of which would be to reinforce the independence of the Parliament—can only progress and develop through the proliferation of practices associated with it. It is only under these conditions that fact-finding missions will be truly effective, that their recommendations will begin to be implemented, that legal proceedings will even be possible—in short, that the executive branch will feel somewhat bound by the work carried out by Parliament.

Translated from French by Ethan Rundell

Notes

1. *Règlement de l'Assemblée nationale*, Paris, December 2009, 90–91, accessible at http://www.assemblee-nationale.fr/connaissance/reglement1209.pdf, last accessed on 8 December 2011.
2. Ibid., 94.
3. *Evénements de Srebrenica. Rapport d'information déposé par la Mission d'information commune sur les événements de Srebrenica*, Paris, 22 November 2001, accessible at http://www.assembleenationale.fr/11/dossiers/srebrenica.asp, last accessed on 8 December 2011.
4. *Evénements de Srebrenica*, 184.
5. Ibid., 185–186.

Chapter 4

A TALE OF TWO COMMISSIONS
Dutch Parliamentary Inquiries During the Srebrenica Aftermath

Christ Klep

"Dutch Members of Parliament were always trying to be in front, almost voraciously, to make the world a better place. But dying for Muslims? No, no, let's not become unrealistic!"

—Dutch member of Parliament Ton de Kok, April 2002[1]

In the Netherlands, Srebrenica has become synonymous with awkward moral questions and self-scrutiny, as well as political pragmatism and even escapism. The shock of Srebrenica gained extra depth because the Netherlands has always taken pride in defining itself as a leading force in democracy and human rights. Along similar lines, Dutch soldiers are traditionally seen as well suited for peace operations, because of their supposed soberness, cosmopolitanism, broad education, and language skills.

The Dutch involvement with Srebrenica centered on the presence of a peacekeeping battalion of United Nations blue helmets. *Dutchbat* III was only weeks from completing its intended tour of duty when the enclave fell in July 1995. After a few days, the Bosnian Serbs allowed *Dutchbat* III to leave.[2] In the Netherlands, the initial reaction was one of relief that the battalion had returned home more or less unscathed.

From the start, the Dutch Government and military authorities claimed that neither *Dutchbat* nor the higher Dutch political and military echelons could have done much to prevent the massacre at Srebrenica: the blame lay squarely at the feet of the Serbs. However, in the years that followed, rumors and media revelations kept popping up. These seemed to indicate that the Dutch soldiers at Srebrenica and the authorities in The Hague had

---

Notes for this chapter begin on page 82.

perhaps not done everything possible to prevent the tragedy. On more than one occasion, officers and civil servants leaked sensitive information to the media, often to help clear their own names.

The aftermath of Srebrenica was thus a long and unpleasant process. Obviously the process is still ongoing, mostly through court cases initiated by Srebrenica victims. Nonetheless, the parliamentary inquiry into the Srebrenica tragedy (2002–2003) serves as an important marking point: from this inquiry onward political and public interest in the Srebrenica affair declined markedly in the Netherlands. As a result, the most intense phase of the aftermath extended over a period of nearly eight years. The moral stakes were high. Human rights organizations, left-wing politicians and progressive opinion makers did not hesitate to stress the gap between the harsh reality of the Srebrenica affair and the pretentions of a nation that had always "seen itself as the protector of Anne Frank and the inheritor of a great tradition of tolerance."[3] Foreign journalists joined in from time to time, like the British reporter Robert Fisk, who wrote scathingly: "Why, one keeps asking oneself, were these Dutchmen in uniform in the first place? Aren't soldiers occasionally expected to fight, even to die?"[4]

The Dutch Parliament and Srebrenica

The moral and political sensitivity of the Srebrenica affair in the Netherlands raises the question of what the role of Parliament has been during the entire eight-year long process. This chapter will develop the thesis that the Dutch Parliament was never able to play its intended autonomous role as powerful overseer of Government policy. It was never an assertive guardian of policy, but instead saw its role diminished by immovable monistic coalition politics. At no time for instance did Parliament call for the resignation of ministers, either as a sign of moral "purification" or as a sanction for providing inaccurate information—deliberately or unintentionally—to Parliament, as happened on a number of occasions. Minister of Defence Joris Voorhoeve, fearing resistance from his civil servants, in turn never sanctioned subordinates vigorously when they leaked information or refused to keep him fully informed about sensitive matters.

All in all, from July 1995 onward, the Government was able to keep a fairly tight *political* hold on the aftermath, based on the strong uniformity between the Cabinet and majority parties. In December 1995, six months after the fall of the enclave, Parliament in fact endorsed Government policy in what was intended to be a "final parliamentary debate" on Srebrenica. Several MPs stated that the time had come to close the book on Srebrenica.[5]

At an early stage the Government drew up strict political boundaries: the Srebrenica affair should not result in the resignation of ministers or a Cabinet crisis. At the end of 1996, the Government chose its own research path by tasking the *Nederlands Instituut voor Oorlogsdocumentatie* (NIOD, Netherlands Institute for War Documentation) in Amsterdam with a large-scale scholarly historical investigation into the Srebrenica tragedy. This was a wide-ranging project, which—as it turned out—would take over five years (until April 2002) to complete.[6] During this period, the Government would consistently weaken the call for a full parliamentary inquiry by stating that the findings of the NIOD team would simply have to be awaited. The Government dreaded a full parliamentary inquiry, if only for the negativity it would entail and the sensitive nature of the intelligence files. It was obvious from the very beginning that important players like the United States and France had no intention whatsoever of sharing relevant intelligence material with the Dutch, reliable allies though they might be.

The resulting stalemate between the Government and bureaucracy on the one hand and between the Government and Parliament (both dictated by coalition politics) on the other hand, seriously undermined the role of Parliament. This applied especially to Parliament's right to initiate its own inquiries. Ultimately, two parliamentary commissions would indeed be set up during the Srebrenica aftermath: the *Tijdelijke Commissie Besluitvorming Uitzendingen* (Interim Commission on Decision Making during Peace Operations) in 1999–2000 and the full (but short) *Parlementaire Enquête Srebrenica* (Parliamentary Inquiry into Srebrenica) in 2002–2003. This chapter will show that both parliamentary commissions were in effect "artificial," i.e. the result of excessive compromise between the ruling majority parties. Both commissions were above all intended to prevent the setting-up of a genuinely in-depth and "all-out" parliamentary inquiry into the Srebrenica affair, as—in the eyes of many critics—should have been the case.

An important observation has to be made at this point. From the very beginning, in fact even *before* the fall of the enclave in July 1995, the Dutch Parliament had manoeuvred itself into an uncomfortable "split" position. During 1993 and early 1994 Dutch parliamentarians had pressed the point that Dutch peacekeepers should be sent to Bosnia, where the humanitarian situation was deteriorating each day. Now, after the fall of the safe area, it would have to inquire into its own role during the Srebrenica debacle. On the other hand, Parliament could hardly be expected to forsake its powers of inquiry entirely, which would have constituted a complete loss of face if we keep in mind the magnitude of the Srebrenica debacle.

What is more, the half-hearted stance of Parliament and the Government left room for the emergence of other, non-parliamentary commissions and reports that deepened, complicated and prolonged the Srebrenica aftermath. Two of these commissions had the effect of strengthening the feeling among journalists, victims, and the public (as well as in Parliament itself) that the Government and military authorities were trying to cover up unpleasant facts.

First, the military set up a so-called *Grote Debriefing* (Major Debriefing), which took about six weeks (from the end of August to early October 1995) to organize and execute.[7] This was in all respects a military operation. Staff officers, civil servants, politicians, and UN personnel were not interviewed. Getting a full picture of human rights violations was not a primary objective of the debriefing. In fact, the controversial principle of "judicial separation" was applied: the *maréchaussée* (military police) were present at all individual debriefings, but they were not allowed to report soldiers' testimony directly when it concerned possible human rights violations at Srebrenica. The police officials could only counsel these *Dutchbat* soldiers to contact a special police team that was not actually part of the debriefing. Few soldiers took that step. As was to be expected, the resulting debriefing report was severely lacking in accuracy and completeness.

Besides the Major Debriefing by the armed forces, a second non-parliamentary commission intensified the general feeling that unwelcome facts were being kept hidden. In 1998, Minister of Defence Frank de Grave asked prominent Social-Democrat politician Wim van Kemenade to inquire into the integrity of top-ranking officials. Van Kemenade fundamentally took on the inquiry alone (with some secretarial support[8]). He was barred from reading the confidential testimonies of the Major Debriefing, nor did he cross-check the information that emerged from the thirty-five hearings he organized himself. Van Kemenade reported within six weeks. His general finding was that, despite the fact that "in some instances the exchange of information at top levels had been remarkably deficient," no deliberate mistakes had been made.[9] Most lapses could be attributed to mere incompetence. De Grave used these conclusions to stay on as Minister of Defence.

The third non-parliamentary report emerged toward the end of the aftermath and was by far the outcome most strongly driven by moral (rather than bureaucratic or political) considerations. Its author was Mient Jan Faber, a former secretary-general of the Dutch NGO *Interkerkelijk Vredesberaad* (Interchurch Peace Council).[10] Faber wanted to fill the moral gap left by the official reports. Much to the chagrin of the Government, Faber published his report only weeks before the NIOD commission presented its findings in April 2002. According to Faber, *Dutchbat* and Dutch authorities had enjoyed more freedom of manoeuvre in 1995 than they cared to admit. For instance, Faber claimed that UN busses could have been arranged to evacuate all Bosniak refugees from the enclave. Faber apparently supposed that *Dutchbat* and the Dutch Government had been overcome by defeatism at an early stage.

A Halfway "Solution": The Interim Commission (1999–2000)

By 1998 at the latest it had become clear that Parliament was stuck between two barriers. On the one hand the Government left the world in no doubt that it rejected a full parliamentary inquiry into the Srebrenica affair. In Prime Minister Wim Kok's view, perhaps mistakes had been made, but the Bosnian Serb attack on Srebrenica and subsequent massacre could not have been foreseen. The Dutch troops had been under UN command in any case, so claims for reparation from the victims of Srebrenica had to be addressed by UN Headquarters in New York. The position that the Netherlands bore no guilt, was also extended to *Dutchbat*: the official point of view was that the Dutch UN troops in Srebrenica had done everything possible.[11] Vital operational support (especially through NATO air power) had however been withheld at crucial moments before and during the fall of the enclave. Further, Prime Minister Wim Kok and political leaders of the majority parties discouraged ministers who might harbor thoughts of resigning over Srebrenica from doing so. Minister Voorhoeve for instance stated (once he had left office in 1998) that he had considered resigning on more than one occasion, but Prime Minister Kok and the leader of Voorhoeve's liberal party (VVD), Frits Bolkestein, had pressured him into retaining office. Kok and Bolkestein feared that Voorhoeve's resignation would be interpreted broadly as an admission of guilt.[12]

In addition to this "we are not to blame" theme, the Dutch Government and majority parties opposed a full parliamentary inquiry because they were afraid of losing control of the Srebrenica aftermath. A full inquiry would judicialize and further mediatize the process, especially in the sense that ministers and civil servants would be forced to appear in public hearings.[13] The focus would automatically be on policy failures and victims, in a very public forum, broadcast live on national television. At the least, it would severely hamper the armed forces, that were already burdened by intense reorganizations and new operations abroad.

The second instrument through which the Government tried to keep control of the Srebrenica aftermath was similarly rooted in political monism. Prime Minister Kok had little difficulty in referring the main effort of investigating the Srebrenica affair to the independent scholarly commission at the NIOD institute in Amsterdam. The Government repeatedly indicated that it would await the NIOD report and not comment on the progress of the work of the commission. Government and majority leaders also left open the question of whether or not NIOD's conclusions would (automatically) open the way to a full parliamentary inquiry. It comes as no surprise that many felt that the referral of the main Srebrenica inquiry to the scholarly NIOD commission was indeed an attempt by the Government to (temporarily) "bury" the affair in a long-term historical investigation. Some pointed to the fact that NIOD was officially part of the Ministry of Education.

These critical (and sometimes cynical) comments gained extra depth when—especially during 1998—new revelations kept emerging about the Dutch involvement in Srebrenica. From the defective military Major Debriefing (autumn 1995) onward authorities had been faced with accusations of cover-up, incompetence, and negligence. In a much-discussed incident, a roll of film shot by a *Dutchbat* officer during the fall of the enclave was destroyed in a Defence laboratory. Both former army commander General Hans Couzy and *Dutchbat*-commander Thom Karremans published memoirs that severely criticized political masters, especially Voorhoeve.[14] Research journalists discovered that Colonel Karremans had performed poorly during training exercises in the run-up to the deployment of his unit to Srebrenica. Doubts expressed by his superiors had apparently been neglected or ignored.

In mid 1998 media pressure was so intense that officials at the Ministry of Defence would later dub this episode "The Hot Summer." At the same time, Van Kemenade's incomplete inquiry into the integrity of top officials backfired. Critical journalists suggested that Van Kemenade himself had become part of the "official" cover-up. A parliamentary majority now finally felt that the House of Commons could no longer stay completely on the political sideline: "something" had to be done to underline Parliament's role as the primary institution in the democratic system. The result, in early 1999, was a political compromise in its purest form: an Interim Parliamentary Commission that would lack the strong powers of a full parliamentary inquiry. Unlike a full inquiry, the Interim Commission could not compel witnesses to appear or search for (and seize) documents under threat of sanctions. Such an investigation is designed to look into and evaluate policy areas in a more general sense.[15]

The investigation became formally known as the "Interim Commission on Decision Making during Peace Operations" and was usually called "The Bakker Commission," after its chairman, Liberal-Democrat parliamentarian Bert Bakker. It was indeed an instrument of compromise. Bert Bakker chose the right words: "This commission is the result of a give-and-take between those who would have liked to start a [full] parliamentary inquiry into the dramatic events of Srebrenica, those who would rather not have seen a Srebrenica inquiry at all and those who did not desire a Srebrenica inquiry at this particular moment."[16] The primary dilemma facing the Interim Commission was obvious: the *true* reason for its existence was the tragedy of Srebrenica, the ensuing media coverage and rumors of cover-up. At the same time, this obvious point could not be stressed too much, if only because that would appear to interfere with the independent NIOD investigation, which by then was in the third year of its existence. NIOD's director Hans Blom in fact left no doubt that he would not accept any "contamination" between the two commissions. Once Parliament had decided to initiate the Interim Commission, both Bakker and Blom—in a nice "one-two" approach—emphatically stressed that they would stay clear of one another's work.[17]

This, as was to be expected, proved impossible in the real world. The Interim Commission addressed both general policy matters (such as: what voice should Parliament have when new peace operations are being considered?) and specific details about Srebrenica that had attracted wider attention because of their controversial nature and media interest.

A vivid example of this selective insistence on detail is the so-called "Zagreb reception." A few days after the demise of the Bosniak enclave, the Dutch battalion arrived at UN headquarters in Zagreb. The general mood was one of relief. A military band and alcohol resulted in a polonaise, soon followed by a cancan-like dance. Critics felt that *Dutchbat* soldiers had been "dancing on corpses." The Ministry of Defence maintained that the "party" had in fact been an understandable relief of tension after months of stress and frustration about the death of a fellow *Dutchbat* soldier at the hands of Bosniak fighters in an incident during the fall of the enclave. The Zagreb reception was in itself a minor episode, but the Interim Commission still decided it should investigate it more closely, mainly because of its mediatized nature. At the same time, NIOD was indeed conducting its own research into exactly the same events, without any apparent mutual exchange of information.[18] In the end, the Interim Commission again chose the road of compromise, stating in the final report that it felt unable, "considering our mandate [which formally stressed wider policy issues, CK] and the ongoing NIOD investigation, to draw any definite conclusions" as to the humanitarian efforts made by *Dutchbat* during the fall of the enclave.[19]

With regard to the Srebrenica aftermath itself, the Interim Commission's report had little direct impact. Government ministers stated politely that they would study the findings, but reiterated the importance of waiting for the NIOD report. From the start, the real significance of the Interim Commission had lain elsewhere: its work would offer Parliament the opportunity—once the proper nostra culpa had been expressed with regard to its own mistakes and negligence in the decision-making process regarding Srebrenica—to generate a tighter grip on the deployment of troops during future peace operations. Parliament did this, above all by stressing the need to modernize and streamline the policy process, because disasters like Srebrenica must never happen again. The Interim Commission's report therefore insisted that Parliament would have to be informed by the Government at the earliest possible moment about new operations. The ensuing debate would then have to be guided by a clear set of criteria, the so-called *toetsingscriteria* or "evaluative framework of criteria." These criteria boiled down to points—most of them fairly obvious—such as sufficient funds, political and public support, military attainability, level of risk, etc. An initial version of the list had been adopted in June 1995.[20] Ironically, this was just two weeks before the fall of Srebrenica! The Interim Commission's report was above all an instrument to (once more) "calibrate" this process.[21] The shock of Srebrenica gave Parliament extra ammunition to make its point: to prevent a Srebrenica-style tragedy, Parliament should be involved in the decision-making process as early as possible. The Government did not agree to a *formal* parliamentary right of approval, embedded in law. It held the parliamentary voice to be more than strong enough already: in any case, no Dutch Cabinet would ever dare to deploy soldiers abroad against the wishes of Parliament.[22]

The Short Full Parliamentary Inquiry into Srebrenica (2002–2003)

The interim Bakker Commission thus served to help transform the shock of the Srebrenica tragedy into a larger Parliamentary voice in the deployment of Dutch troops during international operations. This was essentially the confirmation of a broader and longer-term policy development, sanctioned by a parliamentary majority and with the consent of the Cabinet. The second parliamentary commission on Srebrenica, established two years later (2002–2003), served different purposes. This full (but short) Parliamentary Inquiry Commission was intended primarily to be a "quick fix" for an acute political crisis, caused by the unexpected resignation of the Cabinet of Prime-Minister Wim Kok in April 2002.

As mentioned above, ever since the dramatic events of 1995, Dutch governments and the majority parties had evaded the possibility of a full parliamentary inquiry. The consensus among the ruling parties was that this would have to wait for the independent NIOD report, which in any case was long overdue. It was finally published in April 2002 and political events soon took an unexpected turn. In general, NIOD's conclusions were balanced and not overly harsh. The report was above all a detailed historical study, intended, in the eyes of the authors, to serve as a rich basis for further discussion. According to the report, the Netherlands had fallen into the trap of an ill-considered and indeed impossible mission in Srebrenica—but it had done so out of a combination of sincere political ambition ("showing the flag") and humanitarian compassion. NIOD felt that perhaps Prime Minister Kok could have done more to coordinate policy within the Cabinet. The report also criticized the attitude of the army staff, which had kept vital information from Minister Voorhoeve. NIOD passed a nuanced verdict on the Dutch unit in Srebrenica: despite mistakes, the battalion had operated to the best of its abilities and with compassion toward the Bosniak population.

The initial Government reactions to the NIOD report breathed relief and a willingness to learn from the events. Prime Minister Kok indicated that he could and would defend Government policies—but in the days that followed, however, two Cabinet members hinted that they were considering resignation. Minister Jan Pronk had expressed dissident opinions in the days leading up to the publication of the NIOD report: "In retrospect we have failed. I have failed, Dutch politics has failed."[23] He was referring mainly to the failure of the Government to instruct the battalion unambiguously to protect the Bosniak refugees, especially the men who had sought refuge at the Dutch UN compound. Kok was livid: "We did not ask Mr Pronk, but NIOD, for a scholarly opinion. ... If Pronk thinks he can't shoulder the responsibility, he can resign tomorrow or even today."[24] Along with Pronk, Minister of Defence Frank de Grave indicated that he was seriously thinking about resigning. He was uncomfortable with the NIOD's conclusion that the army staff had been unwilling to fully inform the Government in 1995 (and on numerous occasions in the years that followed), especially by holding back documents that should have been forwarded to the Ministry without any delay.

Wim Kok announced the resignation of his Cabinet on 16 April 2002.[25] On the one hand, he endorsed the findings of the NIOD report in general. On the other, Kok now felt the report should still have serious and highly visible political consequences. By resigning, he stressed that the Dutch Government accepted responsibility, partly on behalf of the international community. At the same time, however, Kok underlined that the resignation should not in any way be interpreted as an admission of guilt. Apologies, for instance to the Bosniak victims of Srebrenica, were out of the question. Kok emphasized that the true culprits of the Srebrenica massacre were still the Serbs. He confirmed his awareness that his apparently unexpected about-turn and resignation might well be interpreted as a form of political escapism, but asked all involved to accept "that the process that has taken place in my head was an independent one, on its own merits."[26]

This was in fact the first resignation of any government in Dutch political history that could not be traced back to a difference of opinion between the Cabinet and Parliament or between members of the Cabinet. The departure of Kok's Cabinet precluded a serious parliamentary debate about NIOD's Srebrenica report. The main practical reason was that nationwide elections had already been scheduled for 15 May—a political reality that simply did not leave enough time to study the 3,200-page report and prepare an in-depth debate. The majority parties decided to move quickly. Three days after Kok had announced the resignation, a parliamentary majority accepted a key motion: NIOD had completed "a sound and balanced inquiry."[27] To improve "the process of finding the truth," however, the House of Commons agreed to hear a (small) number of key witnesses. The short inquiry was not intended to take on any substantial new research. Above all, its purpose was to evaluate and if necessary "complement" the reports of both NIOD and the Interim Commission. The short inquiry would not use the NIOD report as a genuine basis for fundamental debate.[28]

Nonetheless, the report of the short full inquiry was still intended to enable Parliament to pass a final political judgment on its own role and that of the Government, soldiers and bureaucrats in the fateful chapter of Srebrenica! Chairman Bakker made it clear beforehand that the general idea was not to hold individual politicians or civil servants accountable as such. In his report he would write later that the Dutch involvement in the Srebrenica tragedy "ought to be seen as a collective failure in decision-making, for which the political system bears responsibility: the Government as a whole, individual members of the Cabinet, especially those closely involved, as well as the Prime Minister for those elements of the affair that concerned him explicitly, as well as the House of Commons."[29] In other words: where *all* are held responsible, no single individual is really held responsible. One critic wrote: "Apparently, the key players get one more chance to tell their side of the story in the spotlight of the television cameras. ... Establishing the truth is not the starting point, but political theatre!"[30]

On 25 April, one week after Kok's resignation, a somewhat surreal *Hoofdlijnendebat* ("debate on the main points") took place between Parliament and the Government. As well as opting for a short full inquiry, a parliamentary majority—possibly to compensate for the obvious shortcomings of such a skeleton inquiry—had called for this immediate debate. At the same time, however, none of the participants wanted to run ahead of the scheduled inquiry on any of the substantial points. Prime Minister Kok in particular stonewalled proceedings: he had no desire to commit himself to anything yet. He stressed that this would have to wait until the inquiry, a hearing that he wanted to prepare properly in the upcoming months.

The work of the short full inquiry ended in early 2003. Its report, *Missie zonder vrede* (Mission without peace), made some marginal notes with regard to the NIOD's conclusions. The commission felt, for example, that the NIOD team had been wrong in drawing a more or less direct line between the Dutch decision to deploy troops to Srebrenica and the fateful events nearly two years later.[31] In itself, the report added little to what was already known. Chairman Bert Bakker affirmed that the hearings had mainly been intended to provide the parliamentary inquiry with a "public face," i.e. the key players were given one more chance to air their views in a public forum and the public would see the more "human interest" side of the Srebrenica affair through the eyes of the witnesses.

In many respects, the *Missie zonder vrede* report toned down points that had been the source of serious controversies in earlier stages of the aftermath. The NIOD conclusion that the army staff had been "unwilling" to inform the ministry was neutralized by the report: yes, mistakes had been made, but mostly unintentionally or simply out of incompetence. At other points too, the report was mild in its judgments. *Dutchbat* had shown great compassion for the Bosniak population during the fall of the enclave. The Cabinet had "approached the division of responsibilities within the Dutch political system in an adequate manner." Although the Inquiry Commission "regretted the fact that an extensive evaluation of the decision to deploy troops to Srebrenica had not taken place" because of Kok's resignation, it also felt that "by resigning, the Cabinet had properly accepted its own political responsibility for the failure of Dutch and international politics in Srebrenica."[32] These were statements most Parliamentarians could easily live with.

The parliamentary debate on the *Missie zonder vrede* report was finally held in June 2003. Apart from members of the Opposition, all participants—including the new government led by Christian-Democrat Jan Peter Balkenende—consistently interpreted this event not as a genuine debate, but as a form of final political and public catharsis. The Government never tampered with Kok's initial statement that the essential points of the NIOD report were acceptable. Like his predecessor Kok, Prime Minister Balkenende declined any real Dutch guilt for the Srebrenica tragedy and—although he regretted the events—refused to apologize to the victims. The Government and the parliamentary majority furthermore interpreted the *Missie zonder vrede* report as a full and final rehabilitation for the Dutch battalion in Srebrenica. Minister of Defence Henk Kamp chose these words:

> Today, in this long-awaited [parliamentary] debate, I would like to express my deepest respect to all the soldiers of the Dutch battalion in Srebrenica, who dedicated themselves to improving the future of the people in Bosnia. I take pride in what you have done and sincerely hope that your rehabilitation, which today has become a political fact, will prove to be of great meaning to you all. I hope that, from now on, you will be met with respect instead of condemnation and appreciation instead of incomprehension. ... You deserve nothing less.[33]

The opposition parties called for an in-depth written and oral response to the report from the Government, but this call was easily brushed aside.

Without any question then, the report of the short full Parliamentary Inquiry Commission can be defined as a political instrument that served to close the Srebrenica aftermath in the Netherlands expeditiously. In this respect, it was successful. By the end of 2003 the Srebrenica affair had more or less disappeared from the arena of political and media attention. Interestingly and characteristically, several NIOD researchers offered a harsh review of the scope and "toned down" conclusions of the Parliamentary Inquiry Commission. One NIOD researcher for instance pointed to the fact that the army commander General Couzy had given contradictory evidence about the willingness with which he had kept the Ministry abreast of developments during and after the fall of the enclave in 1995. Couzy got away with this and the researcher partly blamed this on the lack of detailed knowledge on the part of the Parliamentary Inquiry Commission.[34]

At this point, it is useful to point to the actual strategy with which the Government and majority parties defused criticism and ended the Srebrenica aftermath. They applied a pragmatic three-pronged strategy. First of all, they would criticize certain fundamental aspects of the reports from the NIOD and the Parliamentary Inquiry Commission. Government ministers for instance stressed that the margins for decision-making had been small indeed at the end of 1993: something had to be done quickly when tens of thousands of Bosniak refugees in Srebrenica were surrounded by Serbs. Sending troops had essentially been a benign act of humanitarianism, and even then no one could have predicted the way in which the thugs of Serb General Ratko Mladić would defy the international community and massacre thousands of Bosniak men. Secondly, and simultaneously, the Government and majority parties would lavish praise on the quality and importance of the work done by the commissions. Finally, the Government and majority parties would emphasize that their conclusions and recommendations were in fact in accordance with the wisdom of policies that had *already* been put in place in preceding years to prevent any future recurrence. The Ministry of Defence, for instance, pointed to the fact that military operations required a substantial level of expeditious organizational adaptability. One could not simply wait for the inquiries' reports to be published. Victims from Srebrenica, their sympathizers, opposition parties, and critical journalists berated this "political opportunism," but to little avail.

An Aftermath in "Splendid Isolation"

Before we conclude, it is appropriate to look at two specific characteristics of the Srebrenica aftermath in the Netherlands.[35] First, it is noteworthy that this was very much a *national* process, almost entirely isolated from foreign influences. This "splendid isolation" also applied to the parliamentary commissions. As mentioned earlier, a consensus soon developed among Dutch majority politicians and officials (including the armed forces) that *Dutchbat* and the Netherlands had been small but benevolent players in a complex and tumultuous world. In this view (supported by the public in general), the Dutch had to a certain extent become victims of unscrupulous realpolitik, the strains of great power politics, and the weakness of the United Nations. This was reflected in the attitude mentioned above: the Netherlands bore no guilt for the Srebrenica tragedy as such. (This also helps to explain why no major arguments emerged between MPs or political parties during and after the inquiries.)

Connected to this self-serving attitude was the tendency *not* to take foreign or UN reports as a starting point for debate or to invite foreign officials to testify before commissions. Out of forty-one witnesses to appear before the full Parliamentary Inquiry Commission only one was a foreign official, UNPROFOR commander General Sir Rupert Smith.[36] Reports would usually refer to foreign and UN reports on Srebrenica only in their introduction or in footnotes.[37] To a certain extent, the work of the ICTY is the exception, particularly the evidence resulting from the trial against Serb General Radislav Krstić, who was convicted in 2001 for genocide at Srebrenica. This material was used extensively by the NIOD commission and, to a lesser extent, by the full Inquiry. The interest in the ICTY proceedings was based in the fact that they offered scarce "objective" primary source material (contrary to the foreign official reports filled with politically or scholarly inspired interpretations). Still, the NIOD report did not concur fully with ICTY's conviction of Krstić for genocide, claiming that—based on contemporary international human rights law—the tribunal could well have come to a different conclusion. NIOD preferred the term *mass murder*.

Criticism against Dutch politics or soldiers from abroad—for instance when the French parliamentary report laid some of the blame at *Dutchbat*'s feet—was invariably met with indignation, a strong denial and the suggestion that the critics should mind their own (national!) business. For instance, former Prime Minister Alain Juppé propounded to the French parliamentary Srebrenica commission that during the Serb attack the Dutch Government had torpedoed UN plans to provide *Dutchbat* with air support and had subsequently blocked a French initiative to recapture the enclave.[38] The disgruntled Dutch Minister of Foreign Affairs Hans van Mierlo replied that "Juppé had got things all mixed up" and that any military action "would only have resulted in a bloodbath."[39]

Interestingly, and critics would stress this point, the official Dutch posture ("We could have done little to avoid the tragedy") automatically implied a certain lack of initiative, even passivity. This clashed with another posture that the Dutch had traditionally been proud of, that of being an active frontrunner in the field of humanitarianism and universal human rights. The official response to this criticism would be that Dutch soldiers and politicians had indeed done all that was possible in extremely difficult circumstances and had in fact prevented even greater loss of life.

This "isolationist" approach also lessened the need to articulate an "official" Dutch point of view with regard to the role of the Bosniaks themselves, especially the sensitive question of whether Bosniak authorities had contributed to the escalation in July 1995. The parliamentary reports mentioned the Bosniak side only briefly, attributing to them a more or less undefined role somewhere between victim on the one hand and active player (e.g., by organizing raids against the Serb besiegers outside of the enclave) on the other. In the end, the Bosniaks of Srebrenica were portrayed above all as the underdog, trying to escape from a deadly trap. The independent NIOD team was most outspoken about the role of the Bosniak side (i.e., "blaming the victim"), attributing to the authorities in Srebrenica some of the guilt for the tragedy, for instance by not disarming and occasionally provoking the Serbs.

At the same time, nearly all commissions and reports felt the urge to recognize the suffering of the Bosniak victims openly in some way. For instance, in a symbolic gesture, the reports of the full Parliamentary Inquiry Commission and the NIOD were presented first to representatives from organizations of Bosniak victims.

A second noteworthy characteristic of all Dutch Srebrenica commissions touches on the problem of writing (contemporary) history as such. In its most elementary sense the problem was this: the witnesses' narratives would soon crystallize into more or less coherent explanations of their own behavior. The pressure to compile this coherent (and preferably credible) story quickly was intensified by the extraordinarily high moral and political stakes of the Srebrenica affair, cranked up even more by the media. To admit to mistakes amounted to admitting—in part—to guilt for one of the worst tragedies in modern history.[40] The armed forces in particular found it extremely difficult to admit structural errors, defending its image of being a "zero-error organization."

Adding to this problem of the hardening of testimonies was the fact that many of the key decisions had never been documented in writing or images. An example may serve to illustrate this. One *Dutchbat* lieutenant claimed that—shortly after the Serbs had taken over the enclave in July 1995—he had noticed a pile of passports and other personal papers taken from captured Bosniak men. Inquiring of a Serb soldier what was happening, he was told: "They won't be needing those papers anymore!" The Dutch lieutenant claims to have informed battalion headquarters without delay about this worrying development, a strong indication that the Bosniak men might well be killed soon. This warning might then have induced his superiors (or even the UN) to intervene. However, Dutch officers present at battalion headquarters were adamant that they had never received the lieutenant's warning. Lacking documentary evidence, the matter still remains unresolved.[41] In any case, all commissions lacked sufficient staff and detailed knowledge to get a definitive grasp on the intricate events at Srebrenica.[42] With the exception of experienced chairman Bert Bakker, MPs simply did not have enough time (commission members always work part-time) or detailed knowledge to be able to oversee and connect all the facts or, for instance, to understand fully the workings of the UN or a military organization.[43]

Conclusion: A Story of Two Parliamentary Commissions

By 1998 it had become clear that the Srebrenica affair would not "go away"—as had perhaps been hoped by the Government and majority parties. The question arose as to whether Parliament should employ one of its most powerful instruments: a full parliamentary inquiry. However, burdened by a stranglehold of monist policies, both Cabinet and majority parties looked for another "way out." Ironically, this approach helped to ensure that the political aftermath of the Srebrenica affair would become lengthy and messy. Temporary "solutions" were found by the Government and majority parties in the scholarly NIOD commission and the politically fairly innocent Interim Commission (1999–2000). The latter was set up with a specific goal in mind: formalizing the already strong voice of Parliament in the decision-making process with regard to deploying

Dutch troops on peace operations. Cabinet accepted this small encroachment on its executive territory without too much protest.

A full Parliamentary Inquiry Commission (2002–2003) was intended to serve as the instrument to bring the painful Srebrenica affair to an expeditious end. Kok's resignation both defused the independent NIOD report and took the political sting out of any future debate. A short inquiry now became the politically motivated way out: the commission did not embark on genuinely new research, nor did it use the NIOD report as a basis for further fundamental debate. The *Missie zonder vrede* report resulted in a skeleton parliamentary debate, which was intended to be a manifestly final catharsis in full public view.

By the time the Srebrenica aftermath ended in the Netherlands after eight long years—always in "splendid isolation" from Srebrenica aftermaths and reports in other countries and at the UN—few Dutch politicians and journalists or the public in general still cared very much. It had never been the intention of mainstream Dutch politics and authorities to pronounce guilt or convict anyone over the Srebrenica affair. If things had indeed gone wrong, the causes could be found in the international community, flawed good intentions or common incompetence; all causes that could be explained away without the need for severe sanctions. In this respect particularly, the parliamentary commissions served their purpose.

Notes

1. Quoted in *NRC-Handelsblad*, 14 April 2002.
2. See, e.g., Jan-Willem Honig and Norbert Both, *Srebrenica: Record of a War Crime* (London, 1996); Norbert Both, *From Indifference to Entrapment: The Netherlands and the Yugoslav Crisis 1990-1995* (Amsterdam, 2000); and David Rohde, *Endgame: The Betrayal and Fall of Srebrenica: Europe's Worst Massacre Since World War II* (New York, 1997).
3. Robert Block, "Dutch troops ignored Bosnia killings," *The Independent*, 21 September 1995.
4. Robert Fisk in *The Independent*, 7 November 1996.
5. Tweede Kamer (House of Commons), proceedings, 7 December 1995, series 22181, number 141, passim.
6. Nederlands Instituut voor Oorlogsdocumentatie (NIOD), *Srebrenica, een "veilig" gebied. Reconstructie, achtergronden, gevolgen en analyses van de val van een Safe Area* [Srebrenica, a "Safe" Area: Reconstruction, Background, Consequences and Analyses with Regard to the Fall of a Safe Area], 4 vols. (Amsterdam, 2002). About the NIOD report, see also Pieter Lagrou's chapter in this volume.
7. The debriefing employed a 24-man team that interviewed a total of 490 *Dutchbat* personel in a three-week period. With the exception of officers from the Military Police, none of the debriefing staff was experienced in interviewing techniques. The interviews took

between one and several hours to complete, the information was then screened and processed by a "core staff." The debriefing report itself defined the timeframe as "extremely limited." (General Onno van der Wind, rapporteur, *Rapport gebaseerd op de debriefing Srebrenica* [Report Based on the Debriefing Srebrenica], Assen, 4 October 1995, 6).

8. Van Kemenade received secretarial support from three officials from the Ministry of Justice, his chief of staff, and two secretaries.
9. Jos van Kemenade, *Omtrent Srebrenica. Rapport over de verzameling en verwerking van informatie door de defensie-organisatie over gebeurtenissen rond de val van de enclave Srebrenica* [Regarding Srebrenica: Report on the Collection and Processing of Information by the Defense Organization Concerning Events with Regard to the Fall of the Srebrenica Enclave] (The Hague, 28 September 2008), paragraph 1.3.
10. Mient Jan Faber, *Srebrenica. De genocide die niet werd voorkomen* [Srebrenica: The Genocide That Was not Prevented] (The Hague, March 2002). Faber's report was above all an individual exercise. He made full use of his personal network to gain information and was able to speak to a number of *Dutchbat* soldiers as well.
11. For a critical review of UN and Dutch policies and arguments, see for instance: Human Rights Watch, Dossier "The Fall of Srebrenica and the Failure of UN Peacekeeping," *Human Rights Watch Publications* 7, no. 13 (October 1995); and Ivan Lupis, "Human Rights Abuses in the Wake of the Collapse of the United Nations-Designated 'Safe Area' of Srebrenica and the International Community," *Helsinki Monitor* 7, no. 1 (1996), 65–72. An interesting analysis can be found in: Liora Sion, "'Too Sweet and Innocent for War', Dutch Peacekeepers and the Use of Violence," *Armed Forces & Society* 32, no. 3 (April 2006), 454–474.
12. See for instance Voorhoeve's testimony during the parliamentary inquiry into Srebrenica, in: Parlementaire Enquêtecommissie Srebrenica, report *Missie zonder vrede* [Mission Without Peace], Tweede Kamer, proceedings, 27 January 2003, series 28506, number 5 (hearings), 638–639. The Inquiry-report, other documents and Parliamentary proceedings are available online at: https://zoek.officielebekendmakingen.nl/kst-28506-3.pdf.
13. Parliamentary hearings were indeed broadcast live on national television and both the reports and transcripts would become widely available, e.g., on the Internet.
14. Hans Couzy, *Mijn jaren als bevelhebber* [My Years in Command] (Amsterdam/Antwerp, 1996) and Thom Karremans, *Srebrenica: Who cares?* (Nieuwegein, 1998).
15. The Parliamentary Interim Commission consisted of seven MPs (the usual number for these inquiries) and seven staff members (nearly all having a social sciences background).
16. Quoted in *De Telegraaf*, 20 May 2000.
17. NIOD researchers felt they were doing the "real" Srebrenica investigation and hinted regularly that the Bakker Commission simply lacked time and expertise to disentangle the complicated Srebrenica affair. In its final report, NIOD referred only sparingly to the work of the Bakker Commission.
18. In its report, the Bakker Commission would distinguish between the closed "welcoming party" of *Dutchbat* on 22 July and the "reception" with Prime Minister Kok and Crown-Prince Willem-Alexander the next day. Tijdelijke Commissie Besluitvorming Uitzendingen, report *Vertrekpunt Den Haag* [Point of Departure The Hague], Tweede Kamer, proceedings, 4 September 2000, series 26454, number 7–8 (main report), 199–201 and 485.
19. Ibid., recommendation 59, 488.
20. *Betrokkenheid van het parlement bij de uitzending van militair eenheden* [Involvement of Parliament in the Decision to Deploy Troops], Tweede Kamer, proceedings, 28 June 1995, series 23591, number 5.

21. The result was a "new" list of criteria that—compared to the original list of 1995—was to some extent supplemented and elaborated, without being amended to any larger extent. Tweede Kamer, proceedings, 8 April 2004, series 29521, number 1.
22. This point was embedded in Article 100 of the Dutch Constitution. The article now reads: "Government will inform Parliament beforehand about the intended deployment or commitment of troops to strengthen the international legal order, including humanitarian assistance during armed conflict."
23. Quoted in television news magazine *NOVA*, 28 March 2002.
24. Tweede Kamer, proceedings, 3 April 2002, 63-4247.
25. A good review of events can be found in: Paul Bartrop, "Assuming Responsibility: The Srebrenica Massacre and the Resignation of the Dutch Government, 16 April 2002," paper presented at the International Association of Genocide Scholars Biennial Conference (Galway, 7–10 June 2003).
26. Tweede Kamer, proceedings, 19 April 2002, 69-4565.
27. Tweede Kamer, proceedings, 17 April 2002, series 28334, number 2.
28. The full Parliamentary Inquiry Commission numbered seven MPs and about fifteen staff members (most of them researchers from the social sciences).
29. Tweede Kamer, proceedings, 4 June 2003, 75-4243.
30. Political commentator Bart Tromp, in *Elsevier Magazine*, 17 April 2002.
31. In a characteristic compromise-ridden response, NIOD's director Blom would deny that his report had in fact drawn a *direct* line between the two events: the massacre could not be reduced to the Dutch Government's decision to send troops in a "linear" sense. Blom also regretted (what he saw as) the Parliamentary Inquiry Commission's excessive focus on "dry" political and administrative processes in The Hague, instead of putting emphasis on Srebrenica's human tragedy as such. See for instance his interview in *VI Nieuwsbrief* [Newsletter of the Veteran's Institute] 2, no. 3 (December 2002), 4–5.
32. Parlementaire Enquêtecommissie Srebrenica, report *Missie zonder vrede*, Tweede Kamer, proceedings, 27 January 2003, series 28506, number 3 (main report), 441, 447, and 452.
33. Tweede Kamer, proceedings, 18 June 2003, 79-4494.
34. Paul Koedijk, "Onwil en onkunde in de polder: de parlementaire enquête Srebrenica," [Unwillingness and Ignorance: the Parliamentary Inquiry into Srebrenica], *Openbaar Bestuur* 13, no. 4 (2003), 2–6.
35. For an extensive discussion see Christ Klep, *Somalië, Rwanda, Srebrenica. De nasleep van drie ontspoorde vredesmissies* [Somalia, Rwanda, Srebrenica: The Aftermath of Three Peace Operations Gone Wrong] (Amsterdam, 2008).
36. Parlementaire Enquêtecommissie Srebrenica, report *Missie zonder vrede*, Tweede Kamer, proceedings, 27 January 2003, series 28506, number 5 (hearings), 675–691. General Smith's testimony added very little to known facts and opinions. In fact, his hearing only obscured the fact-finding process, especially because Smith claimed that—in 1995—Dutch parliamentarians had implored him not to tackle the Bosnian Serbs too strongly out of fear for reprisals against UN soldiers. These parliamentarians subsequently denied vigorously ever having made remarks in that direction. Not a single foreign official was interviewed by the Parliamentary Interim Commission.
37. The NIOD team *did* interview dozens of foreign and UN officials. Most of them agreed because of the scholarly, non-politicized nature of the NIOD inquiry.
38. On the French Parliamentary Fact-Finding Mission on Srebrenica, see Pierre Brana's and Jean-Louis Fournel's chapters in this volume.
39. Quoted in *NRC-Handelsblad*, 2 April 2001.
40. In my opinion, taking an oath made little real difference to the contents of the testimonies. Once in the public domain, witnesses never changed opinions later on.

41. For a review of this affair, see Parlementaire Enquêtecommissie Srebrenica, report *Missie zonder vrede*, Tweede Kamer, proceedings, 27 January 2003, series 28506, number 5 (hearings), 339–341; and NIOD, *Srebrenica, een "veillig" gebied*, vol. 3, 2738–2741.
42. I encountered this phenomenon both as a witness and as an outside expert for the parliamentary commissions. As a military historian at the Ministry of Defence, and having been present at Zagreb when *Dutchbat* returned from Srebrenica in July 1995, it took me several years to master to some degree the intricacies of military organizations and the Srebrenica affair. During hearings, I found myself more often than not explaining basic facts to MPs, instead of providing detailed testimony.
43. Even the NIOD-team (though expanded from three to twelve full-time professional researchers) found it hard to complete its inquiry on time and had to leave important questions unanswered.

Chapter 5

REFLECTIONS ON THE DUTCH NIOD REPORT
Academic Logic and the Culture of Consensus[1]

Pieter Lagrou

In an official ceremony on 4 December 2006, the Dutch Minister of Defense, Henk Kamp, awarded military decorations to the soldiers and officers who had been members of *Dutchbat*, the Dutch battalion responsible for protecting the population of the Srebrenica enclave. This gesture, which provoked a wave of protest, seems incomprehensible given *Dutchbat*'s dramatic failure to carry out its mission, the result of which was the massacre of about eight thousand people confided to its protection. It seems that the Dutch political authorities have never raised the question of the responsibility of Dutch soldiers in the Srebrenica tragedy or, if they have done so, that they have definitively responded by acquitting them.

Yet only a few months after the fall of the enclave in July 1995, the Dutch Government ordered an investigative report to address precisely the question of Dutch responsibility for the tragedy. Published after an enquiry that lasted more than six years, this report is by far the longest and also in several respects the most ambitious of all the reports ordered by national governments or parliaments and international agencies. The white elephant among the various international publications that seek to explain the Srebrenica massacre, the report defies any facile attempt at categorization: it is at once an official report, a product of academic research, an effort at legitimization, an administrative inquiry, a political intervention, and a work of commemoration. Due to its vast size and ambivalent status, its conclusions cannot be easily summarized nor do they lend themselves to an unequivocal critical reading. In attempting to make sense of it, the present chapter will thus rely more on circumstantial contextualization than on internal textual analysis.

Notes for this chapter begin on page 101.

Indeed, in order to understand the report's organization and reception by Dutch society and the research team's working and writing styles, the text must be placed in the context of a very distinctive national tradition of managing public debates by means of commissions of inquiry. The inquiry was confided to the foremost symbol of this tradition, the Netherlands Institute for War Documentation (*Nederlands Instituut voor Oorlogsdocumentatie*, NIOD). In contrast to the burning topicality of the Srebrenica report, the Institute's previous work had consisted of investigations of a historical nature. Yet this text can only be understood from the perspective of institutional continuity and carries all the marks of a "house style." This is reflected in the research team's working method—in particular, the centralized manner in which the collective project was organized—as well as in the positivistic approach they adopted, avoiding interpretive debates and limiting their efforts to reconstructing the facts. However, the interpretive models inherited from the historiography of Nazism, NIOD's principal field of expertise, seem to have played a minor role in the report compared to its unprecedented dependence on legal sources and the very unusual coincidence of a historical-type inquiry with an ongoing legal process. That of course raises the question of the added value of NIOD's work in comparison with the work of the International Criminal Tribunal for the Former Yugoslavia (ICTY). Though NIOD gave itself a pedagogical mission, it is ironic to note that only the Dutch and English versions are available and that the Serbo-Croatian version is still on the drawing board, several years after the report's publication.[2] Was the report thus more a matter of legitimization than of pedagogy? In this connection, one may underscore its specious distribution of responsibility. Focusing on the question of responsibility in high places (The Hague, New York, Zagreb), the report spares the soldiers of the *Dutchbat* themselves. One may also underscore the report's timing, which allowed the Dutch Government to resign three weeks before the end of the legislative session. One may, finally, underscore the forced, consensual character of its conclusions, which clearly seem to seek to put an end to the debate over Srebrenica rather than supply information to fuel it. As I will explain in my conclusion, this culture of consensus and refusal of open debate are at once the central characteristics of this report and of the political culture that produced it.

A White Elephant?

Among the various reports concerning the July 1995 Srebrenica massacre, that presented in April 2002 by the NIOD is in several respects exceptional.³ First, by virtue of its immediate impact: following publication of the report, the Dutch Government accepted its collective responsibility for the criticisms expressed there and resigned. Second, by virtue of its size: more than three thousand pages in three volumes and a large number of annexes, yielding a total of nearly seven thousand pages; a team that, over six years of work, grew from three to twelve full-time researchers⁴; and a nearly unlimited budget that, in 2001 alone, was in the neighborhood of one million Euros.⁵ Third and last, by virtue of the identity of the institute that agreed to carry out this inquiry on behalf of the Dutch Government: the NIOD, an institute created in October 1945 to study the period of the Nazi occupation in the Netherlands. In a half-century of existence, this institute had exclusively devoted itself to producing historical studies of the Second World War and, to a lesser extent, of colonial and post-colonial history. Compared to parliamentary commissions of inquiry and internal audits of international organizations, which operate under more severe time constraints, dispose of limited resources, and depend much more closely on their institutional sponsors, this colossal report could legitimately give rise to expectations of exhaustiveness, impartiality, critical distance, and even historicization of the recent past.

A Pedigree

NIOD's Srebrenica report must be seen as part of a particular national context. This is due, first of all, to the undisputed legitimacy of this institute, which, over the course of a half-century, has practically monopolized historiographical production (and the conservation of sources) on the period of the Second World War. Though they are sometimes compared to similar projects carried out by Soviet bloc academies of science, the twenty-four volumes of *The Kingdom of the Netherlands during the Second World War*,⁶ which appeared in annual installments between 1975 and 1991 and were entirely written by the institute's director at the time, Louis de Jong, were unique in the world for their monolithic and consensual homogeneity. De Jong, moreover, authored the first televised documentary series on the Second World War, which was broadcast in several dozen episodes over the course of the first half of the 1960s, and was the undisputed moral authority in all discussions of the war, collaboration, and the purge. The "De Jong model" subsequently imposed itself as a reliable recipe for consensually managing—and thus depoliticizing—public debates. This practice of managing public debates by means of commissions of inquiry was also criticized for "freezing" them. In 1969, an inquiry into the crimes committed during the repression of the Indonesian uprising (1947–1949) was commissioned. The report, however, was only published in 1994, by which time any chance for controversy had been extinguished and most of the then political leaders had reached retirement age.[7] The question of the seizure of Jewish goods during the Nazi occupation and their subsequent return was confided to no less than six commissions of inquiry over the course of the 1990s. A seventh looked into the non-financial aspects of the return of camp inmates in the context of a research foundation specifically created for this purpose within the NIOD.[8] As its mandate was enlarged—from the return of Jewish camp inmates to other displaced persons from Germany and, later, Indonesia—so, too, did its research team, which ultimately counted fifty members.

Yet, the Dutch Government's 1996 request that the Srebrenica massacre be investigated was totally unprecedented. For the first time, NIOD agreed to produce a report on very recent history, launching its inquiry just sixteen months after the events in question.[9] On several occasions, the institute has been reproached for its slowness and the tardy publication of its research results. Yet, when compared with its earlier work, it is in fact the speed with which the report was put together—just seven years after the fact and six years after the start of the inquiry—that is striking. By way of example, De Jong's first volume was released thirty years after the facts described therein, his last volume forty-six years after them, and the commission on the excesses committed in Indonesia took twenty-five years to make its conclusions public.

When the institute accepted the "Srebrenica mission," the events of which the massacre of the enclave's population were part were still ongoing: although the war in Bosnia had come to an end in December 1995, Yugoslavia continued to tear itself apart, the Netherlands still had troops on the ground, and most Dutch political and military leaders still occupied the same posts. While the inquiry was in full swing, a number of radically new developments took place, including the outbreak of another conflict in Kosovo in 1998, NATO's military intervention there a year later and the first judgments handed down by the ICTY in The Hague. These events cast a new light on the war in Bosnia and led to new paradigms for military and humanitarian interventions. For a center with a long tradition of historical respectability, the decision to take on this research project constituted a transgression of the rules delimiting the exercise of contemporary history, which impose a waiting period at least equivalent to the waiting period for access to public archives (in general, thirty years, though it can be much longer for specific sources in judicial and military archives). Even the French equivalent of NIOD, the *Institut d'histoire du temps présent* (IHTP), which has since the 1960s worked in close cooperation with NIOD and has since 1981 included "history of present time" ("*histoire du temps présent*") in its name, had never ventured so close to current affairs.[10] The temerity of NIOD, the oldest historical institute working on the Second World War in Europe, has been interpreted as a foolhardy mistake that put its scientific legitimacy at risk in order to obtain a new, very large source of funding and enlarge the institute's field of competence. How could NIOD believe that it could adopt the same critical distance and benefit from the same consensual authority with regard to an ongoing conflict when it had taken half a century to obtain this for the period of the Nazi occupation?

Given such expectations, on the one hand, and such misgivings, on the other, how is one to evaluate this unique exercise in both the international and Dutch contexts?

A Healthy Positivism?

Given the unprecedented character of the challenge, the reader is at first glance surprised by the homogenous and carefully honed style of its three thousand pages. At the level of both its structure and its argumentation, the document displays NIOD's "house style" and the framework used very much recalls that of Louis de Jong in *The Kingdom of the Netherlands during the Second World War*. The subject is carefully divided into chapters and paragraphs, with an abundance of intra-textual references. Each question receives detailed introduction, with particular attention devoted to the presentation of sources and the issue of figures, dates, and chronology. The document does not stray into theoretical discussions or interpretive problems and pays no heed to the contributions of other works on the subject beyond the bare reference to sources. The very systematic manner in which the subject is divided between its various parts reveals an unshakeable faith in the explanatory power of well-established facts. The historian's reasoning seems incontestable, as long as it limits itself to reconstructing the *"Wie es eigentlich gewesen ist"* ("how it really was") of Leopold von Ranke.

Several important questions are left open, allowing one to put forward hypotheses and contemplate alternative scenarios as to how the situation might have developed at certain crucial moments. These consist of detailed and very concrete "what if" hypotheses: what would have happened if the Dutch tanks had been equipped with canons rather than machine guns? If the members of *Dutchbat* had fired on the Serbs from their blocking positions? If a part of the enclave's population had not attempted to escape by foot to territory under Bosnian control? These hypotheses and alternatives are then summarized by means of various levels of conclusion. They allow one to take stock of the facts revealed by the research and to demonstrate how the latter suffices to resolve most hitherto unanswered questions. Systematic, exhaustive, and with an eye for the smallest detail, these long approach marches meant to clear the ground for later discussion make reading the three thousand pages of the report seem like a battle of attrition. Like a steamroller, the accumulation of data finishes by crushing the reader.

The introduction characterizes this approach as "fact-finding": it suffices to establish what really happened in factual terms to arrive at a consensual conclusion. The truth, one and indivisible, then becomes self-evident. The delicate question of the relationship to the study's sponsor—the Dutch Government—is swept aside as a false problem that has already been entirely resolved by the terms of the contract, which guarantees the researchers access to the sources as well as scholarly independence. The same goes for the question of the report's date of publication: the six years it took to release the report correspond to the time necessary for carrying out an inquiry of this type, period. The fact that the report was published just three weeks before the end of the legislative session, thereby allowing the Government to resign in a grandiose and perfectly painless gesture of public contrition, was subsequently presented in the various declarations of the team and, in particular, its authorized spokesman, Hans Blom, director of the institute and the inquiry, as pure coincidence and a matter of an entirely inappropriate controversy.

However, the structure of the report carries all the marks of a centralized editing process, that is, one in which, after much discussion, the authors of the various chapters reach agreement on a common text that does not allow for any difference of opinion and expresses a shared interpretation. This inevitably supposes an arbitration mechanism in the event of disagreement, a hypothesis confirmed by the manner in which the institute's director takes responsibility for all of the conclusions and by the fact that the team's researchers were not authorized to participate in the public debate before the final publication of the report.

The solid logic of this framework particularly lends itself to the reconstruction of certain events. To give an example: the description of the exodus on foot toward Tuzla is impressive for the masterful tone of analysis on display, its multiplication of perspectives and sources and the parsimonious but effective use of quotations.[11] This part of the text represents not just a model of reserve in the description of horrific events but also a convincing demonstration of the claim that precisely reconstructing events can supply answers to the central questions put forward by the report concerning the predictable or unpredictable character of certain developments, levels and processes of decision-making, the circulation of information, and the responsibilities that result from it.

Historiographical Models?

In this respect, it seems that the team implicitly shares the renewed confidence in historical positivism that characterizes the recent historiography of the genocide perpetrated by the Nazis. Theoretical debates over questions of guilt, intention, and functionality are for the most part sterile if they are not simultaneously grounded in micro-historical reality. By means of its meticulous chronology and the analysis it offers of command and decision levels, the NIOD's reconstruction of the Srebrenica events seeks to show that, although other massive executions took place in the course of this conflict, the systematic and large-scale killings in the enclave were planned neither well in advance nor in a centralized manner. Rather, the NIOD interpretation holds that this unprecedented turn of events took place on site in a process of radicalization combining historical antecedents and particular local circumstances. This approach overlaps in certain respects with the analyses of the best contemporary historians of the genocide perpetrated by the Nazis, including Christian Gerlach, Dieter Pohl, Christopher Browning, and Florent Brayard. Developed nearly a half-century after the fact, their work concerns the manner in which the Nazis took the decision to carry out massacres, giving particular attention to the activities of the *Einsatzgruppen* on the Eastern Front in the second half of 1941 and the emergence of mass extermination by gassing during the summer of 1942.[12] Relative to older schema, which began with a "naïve" conception of premeditation and the assumption of a strictly hierarchical decision-making process, these recent analyses insist on the exchanges between men on the ground and their hierarchy, the role of the discovery and experimentation of new horizons of possibility in the area of mass massacre as well as on the radicalization of time scales, with the millennium the Reich gave itself for reorganizing the European continent contracting to a single year in which to carry out the totality of its crimes.

It is worth lingering over the question of what influence the historiography of this "other genocide" had on the NIOD team's analysis of the Srebrenica massacre. First of all, the NIOD "house tradition" principally concerns the history of the German occupation of the Netherlands and is centered on questions of resistance and collaboration rather than on the extermination of the Jews or the crimes of Nazism as such. What's more, the publication of the Srebrenica report in 2002 coincided with the creation, in collaboration with the University of Amsterdam, of a Center for Holocaust and Genocide Studies within the NIOD. Holocaust studies thus do not represent a long-standing tradition in the NIOD. Among the team's members, only the chief directors Hans Blom and Peter Romijn are historians of the Second World War, while the researchers who carried out the inquiry on the ground came from completely different backgrounds: military history, the history of the intelligence services, diplomatic history, Balkan anthropology. While the report repeatedly refers to historical and socio-psychological works on human behavior in extreme situations, these do not seem to play a fundamental role in the interpretation.

Its combination of perpetrator history, for the most part based on sources produced by and for the ICTY, and victim history, above all consisting in the (oral) testimony of survivors, suggests that it is mainly at the methodological level that the NIOD team drew lessons from a half-century of Holocaust studies. Over the past fifteen years, the history of the Nazi genocide has been criticized for embracing a dichotomy between a compassionate history of the victim, in large part based on testimony collected well after the fact, and a history of perpetrators heavily indebted to legal sources and interpretations. The representation of Nazism as a "minority" affair ultimately restricted to a clique of criminal leaders around Hitler was in part the product of the Nuremberg International Military Tribunal, which limited itself to judging two dozen high-ranking Nazi dignitaries, and the trials subsequently organized by the Federal Republic of Germany, which, in its refusal to retroactively apply the Nuremberg jurisprudence, requalified Nazi crimes as common-law crimes under the penal code of 1870. The question of the relationship between the interpretive frameworks of the NIOD report and those of the historiography of Nazism can thus in large part be reduced to that of their respective relationships to the legal sources.

A History Dependent on Justice?

The manner in which the ICTY sources are used in the report is unprecedented. The struggle of competencies between judges and historians, about which so much ink has been spilt in the framework of trials held since the 1960s to judge the crimes against humanity committed during the Second World War, here seems transformed. Although the historians of the NIOD underscore how important it was for them to avoid being confused with the tribunal's investigators, it does not seem that the collaboration between international justice and historical research was fundamentally conflictual. That historians were in this case able to consult judicial files—not several decades after they were prepared but, in most cases, before the trials in question had even begun—is a radically new fact that fundamentally challenges the idea that a minimal waiting period and chronological separation are essential to the definition of the discipline of history. It seems crucial to reflect on such conditions of archival access and the destruction of temporal distance they imply. Is the axiom according to which the historian only looks into "old" facts and a set of events that he believes to be "finished" a consequence of the empirical limits on his work or rather an intellectual necessity? In other words, if the legislation governing access to judicial and governmental archives was fundamentally altered—with, for example, the statutory waiting period waved in particular cases and for a specific group of researchers—would the waiting period that historians have until now imposed on themselves necessarily be abandoned? The response to this question is of course inseparable from the identification of these "particular cases" and the conditions that would be imposed on this "specific group of researchers" vis-à-vis public opinion and their colleagues elsewhere in the profession. This question, to which I will return in my conclusion, is not addressed by the NIOD report.

However, in comparison with historians of Nazism, did the suppression of temporal distance between the action of the tribunal and that of the NIOD historians not simply further strengthen their dependence on judicial sources and interpretations? And, when all is said and done, was it ultimately the historian's approach that changed here or rather the action of international justice? The ICTY approach differs radically from that of the Nuremberg Tribunal by virtue of the weight it accorded the testimony of victims and by its use of forensic police methods to establish the facts: the exhumation of mass graves, the identification of victims, cross-checking evidence.[13] In this respect, the qualitative leap that marks the analyses of the NIOD report is just as indebted to the ICTY as the defects of an earlier historiography of Nazism could be attributed to Nuremberg.

At the level of fact-finding, it is thus extremely difficult to distinguish the occasional contributions of the NIOD from the massive contributions of the ICTY. What, then, is the added value of the NIOD's historical approach when set alongside the legal approach? Initially, the ICTY was the object of much criticism and mistrust. Indeed, international justice seemed little more than a fig leaf for an international community that had made it known that it was not inclined to intervene to halt the killings but that it would later appeal to the principles of human rights with all the more conviction by organizing tribunals and trials. The American historian Peter Maguire designated this approach (not without irony) "strategic legalism."[14] Yet, as the judicial process moves forward, the contributions of international justice come to seem ever more crucial. Murky controversies concerning the number of victims, the identity of the perpetrators and even the reality of certain events are in effect important elements in the construction of nationalist mythologies. It is not far-fetched to suggest that, in what concerns the massacres perpetrated during the Second World War on Yugoslav territory, the lack of a critical historiography or any effort to establish the basic facts contributed to the deterioration of relations between population groups, particularly from the 1980s onward. The ICTY, on the contrary, brought a large quantity of irrefutable facts concerning both command structures and the number of victims to light. It identified the guilty and condemned a certain number of them. Moreover, the presence of a representative of the Bosnian Serbs at commemorations of the burial of victims at Potočari on 11 July 2003 would probably have been impossible without the efforts of the international community to incontestably demonstrate the reality of the slaughter.

For a tribunal, the reconstruction of events is subordinated to establishing guilt. For historical research, the approach is in principle just the opposite. While there is debate over whether the verdicts handed down by the tribunal contribute to reconciliation, it seems beyond any doubt that the critical establishment of the factual sequence of events helps pacify relations between the populations. For that to happen, however, historians would first have to give themselves this mission. In the case of the NIOD report, this would entail not only going beyond its mission to determine Dutch responsibility in the massacre—this it does to the point of minimizing Dutch responsibility, as we shall see below—but also setting itself the ambition of initiating dialogue with the populations concerned.

New Paradigms?

The detailed and essentially descriptive reconstruction at which the report aimed also gives a far from flattering sketch of the international intervention. The vivid description of the humiliations experienced day after day by the members of UNPROFOR and the total loss of respect this elicited in the eyes of the local armed forces is much more evocative than rhetorical indignation. By presenting Serb tactics as a fragile combination of heavy artillery and local terror wrought by paramilitary gangs made up of notorious criminals, the same approach efficiently deconstructs the myth of a formidable military adversary.

The accumulation of data concerning the absurd manner in which Dutch soldiers were sent into the trap without protection and under totally contradictory orders resonates like an indictment of the collective incompetence, blindness, and paralysis of nearly all of the national and international bodies involved. Among other problems plaguing the Dutch mission were an opaque command structure split between Tuzla, Zagreb, New York and The Hague, insufficient resources for assuring the protection of the civilian populations for whom they were responsible, a lack of both on-the-ground intelligence and aerial images and the dependence of their supply lines on a Serb army whose hostages they had in fact become. Indeed, the answers to big questions are sometimes hidden in small details. And so it is in the present case, even if it is not always easy for the reader to sustain this conviction throughout the report's three thousand pages.

Yet an historical reconstruction cannot be confined to the simple addition of facts that have been passed through the fine-toothed comb of criticism; it must be developed according to an argument and questions that are posed at the outset of research. A dose of positivism can of course be healthy but it does not in itself constitute a research agenda. Although the NIOD inquiry invalidates the received idea according to which sources are lacking for the study of the very recent past, the framework of interpretation remains a larger challenge. Thus, a large part of the report is devoted to analyzing the Dutch debate over sending troops, including an analysis of the media and a thorough study of the policy debates that took place in Parliament and the public stances adopted by the various political parties, whether in Government or the opposition. It would seem a legitimate topic since what is at stake is the analytical framework by means of which domestic politics is to be decrypted. Yet the very large number of pages devoted to this issue add very little apart from confirming that there seems to have been a national consensus in which each and all seemed to support the same general cause.

The report is more innovative in its analysis of the operation of European policy. The perverse effects of the mechanism of the rotating presidency are portrayed in damning detail. The aim of preserving and even reinforcing national prestige during a presidency leads to a *"union sacrée"* type reflex, temporarily sidelining the normal course of democratic governance. The diplomatic jousting with which the leaders of European governments tried to score points at the national level without a longer-term global vision did not yield convincing results in the area of common agricultural policy. With the first real explosion of violence in Europe since 1945, this same attitude led to a dramatic and unpardonable failure. The report convinces the reader that the analytical models of policy-making traditionally used by historians are no longer up to date. Clearly, the management of the Bosnian crisis by The Hague was not a matter of a partisan national debate opposing, for example, socialists and Christian-democrats, nor a classic issue in international relations, where notions of geopolitical, military, and economic interest take priority. Rather, the militaro-humanitarian policy that was adopted appears to have been a very indirect strategy in pursuit of a dual objective: to position the Netherlands in the concert of European nations and to manage the emotions of the national public. The image presented of the actual European decision-making process is worrisome due to the structural incapacity and democratic deficit it reveals. The example of the pathetic trajectory of a diplomatic telegram would surely transform the biggest Eurosceptic into a tireless partisan of a coherent and effective European Constitution. Given that analyses based on a strictly national perspective no longer suffice to understand the processes driving national developments, historians need new paradigms. While the NIOD report does not offer coherent interpretive models for dealing with this new historical reality, it at least has the merit of offering a diagnosis.

The principal conclusion of the report's international section amounts to an acknowledgement of structural failure in the manner in which Europe is governed. It is a failure magnified by transatlantic misunderstanding and the chronic paralysis of the United Nations. It thus seems that the most urgent lessons to be drawn from the report are to be found at this level. This may seem surprising given that the inquiry was requested by the Dutch Government and the public's expectations specifically concerned the question of Dutch responsibility. At a general level, the report underscores the fact that a small country—part of a larger but dysfunctional European framework—cannot practice geopolitics with impunity. The Dutch Government lacked both the information required for getting involved in this adventure and the military resources necessary for satisfying the responsibilities it had itself requested. In a more general way, it seems that decision-makers lacked the experience necessary to evaluate risks in a realistic fashion. According to the report, Dutch voluntarism was also the product of a certain tradition of self-sufficiency. This was coupled with the missionary spirit characteristic of its foreign policy and a genuine ignorance of the regional context. The lofty conception of the innocence and superiority of this little country in the concert of great powers, with its tradition of tolerance and neutrality, was also a form of blindness concerning its real capacities to intervene in a conflict beyond its frontiers.

A question that the report does not raise but which, it seems, cannot be overlooked concerns the lack of military experience that prevented Dutch troops from meeting their responsibilities. The detailed description of the Dutch soldiers' behavior during the fateful days of July 1995 powerfully raises the question of whether French or British troops, with their experience and code of honor, would have reacted with as little bravery as their Dutch colleagues. The paragraphs devoted to the *Dutchbat* troops are doubtless the report's most disappointing. The Dutch soldiers effectively found themselves in a desperate, painful, and humiliating position that makes it easy to blame them a posteriori and assign them full responsibility for what took place. While the report in no way plays down the action—or rather the inaction—of the Dutch blue helmets, it systematically takes care to avoid drawing conclusions regarding their intellectual and moral qualities. Locating responsibility for what occurred at high levels—specifically, in the malfunction of international and governmental cooperation—the report displays a certain populist solidarity with "our boys" ("*onze jongens*"). Betrayed by the politicians who had irresponsibly gotten them into this trap and left to their own devices in the Bosnian jungle, the soldiers of *Dutchbat* are presented as traumatized by their own impotence.

However, the description of their contacts with the warring parties, the local population, and among themselves reveals their attitude in a crisis situation to have been far from glorious. Of course, a soldier is not a professional hero. Yet the absence of any spirit of resistance or feeling of combative indignation is appalling. It is understandable that an official report hesitates to use the term *cowardice* but avoiding any explicit criticism of the soldiers' behavior verges on complicity. The very long discussion concerning the three meetings that took place between *Dutchbat* commander Thomas Karremans and General Ratko Mladić (pp. 2620–2643) and, more particularly, Karremans's famous toast (he is said to have only drunk water, as if the content of his glass diminished responsibility for the gesture) might be hilarious if the massacre of eight thousand people were not at stake. The passages concerning racist incidents within the *Dutchbat* are handled in an extremely gingerly way. The passages concerning prostitution and the black market are brushed aside in the footnotes.[15] Yet, in the context of an analysis of the hostility that the Dutch soldiers provoked among the population they were supposed to protect—a key element in understanding the events—these would seem to be entirely appropriate matters for discussion. At no moment were the Dutch troops the incarnation of the values that their country considers fundamental to its identity; the result was the death of those who had put their trust in them. Responsibility for the events was also individual, something the report does not admit.

The "Polder-Model"?

The very mild description of the behavior of *Dutchbat* soldiers seems understandable at both a human and a political level. The absence of temporal and social distance between participants and historians has also been detrimental to other efforts at *Zeitgeschichte*, whether in the case of the euphemistic description made by Jean Norton-Cru of the experiences of First World War veterans or a certain type of historiography, sometimes excessively marked by emotion, that is based on the testimony of concentration camp survivors. It seems almost inevitable that cultural and emotional identification would be stronger in interviews with Dutch soldiers than was the case in interviews with their counterparts and certain survivors in Bosnia and elsewhere, a distance only aggravated by the mediation of interpreters in the latter case. Yet this imbalance should have been taken into account when the report was written. That it was not is a choice or omission that has major consequences for the assessment of all three thousand pages.

This returns us to the question with which we began concerning the nature of the postulate of a buffer zone between observation and object of study: is this uniquely inspired by the practical circumstances that have rendered the sources inaccessible until now? Can this distance be abolished as soon as these archives suddenly become accessible or is it rather a matter of intellectual necessity? The NIOD team benefited from an exceptional effort at transparency on the part of the Dutch Government. If the Netherlands in some ways seems a model or "exemplary country," it is doubtless more so for its archival than for its military policies. This transparency nevertheless exclusively applied to members of the team, hand-picked and accredited with the Dutch equivalent of "top secret" access. The documents were collected under special guard on a floor of the NIOD's sumptuous building, the renovated former headquarters of a colonial bank looking over one of the most prestigious canals in Amsterdam.

As a result, the NIOD report is not a contribution to an ongoing debate open to contradiction but rather an end point in itself, the final, closed off step of an autistic process. It is many years before any Dutch, Bosnian, or Egyptian historian, sociologist, or simple citizen interested in the Srebrenica tragedy will be able to obtain access to the same sources. Moreover, these are often cited in cryptic fashion as "confidential sources" (note 14) or "confidential interview" (note 85). This deprives the report of its properly scientific character since, according to Popper's definition, an analysis can only be considered scientific on condition that it can be verified, contradicted, and possibly refuted. A critical reading of the report of the type offered in this necessarily impressionistic chapter is a very imperfect form of peer review. More fundamentally, the NIOD report closes off democratic debate in the same way.

Of course, exclusive access was a conditio sine qua non of the research. The openness shown by the Dutch Government was remarkable in its own right and one cannot expect any organization to open its most recent archives concerning a traumatic failure to the public without further precaution. Such a policy of transparency would be simply inconceivable on the part of the French Government or the UN, for example. For the NIOD team, the choice thus amounted to either accepting these conditions or renouncing the research, leaving the question of Dutch responsibility in the

Srebrenica massacre to slumber in the boxes and cartons of the archives for several more decades.

The decision to accept the investigative mandate required some courage and this must be given its due. Despite the various criticisms made of the NIOD's interpretation, the report made significant contributions to reconstructing the events. It is nevertheless my view that what I have earlier described as the NIOD's "house style" only magnified the perverse effects of this intrinsically problematic situation. Ever since Louis de Jong got down to writing his *The Kingdom of the Netherlands during the Second World War*, it seems that teamwork in the NIOD implies a sort of binding and unanimous democratic centralism, a "one for all and all for one" in which the individual steps aside in favor of the collective and vice-versa. From the moment that one refuses difference of opinion in historiographical production, teamwork and the individual work of writing are constantly confused. In the case of De Jong, the NIOD's collective work disappeared behind his personal signature; in the case of the Srebrenica report, it is the individual signatures of the report's authors that disappear behind a work for which the authors take collective responsibility.

Why should a research report present unequivocal conclusions and interpretations, each fitting into the next like Russian dolls, from the smallest paragraphs up to the final epilogue? Why this irresistible striving for consensus in which the least difference of opinion must be ironed out over the course of interminable internal meetings? The NIOD's "house style" is part of a more general model in the Netherlands, the "polder-model" ("*Poldermodel*"), which is based on a culture of negotiated consensus that has historically marked relations between, variously, Catholics, Calvinists and other Protestants, trade-unions and employers or political parties participating in a governing coalition. The polder-model reposes on a society that is heavily segmented at its base but heavily integrated at the level of its elites. The culture of consensus also implies a discomfort with disagreement, a chronic incapacity to manage dissension. This tradition contributes, for example, to the fact that, to my knowledge, the Netherlands is the only country where one finds the strange practice of submitting critical reviews to the authors under review before publication.[16]

There were nonetheless abundant references in the press to conflicts and disagreements of interpretation within the research team, mainly concerning the question of local responsibilities. In a revealing way, these disagreements were tied to episodes in the private lives of certain members of the team—such as romantic idylls with a *Dutchbat* officer or Serb nationals—as if disagreement were in some way an accident, an anomaly. Yet the idea that disagreements existed within the team is actually rather reassuring, showing that it was composed of researchers capable of thinking autonomously and that, within the group, relations were not placed under an authority that would have rendered such differences of approach unacceptable. So why was this situation, a natural one in a pluralist democracy and in the exercise of scientific criticism, in no way reflected in the report? Even the ICTY often accompanies its publications and judgments with dissenting opinions. Given that the report was conceived to supply an object for parliamentary debate, would not the Dutch Parliament and Dutch public opinion have been better served by a contradictory report in which several authors presented divergent analyses, judging the reader sufficiently adult to form his own opinions? But, above all, would not the fundamental problem that those outside of the team were unable to challenge the analyses or verify the sources have been reduced if internal disagreements had been reflected in the report? This irresistible propensity for consensus appears all the more ironic given the report's insistence on the consensual fashion in which all segments of Dutch political life thoughtlessly pleaded for Dutch troops to be sent. In doing so, no room was left for the debate or objections that might have protected the Government against its own voluntarism and naivety. Is the remedy for this collective and consensual failure to be found in an equally collective and consensual mea culpa, a homogenous verdict pronounced by a team of researchers upon which the prime minister based his conclusions without any other form of discussion? The report thus did not serve the purpose of supplying the debate with critical information but rather served to close it. The NIOD was thus indeed responding to the expectations of the Dutch Government, allowing it, by means of a report and a resignation, to once and for all turn the black page of Srebrenica.

Translated from French by Ethan Rundell

Notes

1. This chapter is drawn from an article first published in Dutch in 2003: "Het Srebrenica-rapport en de geshiedenis van het heden" [The Srebrenica-Report and the History of Present Time], *Bijdragen en Mededelingen betreffende de Geshiedenis der Nederlanden* 118, no. 1–3 (2003): 325–336 (accessible through the online archive of the Koninklijk Nederlands Historisch Genootschap at http://www.knhg.nl/). This article has been completely modified after a critical exchange with Isabelle Delpla and careful rereading on the part of Xavier Bougarel and Jean-Louis Fournel.
2. If there is only one conclusion for the Dutch government to draw from this report, it is that it is important for the Commission's report to be accessible in Bosnia in order to allow research on this war to be pursued by local historians. The experience acquired

and the sources accumulated have to be shared by means of exchange agreements and financial and logistical support in order for independent research to develop in Bosnia itself. Since no community is able to adopt a critical relationship toward its own history as long as it is written abroad—in The Hague or Amsterdam, what is more—it seems logical that a part of the considerable resources put at the disposition of the NIOD team by the Dutch government should be supplied to Bosnian research teams, with the necessary scientific guarantees. It falls under NIOD's responsibility to see to it that its research is followed up in this manner. Unfortunately, several years after the fracas caused by the report's publication on the Dutch political scene, no ambitious outreach project toward Bosnian society has materialized. Given the considerable investment that the publication of the report and all its annexes in Dutch as well as the translation of an English online version represent, it is incomprehensible that the Serbo-Croatian version, partly completed, is not yet available in either paper or electronic form (telephone conversation between the NIOD's director of public relations and the author, 30 November 2006). Such a choice seems particularly revealing of the priorities and objectives that the Dutch government and the NIOD pursued with the publication of the report.

3. Nederlands Instituut voor Oorlogsdocumentatie (NIOD), *Srebrenica, een "veillig" gebied. Reconstructie, achtergronden, gevolgen en analyses van de val van een Safe Area* [Srebrenica, a "Safe" Area: Reconstruction, Background, Consequences and Analyses of the Fall of a Safe Area], 3 vols. (Amsterdam, 2002), 3,392 pages; Directors: H. Blom and P. Romijn; Researchers: N. Bajalica, G. Duizings, T. Frankfort, B. de Graaff, A. Kersten, P. Koedijk, D. Schoonoord, R. van Uwe, C. Wiebes; Assistants: M. van Kessel, E. Meents, J. Vermolen; Editor: P. Bootsma; Appendix: G. Bootsma, *Het officiele NIOD-rapport samengevat* [Summary of the Official NIOD Report] (Amsterdam, 2002), 414 pages; G. Duijzings, *Geschiedenis en herrinering in Ost-Bosnië. De achtergronden van de val van Srebrenica* [History and Remembrance. The Background of the Fall of Srebrenica] (Amsterdam, 2002), 209 pages; B. Naarden, *Beeld en Balkan. Waarneming en werkelijkheid van Zuidoost-Europa* [Image and the Balkans: Observation and Reality of Southeast Europe] (Amsterdam, 2002), 121 pages; D. Schoonoord, *Dutchbat III en de bevolking: medische aangelegenheden. Bevoorrading door de lucht* [The *Dutchbat* III and the Population: Medical Affairs. Air Supply] (Amsterdam, 2002), 239 pages; C. Wiebes, *Intelligentie en de oorlog in Bosnie, 1992–1995. De rol van de inlichtingen- en veiligheidsdiensten* [Intelligence and War in Bosnia, 1992–1995: The Role of the Intelligence and Security Services] (Amsterdam, 2002), 209 pages. The full text is accompanied by a CD containing eight Word documents of around 1,800 pages in total, including debriefing reports, additional media analyses, an annotated bibliography, detailed chronologies, an analysis of the use of chemical weapons, and an analysis of the operation of the Ministry of Foreign Affairs. The full report and its detailed table of contents are available in Dutch and English translation on the NIOD website at http://www.srebrenica.nl.
4. http://www.knaw.nl/organisatie/pdf/Rapport_Evaluatiecommissie_NIOD_2003.pdf
5. http://www.mindef.nl/actueel/parlement/kamerbrieven/2001/4/181201_begroting.aspx, accessed in 2004 and since withdrawn from consultation.
6. Louis de Jong, *Het Koninkrijk de Tweede Wereldoorlog*, 14 vols. (The Hague, 1969–1991).
7. See Jacobus A. van Doorn, *Belast Verleden. Over de historisering van de publicke moraal* [The Bill of the Past: About the Historicization of Public Morality] (The Hague, 2000).
8. See Pieter Lagrou, review of Martin Bossenbroek, *De Meelstreep. Terugkeer en Opvang na de Tweede Wereldoorlog* (Amsterdam, 2001) in *Nieuwste Tijd. Kwartaalschrift voor eigentijdse geschiedenis* 2, no. 5 (December 2002), 72–78.

9. I would like to thank Dick van Galen Last for the press clippings that he kindly sent me on a regular basis.
10. See Pieter Lagrou, "L'histoire du temps présent en Europe depuis 1945, ou comment se constitue et se développe un nouveau champ disciplinaire," *La Revue pour l'histoire du CNRS*, no. 9 (2003), 4–15; Pieter Lagrou, "De l'actualité de l'histoire du temps présent," *Bulletin de l'Institut d'histoire du temps présent*, no. 75 (June 2000), 10–22.
11. NIOD, *Srebrenica, een "veillig" gebied*, vol. 3, 2471–2530.
12. Florent Brayard, *La "Solution finale de la question juive." La technique, le temps et les catégories de la décision* (Paris, 2004); Christopher Browning, *Ordinary Men: Reserve Police Battalion 101 and the Final Solution in Poland* (New York, 1992); Christian Gerlach, *Kalkulierte Morde. Die Deutsche Wirtschafts- und Vernichtungspolitik in Weissrussland, 1941 bis 1944* (Hamburg, 1999); Dieter Pohl, *Nationalsozialistische Judenverfolgung in Ostgalizien 1941–1944: Organisation und Durchführung eines staatlichen Massenverbrechens* (Munich, 1996).
13. I would like to thank Isabelle Delpla here for having suggested this remark.
14. Peter Maguire, *Law and War: An American History* (New York, 2001).
15. The report distinguishes between "frequent misconduct (traffic of drugs and arms, prostitution, black market and contraband)," which passes without particular comment, and misconduct motivated by a particular aversion for the Bosniak population (p. 1550, see also p. 1572). The report is much more explicit concerning the "misconduct" of the *Dutchbat*'s Canadian predecessors and suggests that the Bosniak soldiers commanded by Naser Orić became the principal clients of the enclave's prostitutes only after the arrival of the Dutch troops.
16. Chris Lorenz, "Het 'Academisch Poldermodel' en de 'Westforschung' in Nederland" [The "Academic Polder-Model" and the "West Research" in the Netherlands], *Tijdschrift voor Geschiedenis* 118, no. 2 (2005), 252–270.

Chapter 6

REOPENING THE WOUNDS?
The Parliament of Bosnia-Herzegovina and the Question of Bosniak Responsibility

Xavier Bougarel

"We are not all equally guilty for Srebrenica and that needs to disappear from the agenda, we cannot all be equally guilty and we cannot all decide this question. But we need to ask what are perhaps not really the most attractive questions about what we did on our side."[1]

—Ekrem Ajanović, 1 August 1996

The July 1995 Srebrenica massacre is unanimously seen by Bosniaks as one of the major symbols of the genocide they experienced during the recent conflict and of the passive—indeed, complicit—attitude of the international community while it was underway. Moreover, the majority of works published in the Federation[2] concerning the events in Srebrenica consist either of survivors' testimony or of translations of journalistic inquiries and official reports published abroad that focus on condemning Serb crimes and the passivity of the United Nations. Yet at the same time, the question of possible Bosniak responsibility in the fall of Srebrenica remains the object of heated polemic, mainly concerning the tactical errors that may have been committed by Bosniak military and political leaders and the hypothetical abandonment of the enclave as part of a larger territorial swap. As I will attempt to show in the final part of this chapter, this polemic is indirectly related to larger questions concerning the war aims of Bosniak leaders.

On 1 August 1996, this question was also the subject of debate in the Parliament of the Republic of Bosnia-Herzegovina.[3] It is on this parliamentary debate that I would like to concentrate, starting with a recon-

---

Notes for this chapter begin on page 122.

struction of the dynamics that lead it to be held and moving on from there to consider its participants and content. The aim of this chapter is thus in no way to determine the degree of Bosniak responsibility for the fall of the enclave—a responsibility that, in any case, does not in the least diminish the blame of those who ordered and carried out the massacre. Rather, the chapter seeks to show how rumors and taboos, street demonstrations and backroom maneuvers, personal attacks and official investigations all contributed to shaping what has since become a persistent doubt.

This haunting doubt matters not only for what it will one day perhaps teach us about certain aspects of the events of Srebrenica. Indeed, the manner in which the question of Bosniak responsibility is debated (or not) within the Bosniak community also reveals certain ways in which power is exercised and public space structured there. Even if it ultimately proves to be based solely on unfounded rumors, the debate over possible Bosniak responsibility in the fall of Srebrenica will thus continue to reflect certain essential realities of post-war Bosnia-Herzegovina and deserves in this respect to be taken seriously.

The Demand for Truth versus the Need for Unity: The Origins of a Debate

Questions concerning possible Bosniak responsibility for the fall of Srebrenica and Žepa first arose in the summer of 1995. Indeed, on 13 July of that year, Bećir Heljić, a representative of the Žepa enclave in Sarajevo, stated that "Žepa, Srebrenica and Goražde are bargaining chips for the world but also for our official policy."[4] Heljić's remarks provoked immediate protests from the ruling Party of Democratic Action (SDA). Some days later, Naser Orić, the commander of the Srebrenica enclave who had been recalled to central Bosnia in March 1995, told *Ratna tribina* ("War Tribune"), a newspaper with ties to the populations of eastern Bosnia:[5] "I did not betray Srebrenica, even if many have tried to present me that way. Rather than helping me find weapons and transport them there, they looked in advance for accusations and culprits. I will go before my soldiers when we link up [6] and will tell them what has happened here. I will tell them the truth. Let them then say whether I or someone else is guilty."[7] These remarks reflect a widespread feeling of abandonment among the combatants of the 28th division who succeeded in reaching the "free territories." Just after arriving in Tuzla, some of them forced their way into the building housing the 2nd Corps' headquarters to ask for an explanation. At a late July meeting organized to calm tensions between the representatives of the enclaves, the officers of the 2nd Corps and the authorities of the Tuzla Canton, the former chief of police for the Srebrenica enclave, Hakija Meholjić, requested that an investigative commission be created to look into the responsibility of the UN and the Sarajevo authorities. President Alija Izetbegović, who attended the meeting, opposed this request.[8]

The representatives of the enclaves were not the only ones to raise the question of possible Bosniak responsibility. On 13 July, Nijaz Duraković, the president of the Social Democratic Party (SDP, ex-communist) and sole Bosniak member of the Bosnian collegial Presidency not belonging to the SDA,[9] wondered "why, despite an extremely difficult context, Srebrenica's defense has not been better prepared, why have some actions not been better planned and organized in advance." Duraković expressed his hope that, "when this strong wave of emotion has calmed, these questions will be put on the agenda. The question of responsibility for certain obvious failures has for far too long been passed over in silence."[10] A week later, the SDP stated that it was "unacceptable that the Presidency, as a [collective] organ, has yet to express itself concerning Srebrenica."[11] Though the leaders of the opposition reached an agreement to ask "that the causes of the insufficient efficiency of state, military and political structures in preventing the Srebrenica tragedy be seriously examined and that responsibility be concretely established, where appropriate,"[12] they remained cautious in their interpretation of events. Reacting to Bećir Heljić's statements, they described them as "a logical consequence of a large number of probably unfounded stories concerning a supposed betrayal [by Sarajevo authorities],"[13] and emphasized that "we must not kick the ball of responsibility back to the [Bosnian] authorities."[14]

The ruling SDA for its part sought to soften the political impact of the enclaves' fall. Meeting on 11 July to ratify a number of constitutional amendments, the SDA's parliamentary group was not informed of Srebrenica's fall[15] and, on 4 August, this question was not even included on the agenda of the parliamentary session. When addressing public opinion, SDA leaders strove to minimize the magnitude of the catastrophe, speaking of "the provisional occupation [of Srebrenica]"[16] and asserting that "a large part of the men have succeeded in getting themselves out of this region."[17] Above all, they considered that the questions of enclave representatives and opposition parties threatened the unity of the Bosniak nation, categorically rejected the hypothesis of an implicit territorial swap of eastern Bosnian enclaves for Serb-held Sarajevo neighborhoods and postponed considering the question of possible Bosniak responsibility until war's end. Yet these opinions were not shared by Prime Minister Haris Silajdžić who, finding himself increasingly in disagreement with the leaders of his own party, announced his resignation on 5 August and conspicuously left for Tuzla to meet with representatives of the opposition and refugees from the enclaves. Questioned about the fall of Srebrenica, he responded "I expected this case to be examined during the last parliamentary session. ... The Government does not set Parliament's agenda. I agree with you in saying that, after everything that happened in Srebrenica, things could not remain as they were."[18] In the weeks following the fall of Srebrenica, the emerging debate over the issue of Bosniak responsibility thus took place less in the framework of legal institutions than within the ruling party. Addressing the SDA parliamentary group on 3 August 1995, Haris Silajdžić asked for the resignation of Rasim Delić, chief of the army's general staff and criticized Alija Izetbegović for having "made the task easier for the Serbs in doing what they had intended to do all along" by announcing in the spring plans to break the siege of Sarajevo—a tragic consequence, in his view, of the existence of parallel power networks controlled by Izetbegović and his entourage.[19] SDA officials, on the contrary, tended to put responsibility for Srebrenica's fall on the shoulders, not just of the UN and the great powers, but also of the enclave's political and military leaders. Responding to Silajdžić, Delić thus claimed that Srebrenica "did not fall militarily, but politically, which is to say, psychologically" and accused the leaders of the enclave of not having followed the instructions they had received from Sarajevo.[20] Izetbegović, for his part, considered that "it is not right to use a minor army crisis to launch an attack against the army." For the first time, however, he mentioned the possibility of a parliamentary investigative commission for "if [the enclave] could have defended itself then someone is guilty for the death of several thousand people."[21] Addressing SDA leaders who had come together for a special session two days later, he denounced the "disgraceful behavior of some of our own people, cowards who gave in and began to negotiate with the enemy before deciding to flee, convincing the population that it should also flee."[22]

Beginning in the summer of 1995, the major protagonists of the debate over the question of Bosniak responsibility—representatives of the enclaves, opposition parties, the ruling SDA, and Haris Silajdžić, who was in conflict with his own party—were thus in position. Similarly, the principal points of contention in this debate were already apparent. In its 31 July issue, for example, *Ratna tribina* reproached Sarajevo authorities for the inadequate quantity of weapons that were delivered to the eastern Bosnian enclaves, the recall of Naser Orić and several other officers in central Bosnia four months before the Serb offensive and the absence of any large-scale military initiative to come to the aid of the column that had departed for the "free territories."[23] The paper then portrayed the tensions that had always set eastern Bosnian military units against their own hierarchy as part of a "global plan for abandoning the Drina Valley"[24] and wondered whether "the population and the army needed to be sacrificed in addition to the territory."[25] *Ratna tribina* thus refused to attribute responsibility for the fall of Srebrenica to the people of the enclave, holding instead that "the generals are guilty" and that "Naser Orić is sacrificed in order to save the generals' stripes."[26] In the months that followed, however, Silajdžić's withdrawal of his threat to resign, the discretion shown by the opposition parties, the dispersion of the combatants from the 28th division among different units, the installation of the refugees in housing sites located far away from large urban centers and—last but not least—the NATO air strikes and the victories of the Army of the Republic of Bosnia-Herzegovina (ARBiH) in western Bosnia forced the Srebrenica catastrophe into the background of current events. It would only be with the end of hostilities that the question of Bosniak responsibility was to resurface at the heart of Bosnian political life.

The Search for the Missing, the Women's Movement, and the SDA's Internal Crisis

By attributing the Drina valley to the Republika Srpska and the Serb-held Sarajevo neighborhoods to the Federation, the peace agreements signed at Dayton on 14 December 1995, inevitably reignited rumors of a territorial swap to the detriment of eastern Bosnian enclaves. At the same time, the organization of prisoner exchanges under the protection of the International Committee of the Red Cross (ICRC) once again raised the question of the fate of the thousands of men who had been missing since the fall of Srebrenica and Žepa. Finally, and more generally, the end of hostilities, the demobilization of combatants, the rise of independent media, and the announcement of general elections in September 1996 favored the expression of what had until then been underlying social and political tensions.

It thus stands to reason that the end of the war coincided with the first demonstrations organized by survivors of the eastern Bosnian enclaves. Indeed, on 29 January 1996, the *Aktiv žena*[27] of Srebrenica organized a rally of two thousand people—mostly women—in front of the ICRC headquarters in Tuzla in order to obtain information about the fate of the missing. Infuriated by the silence of this organization, some protesters vandalized the premises. In the days that followed, events took a turn for the worse for those in power as other themes emerged alongside the fate of the missing. On one hand, the leaders of the Srebrenica municipality and Tuzla Canton were accused of having diverted the funds raised during the summer of 1995. On the other hand, rumors resurfaced that the enclave had been abandoned and, while some protesters demanded that Izetbegović meet with them in Tuzla, others declared their intention to vote for Silajdžić, who had just left his position as prime minister and had definitively broken with the SDA. Finally, on 2 February, after the Tuzla canton leaders refused to meet with the protesters, the situation once again worsened, with the windows of the cantonal government's headquarters being destroyed with stones.

These protests, which marked the birth of the Srebrenica women's movement, put the authorities of Sarajevo in a delicate position. On 10 February, Izetbegović thus travelled to Tuzla accompanied by Naser Orić and the governor of Tuzla canton, Izet Hadžić, where they met with between two thousand and three thousand Srebrenica refugees in the town's main gymnasium. In his introductory speech, Izetbegović declared that "for thousands of people, there is no hope they are alive; for a few dozen or a few hundred people, there is still hope." Izetbegović asked his listeners to reject all attempts to "politicize" their demands and announced the creation of a five-member committee—including two representatives from Srebrenica[28]—responsible for supervising all activities linked to the search for the missing and aid to refugees. During the discussion that followed, Izetbegović was sharply criticized by certain speakers, who asked him among other things: "Was Srebrenica sold and, if so, why were ten thousand people sacrificed?" "Will someone in the Government, in the Presidency or in other bodies, some day be held accountable?" "Are you guilty, too?" Izetbegović responded that "it is difficult to give the right answer to nine out of ten of your questions, as there simply is no answer." He then added, "we defended Srebrenica as well as we could," and sought to justify the decision to sign the Dayton agreements.[29]

Izetbegović's visit to Tuzla, together with the announcement of concrete measures in favor of Srebrenica refugees, allowed an end to be put to the demonstrations. But the question of Bosniak responsibility immediately came up again in Parliament, which was thus led to debate the events of the summer of 1995 for the first time. Indeed, on 12 February 1996, Amor Mašović, president of the Commission for prisoner exchanges, presented Parliament with a report concerning the activities conducted by the institution he directed in the framework of the search for those missing from Srebrenica and Žepa. On this occasion, Mujo Kafedžić, a deputy of the Bosniak Muslim Organization (MBO[30]), noted that his party had as early as August 1995 demanded that Parliament examine the circumstances of the enclaves' fall and asserted that "the attempts of some circles to pass over in silence the responsibility of certain local bodies are obvious." SDA deputies countered by announcing that a "neutral" analysis of events was being prepared that would demonstrate that "the concept of safe areas was a death sentence for these territories" and also submitted a ten-point resolution to Parliament concerning Srebrenica.³¹ This resolution, reworked and adopted the following day in committee, provided among other things that:

> 2. The Commission [for prisoner exchanges, renamed the Commission for the search for missing persons] ... will present at the next meetings of Parliament, except in the case that Parliament decides otherwise, a report on what it achieved between the two sessions; ... 4. The services in charge of the study of war crimes will devote their attention to the circumstances of the Srebrenica tragedy in order to identify the war criminals who ordered and carried out the crimes ... ; 5. The Parliament of the RBiH commissions the Government and its relevant agencies to carry out a full report on the problem of missing persons, prisoners and displaced persons, including a report on the part of the armed forces of the Republic of Bosnia-Herzegovina regarding the military circumstances of the fall of Srebrenica; 6. The Parliament of the RBiH will ask the relevant Government agencies for a detailed report on the attitude of the international factor [represented by] UNPROFOR, on the responsibility within the United Nations and NATO, on the International Committee of the Red Cross and the UNHCR before, during and after the Srebrenica tragedy.³²

Over the following months, the debate over possible Bosniak responsibility for Srebrenica's fall once again seemed to subside. In fact, however, multiple factors contributed to bringing about a change in the protagonists involved and the form of the debate. On the one hand, following the transfer of Serb-held Sarajevo neighborhoods to the Federation, the SDA encouraged refugees from eastern Bosnia to come and settle there, once again reigniting rumors of a territorial swap and sparking heated tensions between SDA leaders and local political leaders who supported return. On the other hand, the liberation of Žepa men detained in Serbia since July 1995 fed other rumors according to which thousands of men from Srebrenica had been secretly detained in several mines in Serbia. It was in this troubled context that Ibran Mustafić made his appearance. Elected as a SDA deputy from Srebrenica in 1990, Mustafić had clashed with the leaders of the enclave during the war and was liberated from the Batković camp in the Republika Srpska on 21 April 1996.

Ibran Mustafić's return to the Bosnian political scene lent an even more polemical tone to the debate over possible Bosniak responsibility. At a new parliamentary session on 27 May 1996, Mustafić denounced in the same breath the international community, the Sarajevo authorities, and the enclave's leaders. The following day, he demanded that a commission be created to investigate the fate of the missing and that a fund be set up to centralize aid for Srebrenica refugees, in keeping with the resolution adopted in February. He strongly suggested, what's more, that he was the best candidate for managing these two organizations. The debate was then interrupted by Dževad Mlačo, president of the SDA parliamentary group, who announced that these questions would be dealt with at an upcoming meeting between his group and the representatives of Srebrenica. In doing so, he tried to marginalize Mustafić and once again circumvent legal institutions.

Thwarted in his attempt to reoccupy the position of legitimate representative of the Srebrenica population, Ibran Mustafić joined the Party for Bosnia-Herzegovina (SBiH), which had been created shortly before by Silajdžić.[33] On 14 July 1996, he gave an explosive interview to the weekly newspaper *Slobodna Bosna* ("Free Bosnia"). There, Mustafić claimed that "the Srebrenica enclave ... has been deliberately sacrificed" and that "the Presidency of Bosnia-Herzegovina and the army's general staff have been directly involved in these plots." He then alternated between relatively precise accusations against the Sarajevo authorities and the enclave leaders—described as a "group of mafioso" who created a regime of terror—with more general considerations concerning the failure to demilitarize the "safe area" and extravagant claims that enclave leaders had safely crossed Serb lines and left propaganda tracts behind them inciting the rest of the column to surrender.[34] Yet whatever credit one gives to Mustafić's comments, their importance is elsewhere: for the first time, a political leader originating from Srebrenica had publicly accused the highest reaches of the state of treason.

Introspection or Diversion?
The Parliamentary Debate of 1 August 1996

To understand the impact of Ibran Mustafić's accusations, one must place them within a larger context. On the one hand, the intensification of the electoral campaign and the appearance of the SBiH as the direct rival of the SDA exacerbated the political divides within the Bosniak community. On the other hand, the approach of the first anniversary of the Srebrenica massacre, the exhumation of the first mass graves and the in absentia indictment of Radovan Karadžić and Ratko Mladić by the International Criminal Tribunal for the Former Yugoslavia (ICTY) contributed to returning the events of July 1995—and with them, albeit indirectly, the question of possible Bosniak responsibility—to the center of media attention.

The commemorations of the massacre thus took place in a fairly tense context. On 11 July, several prominent Bosnian and foreign figures attended the first commemorative ceremony to be held in Tuzla while Izetbegović prudently remained in Sarajevo. In a speech broadcast on television, he denounced "the indifference and the hypocrisy of the powerful who could have prevented the catastrophe but continually found reasons not to do so." In response to the question "Who is guilty?" he answered that "the guiltiest are in any case the assassins and those who gave the orders, but we are all guilty, all of us who survived" for "when something happens as terrible as Srebrenica, there are no innocents."[35] At another ceremony organized by the cantonal authorities in Tuzla the following day, the governor, Izet Hadžić, and the mayor of Srebrenica, Fahrudin Salihović, were booed by a portion of the audience despite the interventions of Naser Orić and Ejup Ganić, vice president of the collegial Presidency,[36] who called upon Bosniaks to not let themselves be divided into "political enclaves"[37] and who presented the vote for the SDA as "the means for returning to Srebrenica."[38] Heated controversy then broke out between the SDA and the opposition: the weekly newspaper *Ljiljan* ("The Lily"), closely aligned with the SDA, accused the Tuzla municipality of having orchestrated the incidents of 12 July[39] and the opposition retorted that "the party in power is instrumentalizing the Srebrenica exodus"[40] and that "those who made the Srebrenica population leave can hardly do anything to get them to return."[41]

With six weeks left before the first post-war elections, the parliamentary debate of 1 August 1996, came to seem like a hasty attempt to defuse the question of possible Bosniak responsibility for the fall of Srebrenica. Moreover, this debate was organized in the absence of Ibran Mustafić, who was participating in electoral meetings in Germany, Naser Orić was not invited to participate and Šemsudin Muminović, the officer who commanded the operations to link up with the column[42] and who was initially supposed to present a report on this aspect of the events of July 1995, was in the end asked to remain silent.[43] This debate therefore unfolded in the absence of the elected representatives of Srebrenica and of some of the event's key protagonists.[44] In addition, it must be noted that the most important Bosniak politicians did not participate in the debate: Izetbegović and Silajdžić were absent from the benches of the Parliament and the leaders of the opposition remained silent.[45] Introductory remarks were thus made by the chief of the army's general staff, Rasim Delić, Vice Minister of Foreign Affairs[46] Hasan Dervišbegović and Prime Minister Hasan Muratović, formerly minister in charge of relations with the UNPROFOR. The debate, for its part, saw certain prominent members of the SDA (Dževad Mlačo, Avdo Čampara, Irfan Ajanović, Safet Isović) face off against former SDA deputies who had joined the SBiH (Ekrem Ajanović, Muharem Cero, Smail Ibrahimpašić), two social-democratic deputies originating from the Tuzla region (Mustafa Šehović, Igor Rajner),[47] and some representatives of eastern Bosnian populations present in the Parliament.[48] Finally, the commission in charge of writing the final resolution to be voted on by the deputies was composed of representatives from the major parliamentary groups but included only one representative of the eastern Bosnian populations and no deputies from the SBiH.[49]

In his presentation of the military causes of Srebrenica's fall, Rasim Delić noted that there were objective difficulties in defending the enclave, and insisted on the fact that "the main cause of the fall of Srebrenica was the betrayal of the international community," which had "shamelessly wiped it off the map by abandoning it to the murderous hordes of Serbo-Montenegrin aggressors."[50] This line of argument is also to be found in the presentations of Hasan Dervišbegović and Hasan Muratović, who denounced "the policy of aggression, of ethnic cleansing and of genocide conducted against all of Bosnia-Herzegovina by the Belgrade regime and its [local] quislings,"[51] recounted the chronology of diplomatic activities related to the Srebrenica enclave from March 1993 to July 1995, justified the choice made by the Sarajevo authorities,[52] and accused Yasushi Akashi and General Bernard Janvier[53] of having "sold Srebrenica in exchange for the [blue helmets held hostage by the Serbs in June 1995], presumably with the consent of Mr. Ghali, supreme authority of the United Nations."[54] But, while Dervišbegović only mentioned in passing the fact that "for our conscience and as a lesson for the future, we should also try to evaluate what we ourselves did,"[55] Delić devoted the better part of his presentation to the question of possible Bosniak responsibility for the fall of the enclave and the magnitude of the massacre that followed it.

He immediately asserted that, in his view, the enclave had already fallen, militarily speaking, in March 1993—that is, before his nomination to the head of general staff. He also emphasized that, beginning in April 1994, significant quantities of weapons had been delivered to Srebrenica[56] and that enclave defense and evacuation plans had been developed in coordination with the local authorities, but that the rapid collapse of the enclave and the failure to comply with orders prevented the army from rescuing the column. Delić thus sought to lay the blame for any failure in defending Srebrenica or protecting its population on the enclave's leaders, citing many malfunctions that affected the enclave throughout the siege[57] and during the Serb offensive.[58] As for Naser Orić, Delić asserted that he had been recalled to central Bosnia at his request in order to discuss the internal problems of the enclave and had refused to return to Srebrenica after the helicopter that linked with the enclaves of eastern Bosnia was shot down on 7 May 1995. On this topic, he added: "When it comes to Naser Orić and some others, I will remind you that we are all, together with the media, very much at fault in thoughtlessly creating legends without taking account of the human weaknesses, and not just a few of them, that everyone has within themselves—including Naser Orić."[59] This was, ultimately, the only mistake that Rasim Delić seemed prepared to admit in this affair.

Afterward, the debate solidified around several points. In the first place, SDA deputies insisted on the "question of crime and genocide against the Bosniaks [of Srebrenica]"[60] whereas opposition deputies took a greater interest in the circumstances of the enclave's fall.[61] A second difference of opinion was superimposed on the first regarding the relation between international and local responsibility. In the course of the debate, the denunciation of the massacre and the demand that Serb criminals be judged by the ICTY only constituted a secondary issue as these two points were the object of unanimous agreement. Similarly, all those who intervened accused the international community of having abandoned the population of the enclave and even of being complicit in the massacre, demanding that the main UN leaders appear, either as witnesses or as defendants, before the "Hague international tribunal."[62] But while the SDA deputies drew on these consensual elements in an attempt to dismiss the question of Bosniak responsibility, representatives of the opposition and of eastern Bosnian populations insisted on the necessity of also examining this aspect of the fall of Srebrenica. Irfan Ajanović (SDA) thus rejected the "political speculations concerning the fall of Srebrenica, which are now in the service of the electoral campaign."[63] To this comment, Rajner retorted that "obviously, no one wants to assume any responsibility, and [that] that is the best way to avoid drawing any lessons from this tragedy."[64] A secondary area of contention then appeared on this basis concerning the respective failures of the army hierarchy and enclave authorities and this time pitted the deputies, whatever their political stripe, against the representatives of the populations of eastern Bosnia.[65]

Lastly, a final division appeared concerning the very status of the ongoing debate. For SDA deputies, this parliamentary session should have closed the parliamentary process that had opened six months earlier, putting an end to the controversies that had shaken the Bosniak community since the summer of 1995. They therefore urged the rapid adoption of a resolution designating the international community as "guilty for Srebrenica, for the fall of Srebrenica, for the genocide against the Bosniak enclave of Srebrenica and, in particular, against its civilian population."[66] They also balked at the idea of convening a new parliamentary session in the presence of Srebrenica's political and military leaders, preferring to confide the work of preparing a report on internal developments in the enclave to independent research institutes. For the opposition deputies, by contrast, this session was merely the start of a long overdue soul-searching. They therefore asked that the debate be continued in the presence of representatives of the enclave, on the one hand, and members of the collegial Presidency, on the other, and that a genuine investigative commission be created in place of the ad hoc commission responsible for writing the draft resolution.

As it happened, the resolution presented to the deputies by Irfan Ajanović essentially repeated the positions defended by the SDA. Indeed, it stated that "based on the reports [that have been presented] and the in-depth discussion" during which the Parliament examined "the causes of the genocide against the Bosniak population in Srebrenica and Žepa," the Parliament had concluded that: "The international community is responsible for having allowed the Serb aggressor to commit an unprecedented genocide and massacre against the Bosniak population in the protected and demilitarized areas of Srebrenica and Žepa." The Parliament also observed that the Sarajevo authorities had given UN representatives sufficient advance warning of Serb military preparations, that the armed forces "could do nothing more to protect and defend Srebrenica" and that "the incomplete information according to which not enough has been done for Srebrenica or Srebrenica has been sacrificed is groundless." Based on this, the Parliament asked the ICTY to summon Boutros-Ghali and General Janvier as witnesses, asked the UN to examine the responsibility of Boutros-Ghali, Akashi, and Janvier for the genocide committed in Srebrenica and Žepa, requested that the Institute for Research of Crimes Against Humanity and International Law as well as the Historical Institute of Sarajevo collect information about this genocide and ordered state agencies to investigate "potential illegal practices" within the Srebrenica enclave.[67] After a brief discussion, in the course of which the possibility was raised of requesting the Council of Europe's parliamentary assembly to create its own investigative commission, the resolution was unanimously adopted (with one abstention). Six weeks later, the general elections marked the definitive end of the Parliament of the Republic of Bosnia-Herzegovina, which would therefore never have the opportunity to meet in session in order to examine the reports that the above research institutes and state agencies were supposed to present ... every three months![68]

Political Responsibility in Wartime

In reviewing the debate over the question of Bosniak responsibility, it becomes clear that all of the participants in it distinguished between criminal, political, and moral responsibility, and on this basis sought to establish a hierarchy of responsibility among the various actors in the crisis of summer 1995. This explains why the role of the Serb leaders and, quite often, UN leaders, was treated in terms of guilt (*krivica*) while that of Bosniak leaders was addressed in terms of responsibility (*odgovornost*). In this hierarchy of responsibility, there was at least one point of unanimous agreement: the Serb leaders were criminals (*zločinci*) and must be judged by the ICTY. It only remained to be determined whether this guilt was limited to those who ordered the crime.[69] The international community was also unanimously condemned, leading to a demand that certain UN leaders be indicted or subpoenaed. Yet it was sometimes described in terms of passivity (*pasivnost*) and failure to comply with the UNPROFOR mandate and at other times in terms of treason (*izdaja*) and superpower conspiracies. Finally, the possible responsibility of Bosniak leaders was always seen as a secondary issue since it concerned the fall of the enclave rather than the subsequent massacre and might give rise to demands for resignation but never to demands for legal proceedings. Their possible responsibility was nevertheless sometimes characterized as consisting of errors (*greške*) due to the incompetence (*nesposobnost*) of the Bosniak military and political leadership, sometimes as treason (*izdaja*), in which case the nature of their responsibility was similar to that of UN leaders.

Be that as it may, all those who wanted the attitude of Bosniak leaders in the summer of 1995 to be submitted to critical examination—a group that included survivors, elected officials, and journalists—insisted on the principle of political responsibility. When *Ratna tribina* thus demanded in July 1995 that some of them resign, it was because "the population of the Drina Valley also elected them and it would more than a moral act for them to offer their resignations. That would be the only proof that our 'representatives' place more importance on the population than on their armchairs."[70] At this time, insistence on the political responsibility of Bosniak leaders was also to be found in the remarks of Nijaz Duraković and Haris Silajdžić and the questions addressed to Izetbegović by some Srebrenica refugees in February 1996. It explains the willingness expressed by some opposition deputies on 1 August 1996 "to work in our hearts and minds, as deputies who have taken an oath in this Parliament,"[71] to create a genuine parliamentary investigative commission and convene a new session of Parliament. Implicitly, at least, the question of possible Bosniak responsibility for the fall of Srebrenica was therefore related to a much larger question: What is political responsibility in wartime?

The choice of the frameworks in which this debate should take place depended, among other things, on this question. Indeed, in the months following the fall of Srebrenica, the SDA leaders insisted on the threat that such a debate would represent in a time of war, an argument partly accepted by opposition leaders when they stated, for example, that "we should have confidence in the state in all events."[72] The journalists of *Ratna tribina*, on the contrary, countered this "*union sacrée*" by pointing out the need to draw lessons from the Srebrenica tragedy and make the main Bosniak leaders accountable. It is in this context that one must place Hasan Hadžić's remark that "the Srebrenica tragedy is the most dubious part of the conscience of this state and it is why the state must quickly identify those responsible. If this does not happen, everything will lose its meaning."[73] In addition to the question of the debate's temporal framework was that of its institutional framework. In July 1995, the daily newspaper *Oslobođenje* remarked, for example, that the question of Bosniak responsibility "is not and should not be the object of journalistic analysis but rather of the serious work of state agencies."[74] At the same period, the local representative of the MBO hoped that a special meeting of the political parties of Tuzla would be "the last at which we accuse others instead of speaking of our own mistakes." The president of the meeting, an SDP representative, responded that "this assembly does not have the authority to examine these questions."[75] Therefore, from August 1995 to August 1996, demands for a parliamentary debate concerning the circumstances of the fall of Srebrenica also reflected a willingness to find a legitimate institutional framework for examining this delicate question and, more broadly, to restore executive oversight to Parliament.[76]

In the course of the debate itself, however, some deputies seemed to doubt the relevance of this choice, highlighting its limits and the risks involved. Ekren Ajanović (SBiH), for example, thus concluded his remarks by stating: "Here, I will interrupt myself and if I judge that certain questions need to be asked, I will ask them in writing elsewhere, because apparently some things can't be said here in the Parliament."[77] Likewise, Igor Rajner (UBSD) held that "it is perhaps not the right place [to draw the lessons from Srebrenica]. I am even persuaded that this place and this debate amount to pressure and even to reopen a wound of the Bosnian nation that has not yet healed and that, I fear, will never do so."[78] Nevertheless, Ekrem Ajanović himself requested that "we convene a session during which we can all say face to face what we did or did not do because we will have to do it sooner or later, today or ten years from now."[79] Other deputies, such as Smail Ibrahimpašić (SBiH), also insisted on the necessity of this painful confrontation:

> [Srebrenica] is an open wound for all of us and we who belong to the generation who lived through it will never forget it. ... We will never know the entire truth, we can never say the entire truth, it is not historically beneficial to do so. In history, there have always been things that people have never known about. This will also be true in this case. But ... someone should say the most important things and prove the most important things because if we do not do so then the case of Srebrenica will gnaw away at our generation from the inside, and for the rest of our lives.[80]

The reluctance of some deputies was not only a reflection of the conflict between moral demands and tactical considerations. It stemmed, more essentially, from the question of the link between political and moral responsibility in wartime. Indeed, the deputies who most loudly proclaimed that the leaders of the SDA should be held accountable also justified their attitude by reference to their own moral suffering and doubts. The mayor of Zvornik, Ćamil Ahmetović (SDA), thus stated, "I want to have a clear conscience,"[81] and Igor Rajner almost seemed to apologize when he announced "I must say what torments me."[82] In both cases, the principle of moral responsibility reinforced that of political responsibility. Yet the idea of universal moral responsibility could also dissolve that of identifiable, individual political responsibility. Mustafa Šehović (SDP), for example, remarked that "we are partly to blame, I am partly to blame for Srebrenica as a deputy, sirs, dear friends, you are all in a way partly to blame for Srebrenica."[83] Similarly, in his speech from 11 July 1996, Izetbegović put forward a metaphysical definition of responsibility, stating that: "When something as terrible as Srebrenica happens, there are no innocents, every man and every woman is guilty for the fact that the world is as it is and that a world can exist in which Srebrenica is possible."[84] Finally, and at least implicitly, the debate over the question of Bosniak responsibility was thus a debate about the ways in which power was exercised in territories under Bosniak control. In order to identify those responsible for the fall of Srebrenica, the true centers of power had to be localized and brought out into the open. Furthermore, it is no accident that the debate over possible Bosniak responsibility began within the SDA rather than in the framework of legal institutions or that the conflict pitting Silajdžić against the leading bodies of the SDA over the fall of Srebrenica went hand in hand with his condemnation of the parallel power networks established during the war. Finally, the link between the debate regarding the circumstances of Srebrenica's fall and disputes over the forms of power established by the SDA could be seen in the reactions of the leaders of this party. Asked to explain themselves—whether to the population of Srebrenica or to the Parliament—they generally endeavored to free themselves of this obligation, whether by remaining silent and unapproachable, indefinitely putting off all examinations of the circumstances of the fall of Srebrenica or entrusting this to commissions on which they themselves sat and which they probably knew would never meet. When the social and political pressure became too strong, their strategy consisted of avoiding every encounter between the population of Srebrenica and the opposition parties—as witnessed by the exclusion of Ibran Mustafić on 27 May 1996, and the absence of representatives from Srebrenica at the 1 August 1996 parliamentary debate. They then tried to defuse the situation by drawing on practices inherited from the war and the communist period. So, it was as the "father of the nation"—incarnated in another time and under different circumstances by Marshal Tito—that Izetbegović met with the survivors of Srebrenica and managed to channel their anger in July 1995 and again in February 1996.[85] And it was by mobilizing the old reflexes of political unanimism that, six months later, the SDA succeeded in winning the adoption of the final resolution from an (almost) unanimous Parliament.

Srebrenica and the Question of Bosniak War Aims

The adoption of a resolution denying Sarajevo authorities any responsibility for the fall of Srebrenica allowed this question to be defused. In the end, it does not seem to have played a decisive role in Bosniak voters' choices. But the parliamentary debate of 1 August 1996, which the daily newspaper *Oslobođenje* described as "a collective washing of hands,"[86] did not put an end to the rumors and controversies surrounding the fall of Srebrenica. At the time, it was even accompanied by contradictory new revelations. On 7 August, the weekly newspaper *Ljiljan* published a lengthy study that drew, among other things, on confidential military sources, the aim of which was clearly to ruin the reputation of Naser Orić.[87] This attempt sparked outraged protests from former enclave officers[88] and lead *Oslobođenje* to publish the "confessions of Naser Orić" in which he recounts his own version of events.[89]

In the years to come, controversy over the fall of Srebrenica reemerged at regular intervals, particularly on the eve of ceremonies to commemorate the massacre or important elections. But the configurations were no longer the same. In 1996, the question of possible Bosniak responsibility was linked to that of the fate of the missing and was picked up by a part of the enclave's population, as witnessed in the February demonstrations. Associations representing the Srebrenica population later lost interest in this question, preferring to focus, on the one hand, on the identification and burial of victims[90] and, on the other, on the arrest and trial of Serb war criminals.[91] For their part, most of the former enclave leaders—starting with Naser Orić—took refuge in silence, an attitude that fed new rumors about the manner in which they were "blackmailed" or had been "bought" by those in power. In this context, Ibran Mustafić, who was increasingly isolated on the political scene, and Hakija Meholjić, who had in the meantime become president of the local branch of the SDP, were the only Bosniak figures native to Srebrenica who continued to publicly blame Bosniak leaders of the time for their role in the fall of the enclave.

As it lost its social basis, the debate over the question of Bosniak responsibility became increasingly political. The role played by the independent press in a debate that Parliament had only touched upon in August 1996 and that most politicians carefully avoided from then on is another sign of this politicization. Several former *Ratna tribina* contributors, in particular, continued to investigate the circumstances of the fall of Srebrenica as correspondents for the weekly Sarajevo newspapers *Slobodna Bosna* and *Dani* ("The Days"). In September 1998—that is, on the eve of new general elections—a special edition of *Dani* devoted to the fall of Srebrenica was written by Esad Hećimović, an investigative journalist who had worked during the war for the weekly paper *Ljiljan* and the leading bodies of the SDA but later broke with this party.[92] Just as the proliferation of rumors during the war came to compensate for the absence of reliable information and provided a semblance of public space, the independent press came to replace legal institutions and political parties in the structuring of this same public space. This essential role can easily be explained in a country coming out of fifty years of communism and three and a half years of war and in which institutions do not work, nationalist parties continue to enjoy a strong grip over their respective territories, and political life remains dominated by communal conflicts and personal rivalries. But the press itself often repeated unverifiable rumors and willingly used the vocabulary of treason and conspiracy. Obedient at once to certain reflexes inherited from the communist period and the new laws of the market economy, it did not manage to avoid the sirens of invective and sensationalism and consequently turned out to be largely incapable of encouraging a dispassionate examination of certain fundamental debates.

However, many of the recurrent themes that appeared in the Sarajevo press—from the enrichment of political and criminal elites to the place of Islam in post-war society, from the crimes of the ARBiH to the presence of mujahiddin—in fact stemmed from a more profound doubt concerning the true war aims of the SDA. The Srebrenica tragedy is no exception to this rule. Given this context, it is not surprising that the debate over Bosniak responsibility slowly turned away from the tactical errors that may have been committed on the eve of or during the Serb offensive in order to focus on the hypothetical political choices taken by the Bosniak leadership in the framework of peace negotiations. Indeed, as early as August 1996, several former officers from the enclave claimed in the pages of *Slobodna Bosna* that: "the representatives of Srebrenica at the *Bošnjački sabor*[93] held in fall 1993 returned to Srebrenica with the news that the highest reaches of the Government in Sarajevo had proposed to them an exchange between the Srebrenica territory and certain parts of Sarajevo. Following this, the population was seized with panic, a feeling of betrayal and of the uselessness of all our sacrifices, and it was for this reason that keeping soldiers' morale at the necessary level and motivating them for new actions has been so difficult."[94] This version of events was ultimately taken up in the memoirs of Sefer Halilović, first chief of the army's general staff from May 1992 until June 1993,[95] and was confirmed in an interview given to *Dani* in June 1998 by Hakija Meholjić, one of the nine members of the delegation that attended the *Bošnjački sabor*.[96] In the absence of tangible proof or confirmation from other direct witnesses, however, it remains unverifiable. Moreover, the mention of a possible territorial exchange of eastern Bosnian enclaves for Sarajevo neighborhoods under Serb control during the *Bošnjački sabor* in September 1993 does not necessarily imply the abandonment of these same enclaves in July 1995, especially given that the offensive launched two months earlier by the ARBiH to break the siege of Sarajevo came up against strong Serb resistance and ended in failure.[97] The fact that the debate came to focus on the meeting between Izetbegović and the Srebrenica and Žepa delegation nevertheless attests to the fact that the question of possible Bosniak responsibility in the fall of Srebrenica remained linked to that of the SDA leadership's war aims. Indeed, the *Bošnjački sabor,* a body based on the principle of cooptation and representing only the Bosniak nation,[98] replaced the Parliament elected in 1990 in order to decide on the adoption or rejection of the Owen-Stoltenberg peace plan, and formalized the access of the Bosniak nation to political sovereignty by abandoning the national name "Muslims" for that of "Bosniaks." Moreover, the first session of the *Bošnjački sabor* on 27 September 1993, remains the moment in which the leaders of the SDA most clearly showed that they were tempted to accept a division of Bosnia-Herzegovina in view of creating a Bosniak national state.[99] Yet it must be noted that this debate over the SDA's war aims did not take place and that, for the time being, the debate over possible Bosniak responsibility in the fall of Srebrenica has served no other purpose than to feed the negationist theories of some and the personal quarrels of others.

Indeed, the Serb nationalists and their supporters did not fail to turn the accusations of Ibran Mustafić, Sefer Halilović and Hakija Meholjić to advantage in order to deny the reality of the massacre, present it as a simple act of revenge or the result of an anti-Serb plot. These accusations are to be found on many negationist websites and were used by Slobodan Milošević in the course of his trial. This abuse of the debate over the question of Bosniak responsibility in its turn contributed to its gradual exhaustion. On the one hand, it contributed to giving the debate an even more personal and aggressive tone, as shown by the July 2003 controversy between Sefer Halilović and Alija Izetbegović.[100] On the other hand, it doubtless explains why some protagonists of the events of July 1995 have chosen to remain silent, not wishing to supply grist to the mill of Serb nationalists at a time when the judicial and political sequels to the Srebrenica massacre are far from finished.

Translated from French by Ethan Rundell

Notes

1. *Magnetofonski snimak 20. sjednice Skupštine Republike Bosne i Hercegovine održane u Sarajevu dana 1. avgusta 1996. godine sa početkom u 14 sati* [Tape Recording of the 20th Session of the Parliament of the Republic of Bosnia-Herzegovina held in Sarajevo on 1 August 1996 starting at 14:00], written version, 20/1. The unusual character of the page-numbering is likely due to the fact that the work of retranscribing the audio tapes was given to more than one person.
2. Since the signing of the Dayton agreements on 14 December 1995, Bosnia-Herzegovina has been divided into two constituent entities: the Republika Srpska, a self-proclaimed entity since April 1992 whose existence is legalized by the peace agreement, and the Federation of Bosnia-Herzegovina, created in March 1994 by the Washington agreement.
3. Between March 1994 and September 1996, the institutions of the Republic of Bosnia-Herzegovina and those of the Federation of Bosnia-Herzegovina, created in March 1994 (see note 2), coexisted within the territory under Bosniak or Croat control. Therefore, the Parliament elected in 1990 sometimes held sessions as the Parliament of the Republic of Bosnia-Herzegovina and sometimes as the Parliament of the Federation, in which case only Bosniak and Croat deputies convened. In September 1996, the Republic of Bosnia-Herzegovina disappeared and its Parliament was replaced by a new Parliament elected by the voters of both entities.
4. *Oslobođenje*, 13 July 1995.
5. *Ratna tribina* was published by the Zvornik municipality in exile and followed closely the activity of the military units originating from the Drina valley.
6. Naser Orić alludes to the link-up operation between, on the one hand, the column of soldiers and civilians fleeing in the direction of territory under Bosniak control and, on the other, certain units of the Army of the Republic of Bosnia-Herzegovina (ARBiH) attempting to break through Serb lines in the vicinity of Zvornik. Naser Orić participated in this attempt with a number of volunteers. The link-up with forward elements of the column—mostly soldiers—took place at the front line on 16 July 1995, but several thousand people fleeing with this column were captured by Serb forces and killed.
7. "Naser Orić, ekskluzivno: narod će reći ko je izdao Srebrenicu" [Exclusive, Naser Orić: The People Will Say Who Has Betrayed Srebrenica], *Ratna tribina*, 31 July 1995, 7.
8. Interview with the author, Tuzla, 3 October 2006. For more on this meeting, see Hasan Hadžić, "Bili, ne vratili se" [They Were, but Did not Come Back], *Dani*, 22 June 1998, accessible at http://www.bhdani.com.
9. According to the Constitution in effect until the signing of the Dayton agreements in December 1995, the Presidency of the Republic of Bosnia-Herzegovina consisted of seven members: two representatives of each constituent nation of Bosnia-Herzegovina (Bosniaks, Serbs, and Croats) and one representative of the other Yugoslav nations and

national minorities present in Bosnia-Herzegovina. However, since 1993, the "Yugoslav" Ejup Ganić (SDA) declared himself "Bosniak" and was elected vice president of the collegial Presidency, a position that did not exist in the Constitution.
10. *Oslobođenje*, 13 July 1995.
11. *Oslobođenje*, 20 July 1995.
12. Press conference of the Union of Bosnian Social Democrats (UBSD), which managed the Tuzla municipality in partnership with the SDP, cited in F.S., "Utvrditi odgovornost za pad Srebrenice" [Establishing the Responsibility for the Fall of Srebrenica], *Front slobode*, 28 July 1995, 10.
13. Gradimir Gojer (SDP) comment as reported in *Oslobođenje*, 14 July 1995.
14. Ljubomir Berberović (Serb Civic Council) comment as reported in ibid.
15. On 3 August, during a new session of the SDA parliamentary group, deputy Ekrem Ajanović was outraged that "the last time, on 11 July, we received information in this room according to which Srebrenica could defend itself and had sufficient weapons, and when we left the room our chauffeurs told us that Srebrenica had fallen" (cited in Esad Hećimović, *Kako su prodali Srebrenicu i sačuvali vlast* [How They Sold Srebrenica and Kept Power], Sarajevo, 1998, 62).
16. Ismet Grbo's comments at the press conference organized by the SDA on 20 July in Tuzla, as reported in *Oslobođenje*, 21 July 1995.
17. Izetbegović's comment on Bosnian television, as reported in *Oslobođenje*, 19 July 1995. It is also in this context that one must set the early August announcement of a review parade of the 28th division—in reality, a few thousand combatants out of the twelve thousand men eligible for mobilization in the Srebrenica enclave before its fall—an announcement upon which Serb nationalists were later to draw in their attempts to negate the reality of the massacre.
18. *Oslobođenje*, 6 August 1995.
19. As cited in Hećimović, *Kako su prodali Srebrenicu*, 63. Regarding the set up of parallel power networks during the war, also see Xavier Bougarel, *Bosnie: anatomie d'un conflit* (Paris, 1996); Marko Hoare, *How Bosnia Armed* (London, 2004).
20. Hećimović, *Kako su prodali Srebrenicu*, 62 and 66.
21. Ibid., 66.
22. Ibid., 66–67.
23. See *Ratna tribina*, 31 July 1995.
24. Mehmed Pargan, "Srebrenica se branila sama a izgubili smo je svi" [Srebrenica Defended Itself Alone but We All Lost It], *Ratna tribina*, 31 July 1995, 4–5.
25. Hasan Hadžić, "Da li su, pored teritorije, morali biti žrtvovani narod i vojska?" [Was It Necessary, in Addition to the Territory, to Sacrifice the Population and the Army?], *Ratna tribina*, 31 July 1995, 6–7. This article is actually a text that Hasan Hadžić was unable to read in front of the Parliament of the Tuzla canton on behalf of the Bosnian Drina Valley Alliance (*Savez bosanskog Podrinja*), which brought together the exiled municipalities and the refugee associations originating from this region.
26. Sead Numanović, "Krivi su generali" [The Generals Are Guilty], *Ratna tribina*, 31 July 1995, 3.
27. The *Aktiv žena* ("women's active") is a structure inherited from the communist period, and played a role similar to civil defense in the enclave.
28. The three other members of this committee would represent the Republic of Bosnia-Herzegovina, the Federation of Bosnia-Herzegovina and the Tuzla canton.
29. *Oslobođenje*, 11 February 1996.
30. The MBO is a small party created in September 1990, following an internal split within the SDA.

31. *Oslobođenje*, 13 February 1996.
32. *Oslobođenje*, 14 February 1996. The other points of the resolution provided for the appointment of one person responsible for representing the Drina valley population before Bosnian institutions, the presence of Srebrenica population representatives within the Commission for the search of missing persons, the dispatch of a Srebrenica women's delegation on the ground, the publication by the finance inspection service of a report on the use of funds collected for the refugees of Srebrenica, the monthly payment of fifty Deutschmarks to school children originating from the Drina valley, and, more generally, material assistance for displaced populations.
33. Amongst the SDA officials who joined the SBiH were several other people who had criticized the Sarajevo authorities for their attitude during the crisis of summer 1995, starting with Ekrem Ajanović and Bećir Heljić.
34. Ibran Mustafić, "Predsjedništvo i generalštab su žrtvovali Srebrenicu!" [The Presidency and the General Staff Have Sacrificed Srebrenica!], *Slobodna Bosna*, 14 July 1996, 6–10.
35. Alija Izetbegović, "Kada se dogodi nešto tako stravično kao što je Srebrenica, tada nema nevinih" [When Something as Dreadful as Srebrenica Happens, Nobody Is Innocent], in *Godina rata i mira. Odabrani govori, intervjui i pisma* [The Year of War and Peace: Selected Speeches, Interviews and Letters] (Sarajevo, 1997), 116.
36. See note 9.
37. *Oslobođenje*, 13 July 1996.
38. As cited in *Oslobođenje*, 26 July 1996.
39. Alosman Husejnović, "11 000 neklanjanih dženaza" [11,000 Non-Accomplished Burials], *Ljiljan*, 17 July 1996, 12–13.
40. Sead Avdić (SDP) comment, as reported in *Oslobođenje*, 18 July 1996.
41. Fikret Jahić (SBiH) comment, as reported in *Oslobođenje*, 16 July 1996.
42. See note 6.
43. Interview with the author, Tuzla, 12 October 2006.
44. Apparently, the only political leader from Srebrenica present in the Parliament was Zulfo Salihović, who became president of the local SDA chapter during the war. Deputy Ekrem Ajanović (SBiH) protested against this fact, asserting that, "in order that we know everything that happened there and how it happened, it is necessary that Naser Orić, and the deputy Ibran Mustafić, and representatives of Srebrenica, of the population of Srebrenica, elected by the population, be present at this session so that we can then truly ask ourselves as individuals whether we made sufficient efforts to prevent this tragedy" (*Magnetofonski snimak 20. sjednice*, 20/1).
45. At the same time, HDZ Croat deputies were gathering in Neum on the Adriatic coast. This attitude is due to the fact, among others, that, since the creation of the Federation in March 1994, the majority of HDZ deputies no longer recognized the Parliament as legitimate when it met as the Parliament of the Republic of Bosnia-Herzegovina (see note 3).
46. As a member of the HDZ, the minister of Foreign Affairs Jadranko Prlić did not attend this session of the Parliament of the Republic of Bosnia-Herzegovina.
47. It should be observed that the only non-Bosniak deputy participating in the debate, Igor Rajner, was the president of the Tuzla Jewish community. The fact that he did not belong to any of the three constituent nations of Bosnia-Herzegovina allowed him a certain liberty of speech. It is also interesting to note the manner in which the geographical origin of the deputies influenced their positions. Ekrem Ajanović (SBiH), for example, originates from Tešanj, a city that was also besieged for several months. As he himself emphasized, "I spent eleven months in Tešanj which was besieged and I know

what sort of psycholocial situation it represents and I know that sometimes, even well-intentioned suggestions coming from the outside can do more harm than good on the ground. ... After all these discussions today, I can say, and the majority of the people of Tešanj would agree, thank God we have had enough force and wisdom at certain moments to not listen to the people from the outside and even to disobey some of their orders and to decide that O[perational] G[roup] 7 would not become a UN safe area, although there had been propositions and requests to do so" (*Magnetofonski snimak 20. sjednice*, 20/1).

48. Apart from Zulfo Salihović, SDA president from Srebrenica, the two other representatives of eastern Bosnian populations intervening in the course of the debate were Ćamil Ahmetović, mayor of Zvornik, a SDA member who was nevertheless very critical of the Sarajevo authorities, and Veiz Šabić, a SDA town councilor from Bratunac and brigade commander who spent the war in the Srebrenica enclave.
49. The members of the commission were Irfan Ajanović (SDA deputy, Doboj), Avdo Čampara (SDA deputy, Sarajevo, Secretary of the Parliament of the Republic of Bosnia-Herzegovina), Mirsad Đapo (SDP deputy, Brčko), Rasim Kadić (Liberal Party deputy, Sarajevo), Igor Rajner (UBSD deputy, Tuzla), Veiz Šabić (SDA town councilor, Bratunac), and Pero Vasilj (HDZ deputy, Tuzla). Following a question posed by Muharem Cero (SBiH) about a possible report prepared by this commission, the president of the Parliament, Miro Lazović (SDP), specified that "we have not had a parliamentary commission charged with preparing [in advance] its position about this point of the agenda. This is a commission responsible for following today's discussions and proposing a conclusion to the Parliament. It has not finished its work and it is an *ad hoc* commission only for today's session" (*Magnetofonski snimak 20. sjednice*, 10/1).
50. Ibid., 12/2.
51. Ibid., Hasan Dervišbegović's presentation, 1. The presentation by Hasan Dervišbegović is an internal document of the Ministry of Foreign Affairs or the collegial Presidency, with some minor correction, and whose original title ("Analysis of the causes of the fall of Srebrenica and Žepa and of the ensuing massacre") has been crossed out. It is inserted as such in the transcriptions of the parliamentary debate and therefore preserves its separate page numbering.
52. Hasan Dervišbegović declared for example that "all of us, and not only the safe areas, have been the victims of the great deception which consisted in keeping the political and other consequences of the war under control but not resolutely opposing [Serb] aggression. We knew it but we hardly had the possibility to reveal this in broad daylight or to try to overcome this deception because, at the end of the day, one of its results has been humanitarian aid and the lowering of the intensity of fighting which were important for the survival of Bosnians" (ibid., 3). These comments bring to mind those made by Alija Izetbegović on 11 July 1995, before the SDA parliamentary group concerning the demand presented by certain deputies that the UNPROFOR be expelled from Bosnia-Herzegovina: "A word about the UNPROFOR; no one likes it but it is a sort of necessary evil, you have to understand this. Look at Srebrenica. If we had said 'out with the UNPROFOR,' there would not have been these bombings. If it had not been there, NATO would not have been used. The UNPROFOR is a means to get the international community involved. The UNPROFOR is necessary for us as long as we cannot do what they do. They hold the [Sarajevo] airport and in doing this they protect the tunnel [between Sarajevo and Mount Igman], they protect Srebrenica, Bihać, they drive convoys to Goražde. ... The international community also controls the air-exclusion zone above Bosnia-Herzegovina. In this way, 20 to 30 planes and helicopters are

kept on the ground. Whatever we may feel, it is necessary to keep this in mind. Let us hope that beginning next November, we will not need to extend their mandate" (as cited in Hećimović, *Kako su prodali Srebrenicu*, 13).

53. In July 1995, Yasushi Akashi was the special representative of the secretary general of the UN for ex-Yugoslavia and General Bernard Janvier was the commander of the UN-PROFOR for former Yugoslavia (not to be confused with Rupert Smith, commander of the UNPROFOR for Bosnia-Herzegovina).

54. *Magnetofonski snimak 20. sjednice*, 16/1. Hasan Muratović specified that "there is no proof that such an agreement has been signed but everything suggests that Akashi and Janvier accepted this agreement." In this context, he added, "there is a question that remains unanswered. Did Akashi and Janvier have an agreement with Mladić so that the people leaving Srebrenica for Tuzla would be allowed to pass? This question still needs to be investigated. Insofar as it has been written about many times in the western press and UN leaders themselves suggested that all of the people from Srebrenica who wished to peacefully go to Tuzla had to be allowed to leave and that the Serbs would let them pass, it is quite likely that this part of the agreement existed. In my contacts with certain people from Srebrenica, I tried to find out if they had been informed of this possibility, and the fact is that our people were not fired at when they crossed the front lines surrounding Srebrenica. Therefore, this remains something to be considered, but in this scenario the guilt of the UN is all the greater because [this means that] it entirely oversaw the lead-up to the capture of Srebrenica." At another point in his presentation, Muratović nevertheless affirmed that "we knew everything that was going to happen if we let the Serbs transport [the inhabitants of Srebrenica] to Kladanj; at this point, the UN could have contributed to providing protection while waiting for the moment when the UN could organize the transport [itself]. If this had been done, it is certain that several thousand fewer people would have been sacrificed." Finally, Muratović paid homage to the attitude of General Rupert Smith, commander of the UNPROFOR in Bosnia-Herzegovina, who "has warned Akashi and Janvier that the Serbs were certainly going to attack the three enclaves [Srebrenica, Žepa, and Goražde], that they were going to take them if they did not receive air support and that a serious tragedy would ensue. He said that it was a firm decision on Mladić's part that he had learned of through the [British] secret services" (ibid., 16/1 to 18/1).

55. Ibid., Hasan Dervišbegović's presentation, 1.

56. Rasim Delić specified that arms deliveries to the Srebrenica enclave began in April 1994, after the end of the Croat-Bosniak fightings had permitted a resumption of the weapons supply and the Serb offensive against Goražde had demonstrated that the international community was not ready to defend the safe areas with the necessary determination. Next detailing the quantity of weapons transported to the Srebrenica enclave, he reckoned that "Goražde did not receive half of these [military] means in the course of the same period, and [that] Sarajevo defended itself with many fewer means in 1992 and 1993" (ibid., 11/2). This evaluation contradicts that of Naser Orić, who held that the low level of arms deliveries contributed to the spread of a defeatist attitude within the enclave (*Oslobođenje*, 26 August 1996).

57. Among these malfunctions, Delić mentioned "an unfair fight for power and [political] divisions on this basis; poor relations between the police and the Territorial Defense and, later, the army; the assassination of opponents and political competitors, or attempts on their lives; the use of war for the purposes of personal enrichment and criminal activities; poor organization of the armed forces of the Territorial Defense and, later, the army and a struggle for command posts" (*Magnetofonski snimak 20. sjednice*, 11/2).

58. In regard to the weak resistance of Bosniak forces, Delić stated that "we expected a higher level of resistance, which would have allowed external forces to regroup towards Srebrenica. ... We were in permanent contact with Srebrenica [until 10 July] but they did not listen to our suggestions and orders, they did not act in accordance with the plans that had been drawn up in advance and by means of which Srebrenica may not have been preserved but the population would at least have escaped. What can one say about the resistance when not a single [Serb] tank was destroyed despite the large quantities of anti-tank weapons. At one point, three tanks were directed from Zeleni Jadar towards the city and if just one had been destroyed, the Chetniks would not have entered the city, but not a single one was destroyed" (ibid., 12/1).
59. Ibid., 12/1.
60. Dževad Mlačo (SDA), ibid., 19/2.
61. From this point of view, Dževad Mlačo (SDA) and Igor Rajner's (UBSD) questions concerning the nature of the massacre played a pivotal role. Dževad Mlačo emphasized that "we have had cases where cities have been captured by the aggressor but the crimes against the population have not been committed to a comparable extent, not even close to [what happened in] Srebrenica and Žepa," and concluded from this that "this is truly completely calculated, from start to finish set up with the support of the international community which did nothing to protect, not the area, but the civilian population" (ibid., 19/2 and 20/1). Igor Rajner was more hesitant about the singular character of the massacre, not knowing if it was "the greatest [Bosnian] defeat" or a defeat "similar to April and May 1992, when the Bosnian population suffered terrible losses." Above all, he relied on Mlačo's comments to raise different questions: "This gentleman from Bugojno made a very good observation about one thing. [The Serbs] occupied and captured other cities, but with a lot less bloodshed. What hardened them so much? For they had certainly become hardened. Think about it, they let the women and children go, they let the elderly go, but they mercilessly killed the soldiers. Without mercy. Why? What does it mean? I say it again, it is perhaps not a question for this place or for public opinion but it is a question from which we must draw lessons" (ibid., 23/2). Lastly, Mevludin Sejmenović, SDA deputy from Prijedor, a western Bosnian town where several thousand Bosnian civilians had been killed at the beginning of the war, opposed this presentation of the Srebrenica massacre as a singular case and asked that the Parliament also devote a session to the western Bosnian case (ibid., 25/2 and 26/1).
62. Dževad Mlačo (SDA), ibid., 19/2. It is not always clear whether the deputies are referring to the International Criminal Tribunal for the former Yugoslavia (ICTY) or to the International Court of Justice (ICJ), both based in The Hague, and some deputies seem to confuse the two institutions.
63. Ibid., 22/2 and 23/1.
64. Ibid., 23/2.
65. In a general way, the representatives of the eastern Bosnian population asserted that a longer resistance would not have changed the ultimate fate of the enclave and its population, and that the use of the evacuation plans prepared by the general staff would have lead to an even larger catastrophe. By contrast, the opposition deputies shared a certain number of doubts with SDA deputies concerning the conduct of civilian and military authorities in the enclave. Igor Rajner declared for example that "all of us who spent the war near Srebrenica know that there were problems" (ibid., 24/1), rejecting the idea that a longer resistance would not have changed the final outcome for the enclave: "I accept, with no reservations, [the idea of] the international community's responsibility; it is so powerful that it could have done a lot more, had Srebrenica defended itself

for three more days, it could have perhaps saved the population of Srebrenica. You know how much time they need to react but once they do react, it works. This automatically means that I do not accept the idea that resistance was useless" (ibid., 23/2).
66. Irfan Ajanović (SDA), ibid., 23/2.
67. Ibid., 29/1 and 29/2.
68. Between 1998 and 2000, the Institute for research of crimes against humanity and international law published three edited volumes devoted to the Srebrenica massacre. These include the proceedings of an international conference organized in July 1997, the ICTY's indictments of Radovan Karadžić, Ratko Mladić, Radislav Krstić, and Dražen Erdemović, an annotated translation of the UN report on the fall of Srebrenica, as well as various documents and testimonies, but none of these addresses the question of Bosniak responsibility.
69. During the 1 August 1996 parliamentary debate, the deputy Safet Isović (SDA) was shocked by "the inertia of our institutions in identifying and publishing the names [of war criminals] and transferring war crimes documentation to The Hague. In the end, it will turn out that the only guilty people are Mladić, Karadžić and Dušan Tadić [*sic*; Safet Isović is probably thinking of Dražen Erdemović here—*trans.*], and that they killed all of these people by themselves. I beg this parliamentary commission and I beg this Parliament as the supreme organ of power to order this commission or to the government and, through it, all institutions responsible for collecting information about war crimes, to send proof as quickly, efficiently and completely as possible concerning the enormous number of people who took part in war crimes in Bosnia-Herzegovina" (*Magnetofonski snimak 20. sjednice*, 28/2).
70. Pargan, "Srebrenica se branila sama."
71. Muharem Cero (SBiH), *Magnetofonski snimak 20. sjednice*, 26/2.
72. Alija Behmen (SDP) comment as reported in *Oslobođenje*, 14 July 1995.
73. Hadžić, "Da li su pored teritorije."
74. *Oslobođenje*, 16 July 1995.
75. B. Skoković-Tomić, "Parlamentarne stranke Tuzle i pad Srebrenice: ne dozvoliti anarhiju" [The Parliamentary Parties of Tuzla and the Fall of Srebrenica: Not Tolerating Anarchy], *Front slobode*, 28 July 1995, 2.
76. On the role of the Parliament during the war, see for example Senad Slatina, "Da li je Skupština vlast ili alibi za vlast?" [Is the Parliament the Power or An Alibi for the Power?], *Slobodna Bosna*, 29 December 1995, 10–11.
77. *Magnetofonski snimak 20. sjednice*, 21/1.
78. Ibid., 23/2.
79. Ibid., 21/1.
80. Ibid., 24/2 and 24/3.
81. Ibid., 25/2.
82. Ibid., 23/2.
83. Ibid., 19/1.
84. Alija Izetbegović, "Kada se dogodi nešto tako stravično," 116. The metaphysical guilt about which Izetbegović spoke in his 11 July 1996 speech brings to mind that evoked in 1946 by Karl Jaspers, for whom "each finds himself co-responsible for all injustice and all evil committed in the world" and the simple fact "that I still live, after such things have happened, bears down on me like unpardonable guilt" (Karl Jaspers, *La culpabilité allemande*, Paris, 1990, 47). It is likely that Izetbegović's speech was inspired by his philosophy readings in the 1980s, including Jaspers and other Christian philosophers (see Alija Izetbegović, *Moj bijeg u slobodu. Bilješke iz zatvora 1983–1988* [My Flight into Freedom: Notes from the Prison 1983–1988], Sarajevo, 1999).

85. It is also in this context that Izetbegović's capacity to prevent any act of revenge against the Serb population of Sarajevo must be situated. Miro Lazović, president of the Parliament, recounted in an interview to *Radio Free Europe* that, in July 1995, "we received a threatening letter from a group of people from Žepa and Srebrenica who then lived in Sarajevo, saying that the Serb population of Sarajevo would suffer if Žepa or Srebrenica fell. Mirko Pejanović [a Serb member of the collegial Presidency] and I both received this letter and, worried about the situation of Srebrenica and Žepa as well as what could happen in Sarajevo, we met with Izetbegović and informed him of the letter's contents, and I must say that during our meeting with the representatives of Žepa and Srebrenica, he clearly said that not a single hair of a Serb or a Croat from Sarajevo should be touched. He was really firm on this point and I must say that, after that, the anger shown by this group subsided" ("Miro Lazović: utopisti i buhe" [Miro Lazović: Utopians and Fleas], in *Svjedoci raspada* [Witnesses of the Breakdown], Prague, RFE/RL, accessible at http://www.slobodnaevropa.org).
86. *Oslobođenje*, 7 August 1996.
87. Nedžad Latić, "Svjedoci tvrde da ljudi Nasera Orića stoje iza 19 atentata u Srebrenici," [Witnesses Claim that Naser Orić's People Stay Behind Nineteen Assassination Attempts in Srebrenica], *Ljiljan*, 7 August 1996, 18–22.
88. "Zlatni ljiljani brane istinu i Nasera Orića" [Golden Lilies Defend the Truth and Naser Orić], *Slobodna Bosna*, 25 August 1996, 37–38.
89. "Ispovijest Nasera Orića" [The Confessions of Naser Orić], *Oslobođenje*, from 24 August to 29 August 1995. These "confessions" are, in fact, a transcription of a conversation recorded shortly after the fall of the enclave between Naser Orić, Sefer Halilović, the first chief of the army's general staff, and Rusmir Mahmutćehajić, former minister of war industry who broke with the SDA during the war. *Oslobođenje* presented this document as a third version of events in Srebrenica, after those presented by Ibran Mustafić in *Slobodna Bosna* and Rasim Delić before the Parliament, but did not specify whether it had been published with the consent of the interested party.
90. See for example Creg E. Pollack, "Intentions of Burial: Mourning, Politics, and Memorials Following the Massacre at Srebrenica," *Death Studies* 27, no. 2 (February 2003): 125–142; Isabelle Delpla, "Incertitudes publiques et privées sur les disparus en Bosnie-Herzégovine," in *Crises extrêmes. Face aux massacres, aux guerres civiles et aux génocides*, eds. Marc Le Pape, Johanna Siméant, and Claudine Vidal (Paris, 2006), 287–301.
91. See for example Isabelle Delpla, "In the Midst of Injustice: The ICTY from the Perspective of some Victim Associations," in *The New Bosnian Mosaic: Identities, Memories and Moral Claims in a Post-War Country*, eds. Xavier Bougarel, Elissa Helms, and Ger Duijzings (Aldershot, 2007), 211–234.
92. Hećimović, *Kako su prodali Srebrenicu*. In this well-documented dossier, Esad Hećimović minutely reconstitutes the attitude of the SDA leadership during the crisis of summer 1995, then uses the former to reveal the informal practices thanks to which the SDA established its hegemony in the territories under Bosniak control.
93. The *Bošnjački sabor* (Bosniak assembly) brought together the major political, intellectual, religious, and military leaders of the Bosniak nation. Its first session, on 27 September 1993, was mostly devoted to the examination of the Owen-Stoltenberg peace plan and its second session, on 18 July 1994, to the examination of the Contact Group peace plan.
94. "Zlatni ljiljani brane istinu."
95. Sefer Halilović, *Lukava strategija* [A Cunning Strategy], (Sarajevo, 1997), 109.
96. In this interview, Meholjić asserted that "President Izetbegović received us and, immediately after greeting us, asked: 'What do you think of an exchange between Srebrenica

and Vogošća?' There was a silence, then I asked to speak and I said: 'President, if you called us to present us with a fait accompli then it wasn't worth the trouble because you have to present yourself before the population and carry the weight of this decision concerning us'" (Hadžić, "Bili, ne vratili se").

97. For a critical discussion of the various conspiracy theories surrounding the fall of Srebrenica, including those blaming Bosniak authorities, see, among others, David Rohde, *Endgame: The Betrayal and Fall of Srebrenica, Europe's Worst Massacre since World War II* (Boulder, CO, 1997).

98. See note 93.

99. On the national project of the SDA leadership, see, for example, Xavier Bougarel, "L'islam bosniaque, entre identité culturelle et idéologie politique," in *Le Nouvel Islam balkanique. Les musulmans, acteurs du post-communisme (1990–2000)*, eds. Xavier Bougarel and Nathalie Clayer (Paris, 2001), 79–132.

100. In early July, Izetbegović accused Halilović of having made remarks before the ICTY that could have helped Milošević develop his own version of events. A few days later, Halilović counter-attacked, claiming that "Milošević unfortunately has enough material to establish the 'betrayal' of Srebrenica on the basis of many public declarations by protagonists in the events and secret agreements that you yourself signed" (*Oslobođenje*, 11 July 2003). The following day, Izetbegović stated that "one of my greatest mistakes had been to name Halilović chief of the general staff " and then left his readers free "to believe Milošević and Halilović or to believe me" (*Oslobođenje*, 12 July 2003). Halilović then once again upped the stakes by declaring that his own mistake had been to negotiate Izetbegović's liberation in May 1992 while he was detained as a prisoner by the Yugoslav People's Army. Eight years after the Srebrenica massacre and four months before the death of Izetbegović, the debate over the question of Bosniak responsibility thus found itself reduced to a pathetic settling of personal accounts.

Chapter 7

THE LONG ROAD TO ADMISSION
The Report of the Government of the Republika Srpska[1]

Michèle Picard and Asta M. Zinbo

This chapter presents the origins and aftermath of the June 2004 report in which the Republika Srpska (RS) acknowledged responsibility for the gross violations of international humanitarian law in Srebrenica in July 1995. On 7 March 2003, the Human Rights Chamber for Bosnia-Herzegovina issued the "Selimović" decision (no. CH/01/8365 et al.) in response to an application filed by families of missing persons. The decision dealt with forty-nine cases relating to Srebrenica and ordered the RS to launch an investigation into the events.[2] Following this decision, the RS Government set up a commission of inquiry and the chief of staff of the International Commission on Missing Persons (ICMP)[3] participated as an international community representative. Indeed, created in 1996 for the former Yugoslavia, the ICMP developed programs for locating and identifying nearly forty thousand missing persons and for supporting associations of families of missing persons across the region, including from Srebrenica. As the Human Rights Chamber did not take part in the commission's work, this chapter will first consider the Chamber's point of view concerning the "Selimović" decision, before turning to examine the establishment, work, and results of this commission.

However different in nature, both the Human Rights Chamber for Bosnia-Herzegovina and the ICMP operated according to the principle of defense of human rights, that is, defense of individual rights against the violations committed by state authorities. The Human Rights Chamber for Bosnia-Herzegovina and the ICMP are both distinct from and complementary to criminal courts in as much as they consider victims on an individual basis while emphasizing the collective responsibility of governments and states or their agents for their citizens. Unlike the war

---

Notes for this chapter begin on page 145.

crimes trials and judgments of the International Criminal Tribunal for the Former Yugoslavia (ICTY) or the Court of Bosnia and Herzegovina, the Chamber and the ICMP mainly deal with the individual rights to information about the fate of missing persons, whether dead or alive, and with the responsibility of the relevant government authorities.

The "Selimović" Decision of the Human Rights Chamber

The Human Rights Chamber for Bosnia-Herzegovina

Signed in December 1995, the Dayton agreements established a judicial body, the Human Rights Chamber, in charge of implementing the European Convention on Human Rights (ECHR) and all its protocols in Bosnia-Herzegovina. This made it a country where, on paper at least, human rights were protected better than anywhere else in the world. Created in the aftermath of a war, the Human Rights Chamber represented an unprecedented experiment. It was composed of eight foreign judges appointed by the Council of Europe and six local judges (two for each constituent nation) appointed by the two constituent entities of Bosnia-Herzegovina (the Federation of Bosnia-Herzegovina and the Republika Srpska). The Chamber had jurisdiction over the whole territory and all the authorities of Bosnia-Herzegovina. Any person deeming himself or herself a victim of human rights violations could file an application with the Chamber. The application was examined according to the adversarial proceedings.

The first application for missing persons filed with the Chamber concerned Father Matanović, a Catholic priest in Prijedor, in Western Bosnia, who had disappeared with his parents in September 1995. He had been seen for the last time when in the custody of the Serb police. The application was filed on his behalf and that of his parents by the Ombudsman for Bosnia-Herzegovina.[4] It was on this occasion that the Chamber defined its temporal competencies. Indeed, an international convention has no retroactive effect and only applies to events subsequent to its entry in force. Thus, the Chamber's jurisdiction could not cover events preceding the Dayton agreements of 14 December 1995. There is, however, an established case-law by the European Court of Human Rights that defines the notion of continuous violation of human rights, that is a violation that may have begun before the entry into force of a convention but continued after it. Father Matanović and his parents had been seen for the last time in September 1995, before the entry into force of the agreements, but their names could be read on lists of prisoners established after the agreements. The Chamber, which, at the time, did not know what happened to them, considered that it was a case of continuous violation of human rights and the RS was sentenced for violation of article 5 of the ECHR and ordered to conduct an investigation.[5]

Later, in the Unković case,[6] a Serb couple filed an application against the Federation because of the disappearance of their daughter and her family. On that occasion, the Chamber redefined its jurisdiction by holding that the suffering those people were undergoing, due to the lack of information concerning their daughter, made them victims too. Thus, the application was not filed on behalf of the missing persons but in their own name. In that case, the Human Rights Chamber followed the case-law established by the European Court of Human Rights, notably in the "Cyprus vs. Turkey" case. In that case, the Court had noted that, twenty years after the Turkish military operations in the north of the island, about 1,500 Cypriots were still reported missing. The missing persons had last been seen alive in the hands of the Turkish army, but Turkey never tried to find out what had become of them, thereby rendering it an ongoing violation of family rights.

The agent of the Government of the Federation then challenged the Chamber to examine complaints of thousands of Srebrenica families. As a result, large numbers of applications were submitted to the Chamber by Srebrenica associations. We may wonder why such a mass of applications was referred to the Chamber. The reason is that the victims are deprived of any status before the ICTY and thus cannot file a complaint in that court. In fact, the status of victims was hotly debated when the ICTY and the International Criminal Court were created. Given the deplorable state of the Bosnian judicial system after the war, moreover, it was very difficult to file an application to the local courts. Prompted by the Federation's authorities for political reasons, the families turned toward the Chamber. The latter were all the more at a loss as to what to do as there were still rumors in Bosnia according to which the Bosniaks of Srebrenica were being held prisoner in mines in Serbia or elsewhere.

The "Selimović" decision of 7 March 2003

The applications linked to the Srebrenica massacre were introduced from November 2001 to March 2002. Due to their number, the Chamber, which had only limited means at its disposal and could not possibly treat them one by one, had to screen them to examine them in a single decision according to a procedure that had already been used many times before. Applications had to meet the same criteria: the victims had to be family members of the missing persons and not the missing person themselves; the missing persons had to be registered in keeping with the procedures of the International Committee of the Red Cross (ICRC) and also declared as missing to the competent governmental commissions; finally, according to the judges, the victims had to be civilians and not soldiers.

Having reached its first judgment ("Selimović"), on 20 June 2002, the Chamber transmitted forty-nine applications (out of 1,800 introduced) to the Government of the RS and requested the latter to give its observations regarding articles 3, 8, and 13 of the ECHR concerning the prohibition of inhuman and degrading treatment (article 3), the respect for private and family life (article 8) and discrimination (article 13), and regarding the 1948 Genocide Convention. The latter had been ratified by Yugoslavia in 1950 and by the Republic of Bosnia-Herzegovina on 29 December 1992 (where it figures in the Constitution). The Convention compels state signatories to punish persons guilty of genocide.

The observations transmitted by the RS in August 2002 dealt with the admissibility and not the merits of the cases. In particular, the RS pointed out that domestic remedies had not been exhausted since applicants had not applied to the RS Commission for Missing Persons. The RS also argued that the definition of the United Nations for missing persons, according to which they had to have been arrested, kept as prisoners or kidnapped against their will, did not apply to the men of Srebrenica, since the latter had voluntarily fled into the woods. Lastly, the RS maintained that the applications were incompatible *ratione temporis*, since the violations preceded the entry into force of the Dayton agreements.

In its screening of the admissibility of the applications, the Chamber upheld the fact that, as regards the exhaustion of domestic remedies, all the applicants had followed the proceedings set up by the ICRC, according to which all the applications transmitted to one party must be transmitted to the other parties. In that case, the applicants had filed requests to the Federal Commission for Missing Persons and sometimes to the ICRC, which was in agreement with the proceedings mentioned above. The domestic remedies had thus been exhausted. As to the definitions of missing persons, the Chamber dismissed the RS argument, since it was clear from the ICTY Krstić judgment that the persons concerned had been captured and detained by the Serb forces before disappearing.

Concerning its temporal jurisdiction, the Chamber pointed that, for the families, it was a matter of continuous suffering that had stopped neither with the Dayton agreements nor with the ICTY judgments, which only offer a global description of events. Such judgments, therefore, did not put an end, at the individual level, to rumors and to families' expectations. In fact, during the war, a number of warlords and militia had opened their own prisons and turned their prisoners into slaves, which fostered rumors concerning the fate of missing persons.

Regarding the merits, the Chamber found a breach of article 8 of the ECHR, since the state has a positive obligation to supply all information concerning a person when it has it or controls it and refuses to supply it on arbitrary and unjustified grounds. The Krstić judgment made it clear that the Army of the RS had separated women, elderly people, and children from men of fighting age, with the latter being taken into custody in Bratunac. The Army of the RS also captured a number of men who tried to flee across the woods and took them to Bratunac, as well. They took their personal documents and belongings from them and burnt them. The men were then killed during mass executions and buried in mass graves. Later, the army dug up the bodies and reburied them elsewhere. These facts, which are indisputable, show that the RS authorities had in their possession or in their control all the necessary elements to find information about the missing persons, even after the Dayton agreements. Moreover, the RS authorities had not tried to find the information, had not taken any steps to help the search for the missing persons, had not conducted any investigation to determine the dates or the places of detention, or to identify the places where the bodies were buried.

As regards article 3 of the ECHR, the Chamber applied the case-law of the European Court of Human Rights in the case "Cyprus vs. Turkey." The level of gravity of the suffering endured by the families of those persons was such that it could be defined as inhuman treatment, in the sense of article 3 of the ECHR. The Chamber applied the principle of non-discrimination, which applies whenever one person is treated differently from others placed in an identical or similar position, with no reasonable or objective reason for it (which must be supplied by the state). In our case, the report concerning the Srebrenica events presented on 3 September 2002 by the office of the RS in charge of the relationships with the ICTY was clearly discriminatory by insisting on the fact that:

> "roughly 1,800 Muslim soldiers are estimated to be killed during combats in fleeing ... and probably another 100 persons had died of physical conditions while fleeing ... the number of Muslim soldiers who were executed by Bosnian Serb forces for personal revenge or for simple ignorance of international law ... would probably stand less than 100."[7]

No mention was made of the Bosniak civilian victims during the July 1995 massacre.[8]

The Chamber thus found a violation of articles 3 (prohibition of inhuman or degrading treatment) and 8 (respect of private and family life) of the ECHR and of the obligation of non-discrimination according to these provisions. It ordered the RS to take four measures. The first was to transmit all information in their possession or under their control concerning the fate of the missing persons and the place where they were, to free them immediately if they were alive or detained and, if deceased, tell where their mortal remains lay. The second measure was to conduct investigations into the Srebrenica events and to present a report on those events. The third measure was to publish the decision of the Human Rights Chamber in the official journal of the Republika Srpska. Finally, the authorities had to pay the Foundation of the Srebrenica-Potočari Memorial and Cemetery[9] the first two million convertible Marks (KM) out of a total of four million KM (2,045,168 Euros).[10]

The decision can be accounted for without violating the secrecy of deliberations. The judges of the Chamber reflected for a long time about what reparations might mean confronted with such an awful tragedy and the impossibility of ever satisfying the victims. They first considered giving out the money directly to the associations that represent and help the Srebrenica victims. But such conflicts stand among these associations that it is impossible to appoint a single legitimate representative of the victims. In what concerns the obligation to conduct an investigation into the events, the judges did not mention the creation of a commission but had in mind the Truth and Reconciliation Commission of South Africa. As a matter of fact, Bosnia lacked a public, non-criminal commission, which would not establish penal responsibilities, in view of making a real, uncontroversial investigation. Following the Chamber's suggestion, the RS proposed to set up a commission. During the examination of the follow-up of the decision, the Chamber insisted with the High Representative on the necessary transparency of the commission's work and especially on the holding of public hearings, which was in fact not the case. It must be borne in mind that the ICTY already existed and a number of local courts also had jurisdiction to adjudicate war crimes. It was thus unnecessary to repeat their work, and the commission the Chamber wished for was different in its principle. A criminal court examines the individual penal responsibilities and, notably, as was the case for Srebrenica, considers the fate of victims in a global way only. By contrast and in keeping with the principle of defending human rights, the judges in the Chamber wanted a real investigation to take place and the RS Government to acknowledge collective responsibility. The problem was to determine to what extent the RS Government, and not this or that individual, was responsible. Incidentally, it was easy for the RS to take cover behind the individual responsibility of this or that soldier and to hear him talk about the events, which would only result in holding back the commission in its work indefinitely.

The Aftermath of the Human Rights Chamber's Decision

The decision met with mixed reactions. The reactions of the international community, NGOs defending human rights, and the Anglo-Saxon international press were positive, while the French press showed no interest. The most severe criticism came from the Association of the Mothers of Srebrenica and Podrinje, who opposed the Dayton agreements and whose leader was Ibran Mustafić.[11] The association blamed the Chamber for missing the point, on the ground that the real victims were not relatives but rather those who had gone missing, since the violation of human rights was the massacre itself and not the fact that the RS did not say where the corpses lay. Moreover, it was opposed to accepting money from the RS for the cemetery and the memorial of Potočari. Such reactions are understandable to us as human beings, even if the grounds for judicial reasoning are different. The Federation's daily newspapers, *Dnevni Avaz* and *Oslobođenje*, repeated the same arguments and the weekly *Dani* asked whether it was normal to require criminals to investigate their own crimes. Those newspapers, however, approved the fact that Serb tax payers had to pay for Bosniak victims, whereas many women in Srebrenica considered that it would have been preferable to pay compensation individually and not collectively.

As regards the implementation of the decision, the Chamber had no coercive power, especially since it delivered that decision in March 2003 and ceased to exist in late 2003; however, it cooperated with the High Representative in that matter. The first financial installment amounting to two million KM was made on 4 September 2003. The decision was published in the official journal of the RS. Following the Chamber's decision, the RS Government presented two reports. The first interim report was published on 3 June 2003 and the second on 5 September 2003. The RS highlighted difficulties in complying with the request to investigate and it was concluded that the Government of the RS, within the set deadline, was not able to provide all the requested answers.[12]

The RS Commission of Inquiry and the RS Report on the Events of Srebrenica

The Commission's Work

With the Human Rights Chamber having concluded that these two interim reports did not fulfill the obligations of the RS, the High Representative in Bosnia-Herzegovina, Paddy Ashdown, announced at an 15 October 2003 press conference that the president of the RS, Dragan Čavić, was to put together a commission responsible for submitting a complete report within six months. Victims and other members of the Bosniak community expressed their great concern and fear that this commission would act in bad faith and that their participation would give undesirable legitimacy to the process.[13] In December 2003, after much discussion concerning the composition of the commission, Marko Arsović, Milan Bogdanić, Milorad Ivošević, Đorđe Stojaković, and Gojko Vukotić were finally named as representatives of the RS; Smail Čekić, director of the Institute for Research of Crimes Against Humanity and International Law, was named as representative of the victim community; and Gordon Bacon, chief of staff of the ICMP, was named as representative of the international community. Mr. Bacon was a member of the commission on a personal basis. On 25 December 2003, the Government of the RS confirmed the appointment of the members of this commission, the exact title of which was the "Commission for Investigation of the Events in and around Srebrenica between 10 and 19 July 1995."

After a slow start, the Commission settled on its procedural rules (including a decision-making procedure by consensus), strategy, and working plan in early 2004. The members of the Commission addressed requests to various institutions, such as the army and the police, and tried to obtain archival materials, but sometimes found themselves with nearly empty dossiers, and were told that no one seemed to have the relevant documents in their possession. They thus became aware of the secret influence of certain RS officials. Several members of the Commission and their families were threatened, spit on, or dubbed traitors to the Serb people and their country. The combination of political manipulation, a hostile public opinion, a lack of resources, and official support and threats against the security of members of the Commission represented an obstruction to its work.[14]

In response to concerns expressed by the High Representative, the Government of the RS itself, and the interim report of 5 April 2004, the High Representative announced that the Government of the RS should dismiss Marko Arsović, the acting president of the Commission, and that the latter should receive appropriate support in its work. Moreover, the High Representative announced the dismissal of Dejan Miletić, RS liaison officer with the ICTY, and General Cvjetko Savić, chief of the general staff of the Army of the RS, due to their obstruction of the Commission's work.[15] Finally, the High Representative publicly reprimanded the Commission and held the president of the RS, Dragan Čavić, and the prime minister, Dragan Mikerević, personally responsible for the success of its work. These events were widely covered in the media.

The Commission was instructed by the High Representative not to elaborate on historical facts that preceded the massacre and instead concentrate on the search for new information, in particular to locate new mass graves and to compile the list of individuals executed between 10 and 19 July 1995.[16] The Commission thus revised its strategy and working plan. A series of two-member teams were formed: Milan Bogdanić and

Gordon Bacon were put in charge of seeking the location of mass graves; Smail Čekić and Đorđe Stojaković were put in charge of obtaining documentation from the minister of the interior and the police; and Milorad Ivošević and Gojko Vukotić were put in charge of investigating the role of the army (or armies). At the end of May, the Government of the RS appointed a seventh member, Željko Vujadinović.

During the preparation of the final report, the Commission received a large number of RS police and army documents. Some of its members, in coordination with the RS and Federation Commissions for Missing Persons, traveled to the field to verify the supposed location of the new mass graves. The Commission's final report was submitted to the RS Government on 4 June 2004. On 11 June 2004, the Government adopted it.[17] The report was divided into four sections: the fate of Bosniaks in and around Srebrenica, the location of mass graves, the fate of those unaccounted for, and information on cases submitted to the Human Rights Chamber. The report contained information on the location of thirty-two mass graves, including eight previously unknown ones and three which the Commission had been unable to locate due to insufficient data. One of the priorities of the Commission was to create a list, as accurate as possible, of the persons who went missing during the events in Srebrenica between 10 and 19 July 1995, with an emphasis on the fate of the persons named in the Human Rights Chamber Decision of the 3 March 2003. It reported on the status of 1,849 persons for which applications were submitted to the Human Rights Chamber and the Constitutional Court of Bosnia-Herzegovina, including 1,135 individuals believed to have gone missing between 10 and 19 July 1995.[18] The report itself highlights inconsistencies in the number of applications submitted, the number of persons represented in these applications, the number of persons unaccounted for, and the number of persons unaccounted for between 10 and 19 July 1995, and data-collection weaknesses.[19]

The report and attachments closely examined the role of the RS Ministry of Defense, RS Ministry of Interior and the relevant RS Ministry of Interior's police stations, in particular the actions of the RS army and police. It included documents that clarified the three phases of operation "Krivaja": the attack, the separation of women and children, and the execution of the men. It also included the orders for the participation of police units of the Republic of Serb Krajina (RSK) and Serbia.[20] The documentation that was received by the Commission, portions of which were contained in confidential annexes, mostly came from RS institutions as well as some state, federal, and international institutions. In addition to lists of missing persons, the data collected during the Commission's work consisted of documents from RS army and police structures, such as the Ministry of Defense and the Ministry of the Interior. They included movement orders for military units, procurement orders with companies to supply vehicles, busses and equipment on particular dates as part of "Krivaja 95," and witness interviews and statements (for example, descriptions by bus and truck drivers of the number of people they had transported, the places they had dropped them off, and how, following this, they had heard gun shots and then nothing more). Killed prisoners were immediately buried in mass graves, which were later relocated by the RS Army. But not all of the information requested was received; it was only on 16 June 2004 that the RS Ministry of the Interior supplied sixteen boxes of documents. The Commission was thus granted an extension until 15 October 2004 for the preparation of an addendum to the report.[21]

According to statements made by one of the participants, members of the Commission reacted with shock, surprise, and fear to the detailed documentation they had uncovered. They had unofficially found evidence concerning 8,200 individuals reported missing after the fall of Srebrenica. Renowned Serb lawyers, judges, and historians who participated in the Commission's work had already received threats. They wondered how it would be possible to publish this information while continuing to live in Banja Luka.[22]

The addendum to the final report was completed and submitted on 15 October 2004. It included a section on mass graves, an effort to establish a complete list of missing persons, and recommendations. All information on mass graves was passed to the Federal Commission for Missing Persons for further action. The Commission of inquiry created a special database where it registered thousands of entries from multiple preexisting lists of missing persons. Many obstacles had already been encountered during the course of earlier attempts to cross-check such lists compiled by different sources. The difficulties in doing so stemmed in some cases from the similarity between certain proper names and the incomplete or erroneous character of some data. The report emphasizes that the lists were not final or definitive.[23] The multiple lists were divided into several sub-categories, but the report indicated that the data varied between 7,000 and 8,000 individuals for the period of July 1995[24] and that 13,569 individuals were represented on the lists covering the period from 1992 to 1995 from the Srebrenica region.[25] According to some sources, the data was intentionally segmented for fear of public reactions and the unfortunate consequences that it might have for members of the Commission. The Commission concluded that efforts should be made to continue collection of documentation and relevant facts, particularly in connection with possible new individual and mass graves, and to improve and speed up the process of the exhumation and identification of bodily remains, which is of high importance in providing the answers to the families of victims on the fate of their relatives.[26]

At its session on 28 October 2004, the RS Government accepted the report, which "demonstrates that, at the area of Srebrenica in July 1995, were committed crimes of huge extent, by means of rude violation of the international humanitarian law."[27] The Government also declared that it sympathized with the pain felt by all of the Srebrenica victims' relatives and expressed its sincere condolences and apologies for the tragedy they had experienced. It affirmed its commitment to bring all who had committed war crimes to justice and declared that the Commission's working method should serve as an example for later inquiries into crimes committed in other regions, no matter who the perpetrators.

The Follow-Up of the Report and Political Prospects in Bosnia-Herzegovina

Following the High Representative's request to the prime minister of the RS in January 2005, an eight-person working group was named to implement the conclusions of the final report of the Commission on the Srebrenica massacre. This group was to analyze the report's documentation and identify all officials whose names appeared in the confidential annexes as possible perpetrators, particularly those who were still employed by the institutions of the RS. In its 1 April 2005 report, the working group identified 892 individuals who, despite their involvement in the events of Srebrenica, were still employed as officials at the level of municipalities, entities, or the central state, above all in the services of the minister of the interior and of the police. This information was transmitted to the office of the prosecutor of the Court of Bosnia-Herzegovina and the Office of the High Representative on the understanding that the list of names would not be made public until official proceedings had been opened.

On several occasions, the members of Srebrenica associations of missing persons and other groups called for the list of those involved to be made public. The controversy continued until 24 August 2006, when the names of 69 out of the 892 individuals mentioned on the list were published in the press (followed by 59 more names the next day) despite objections from the office of the prosecutor of the Court of Bosnia-Herzegovina, which opposed publishing the names due to the ongoing nature of the investigation into war crimes in Srebrenica and the right of the accused to a defense.[28] Srebrenica Commission member Smail Čekić met with Srebrenica women informing them that a list of 19,473 persons belonging to the Drina Corps of the RS Army in July 1995 had been compiled and added that 892 of them were employed in state, entity, and municipal institutions.[29] The ICTY prosecutor's office also had to publicly underscore the fact that, while the Commission's report was to be made public, certain parts should definitely not be—those containing the names of those involved, for example—without the consent of judicial institutions.[30]

On 6 April 2005, the new prime minister of the RS, Pero Bukejlović, stated that the adoption of this report showed the RS Government's determination to shed full light on the events of Srebrenica. The High Representative recognized the seriousness of the Commission's work, but regretted that it was not complete. Indeed, the RS Ministry of the Interior did not furnish information on hundreds of individuals who had been deployed in July 1995 under the authority of the Army of the RS in Srebrenica.

At the same time, Pero Bukejlović stated in March 2005 that the genocide committed against the Serbs in Sarajevo was perhaps larger than that of Srebrenica.[31] Some saw this statement as a political provocation intended to turn attention away from the failure of the RS authorities to arrest Radovan Karadžić and Ratko Mladić. The representatives of several NGOs strongly condemned this declaration.[32] According to Sulejman Tihić, member of the Presidency of Bosnia-Herzegovina, such statements proved the need for establishing a Truth and Reconciliation Commission in Bosnia to examine the suffering of all civilians. The Chamber of Representatives of the Federation's Parliament adopted a motion condemning these statements as "horrible lies."[33]

After the appearance in the streets of Banja Luka of posters denying the crimes committed by the Army of the RS in Srebrenica, Dragan Čavić, president of the RS, stated on 9 June 2005 that "there is no basis for speaking of genocide" in regards to Srebrenica.[34] Despite the reports submitted by the RS Commission, the ICTY Krstić judgment, which resulted in a conviction for genocide, and the June 2005 revelation of videotapes of the executions carried out by the paramilitary unit known as the "Scorpions," RS officials continued to play down the gravity of the crimes that had been committed.

While it is difficult to say that a revolution took place in the conscience of Serbs, the creation of the Commission and the fact that its report was based on sources that were for the most part supplied by RS authorities give credence to the report's claim that it showed the maturity of the Serb people.[35] The most positive point remains the personal commitment of the majority of the Commission's members. The courage they showed in the face of pressure and threats saved this Commission from becoming the farce some feared it would be. Although most of the facts were already well-documented, it was important for the RS itself to create an authority that would reach its own conclusions. This task was all the more delicate given the twofold task expected of the Commission by the Government of the RS: to cooperate while ensuring that whatever facts revealed not be too damaging for the RS. It is to be regretted, however, that the work of the Commission was the result of strong pressure exercised by the High Representative, the public interventions of whom were seen as a new case of discrimination against the Serbs at the hands of the international community. This pressure weakened the legitimacy of the report's conclusions in the eyes of Serb public opinion in the RS. The fact that the text of the report was not distributed to the public, that ordinary citizens were not informed of the details of its conclusions, and that its annexes remained strictly confidential only exacerbated this state of affairs.

As the spring 2005 accusations of genocide against the Serbs of Sarajevo show, moreover, the work of the RS Commission on Srebrenica gave rise to denial, very violent claims of greater victimhood, and attempts to equalize suffering of various groups. Growing recognition of the crimes in Srebrenica in 1995 against the Bosniaks fed demands on the part of Bosnian Serbs and Croats, as well as other Bosniaks. Concerned by the focus on the Srebrenica massacre and the lack of attention accorded to their loved ones—whether victims of events that took place prior to 1995 or those that occurred in other parts of the country—these groups demanded that they, too, be recognized as equal victims. This Commission can thus be seen either as a model for the future or, on the contrary, an example of what must not be done—for reasons of principle, not of persons. Indeed, if the society genuinely wishes to overcome the bloody past of recent conflicts, separate Bosniak, Serb, and Croat commissions must not be created for each region or event. The method of examining the actions of a single national group on a restricted geographical territory gave rise to hostile reactions on the part of other national groups—in the present case, the Serbs—and led to unfortunate competition among victims. Following later decisions by the Human Rights Chamber and the Constitutional Court, there were calls for the creation of similar commissions for Sarajevo, Bratunac, Višegrad, Foča, Rogatica, Vlasenica, Mostar, and yet other regions.[36]

On 25 May 2006, after calls from groups in the RS and a blockage of Parliament by all Serb representatives, the Council of Ministers of Bosnia-Herzegovina decided to create a state commission to look into the suffering of Serbs, Croats, Bosniaks, Jews, and other groups in Sarajevo between 1992 and 1995. With very wide media coverage both for and against the decision, the members of this commission were named in June 2006 and given responsibility for publishing a final report in the twelve months that followed.[37]

At the same time, the idea of creating a Truth and Reconciliation Commission for all of Bosnia-Herzegovina reemerged in various circles. However, there was very little participation on the part of victims' groups in this debate and they were not given an opportunity to submit their own proposals.[38] Since 2006, civil society organizations from the post-Yugoslav countries have actively discussed the need for establishing a regional truth-telling mechanism. A coalition for a regional truth commission remains engaged in discussion to establish such a commission.[39] Yet, whatever form they take, such efforts must be focused on the needs of victims and the search for truth and justice, not criteria of nationality. The ICMP is seeking to work in this direction.

The Work of the ICMP Concerning the Victims of Srebrenica

At the end of the conflicts in former Yugoslavia, the fate of forty thousand people—71 percent of whom had disappeared in Bosnia-Herzegovina— was unknown. The ICMP believed that many of them had been victims of a policy of forced disappearance and that finding and identifying them would allow their loved ones to mourn their loss, thereby contributing to a larger process of reconciliation. The ICMP divided its activities between two main programs[40]: forensic sciences and civil society initiatives. As a result of attempts by perpetrators to conceal evidence, bodies were removed from their initial mass graves and reburied in other locations. As a consequence body parts are found disarticulated in numerous primary and secondary mass grave sites. Due to the thousands of skeletons that were found in secondary mass graves, it was nearly impossible to engage in the "classic" identification of bodies on the basis of clothing and physical characteristics. The ICMP thus developed a large-scale DNA identification program. It opened a special forensic facility in Tuzla, the Podrinje Identification Project (PIP), where hundreds of human remains from the Srebrenica region were collected, as well as the Lukavac Reassembly Center (LRC), which had the difficult mission of returning the most complete mortal remains possible to families. With the help of scientific methods, it endeavors to reassemble body parts that have been dispersed between several sites related to the Srebrenica massacre. Indeed, in late 1995 and early 1996, the authorities of the RS had moved the bodies in order to hide the evidence of mass murder. Bodies in secondary graves are commingled. It was thus only by means of DNA identification that anthropologists were able to establish a link between the various bones they had found and reliably reconstitute victims' bodies. In the process of identification, the use of DNA tests involved obtaining and analyzing bone samples from the individuals who had been unearthed and blood samples from surviving relatives. Without these two elements, it is impossible to establish a DNA match. For the single case of Srebrenica, the ICMP collected 22,135 blood samples, corresponding to 7,723 missing persons,[41] and 22,111 bone samples, which were transmitted by the relevant authorities to the ICMP

Identification Coordination Center in Tuzla. As a result, the ICMP was able to establish 15,398 match reports between blood and bone DNA sequences (not including 197 negative match reports on presumptive cases), covering a population of 6,683 different individuals, and succeeded in re-associating 8,715 separated skeletal elements. As of December 2011, 5,642 Srebrenica identification cases have been closed and 5,224 identified bodies have been buried, 5,011 of them at the Potočari memorial.[42]

Through its program to support civil society initiatives, the ICMP works with more than a hundred associations of families of missing persons in the former Yugoslavia. ICMP's goal is to encourage effective engagement of family members of the missing in representation of their interests, particularly in order to put pressure on the authorities and ensure that their rights are recognized. Since 1998, the ICMP has awarded many grants to the associations of families of missing persons of Srebrenica for projects, training workshops, and other forms of support to help them reach their objectives. Association activities have centered on the search for truth and justice, the development of the Foundation of the Srebrenica-Potočari Memorial and Cemetery and bringing war criminals to justice. For the ICMP, it is imperative that the various survivor groups be able to express their views concerning the path to be taken in the search for truth, justice, and reconciliation in former Yugoslavia.

Translated from French by Ethan Rundell

Notes

1. The two authors of this chapter are responsible only for the presentation of the work of their respective institutions, i.e., Michèle Picard for the Human Rights Chamber (in the first part of the text) and Asta Zinbo for the International Commission on Missing Persons (in the second part of the text).
2. Human Rights Chamber for Bosnia-Herzegovina, *The "Srebrenica Cases" (49 Applications) against the Republika Srpska (case n°CH/01/8365 et al.)*, decision on admissibility and merits of 7 March 2003, accessible at http://www.hrc.ba/database/decisions/CH01-8365%20Selimovic%20Admissibility%20and%20Merits%20E.pdf, last accessed 8 December 2011.
3. ICMP endeavors to secure the cooperation of governments and other authorities in locating and identifying persons missing as a result of armed conflicts, other hostilities, or violations of human rights and to assist them to do so. See http://www.icmp.org/mandate/.
4. An international ombudsman appointed by the Organization for Security and Cooperation in Europe (OSCE). He and the Human Rights Chamber composed the Commission on Human Rights provided for in Annex 6 of the Dayton agreements; the Ombudsman had the ability to lodge applications to the Chamber.

5. Human Rights Chamber for Bosnia-Herzegovina, *Josip, Božana and Tomislav Matanović against Republika Srpska* (case no. CH/96/1), decision on admissibility of 13 January 1996 and decision on the merits of 11 July 1997.
6. Human Rights Chamber for Bosnia-Herzegovina, *Đorđo Unković against the Federation of Bosnia-Herzegovina* (case no. CH/99/2150), decision of 12 April 2002.
7. Bureau of Government of the Republika Srpska for Relations with the ICTY, *Report about Case Srebrenica* (Banja Luka, September 2002), 33–34, quoted in paragraph 94 of the Chamber's decision. See also the declaration of Dejan Miletić, head of the Office of the RS in charge of the relations with the ICTY, during a press conference in Banja Luka on 3 September 2002.
8. This report was firmly condemned by the international community, political officials, and NGOs (see *Oslobođenje*, 4 September 2002; *Dnevni avaz*, 4 September 2002). The office of the prosecutor of the ICTY expressed his bitterness about this "scandalous and shameful report, in which the well established evidence introduced before the ICTY was totally ignored" (declaration of Graham Blewitt, in *Dnevni avaz*, 5 September 2002; *Jutarnje novine*, 5 September 2002).
9. Foundation established by a decision of the High Representative on 10 May 2001 (see the press release issued on by the Office of the High Representative (OHR) on 10 May 2001, accessible on http://www.ohr.int).
10. *The "Srebrenica Cases" (49 applications) against the Republika Srpska* (case no. CH/01/8365 et al.), IX. Conclusions, article 220.10, asking the RS to pay 2 million KM no later than 7 September 2003 and four yearly installments of five hundred thousand KM to pay on 7 September 2004, 2005, 2006, and 2007.
11. *Jutarnje novine*, 10 March 2003.
12. According to the principle of the universality of human rights, the Chamber subsequently delivered other decisions in relation with other regions of Bosnia-Herzegovina involving the responsibility of the Federation. For all the decisions of the Human Rights Chamber see http://www.hrc.ba, last accessed 8 December 2011.
13. The names of several well-known survivors, such as Hasan Nuhanović, and other public figures, such as Amor Mašović, president of the Federal Commission for Missing Persons, were put forward but they refused to participate in the Commission (Asta Zinbo's interview with Hasan Nuhanović, 20 November 2003).
14. Letters from the Commission to the government of the RS, 19 March and 8 April 2004.
15. Decisions of the High Representative nos. 203/04 and 204/04, 16 April 2004, accessible at http://www.ohr.int, last accessed on 8 December 2011.
16. Remarks by Milan Bogdanić, president of the Commission, during the ICMP conference *Mechanisms for the Research and Documentation of the Truth*, held in Jahorina on 20 October 2004.
17. See Republika Srpska Government—The Commission for Investigation of the Events in and around Srebrenica between 10th and 19th July 1995, *The Events in and around Srebrenica between 10th and 19th July, 1995* (Banja Luka, 11 June 2004). The RS reports on Srebrenica are accessible at http://www.domovina.net/srebrenica/page_006.php, last accessed 8 December 2011.
18. *The Events in and around Srebrenica between 10th and 19th July 1995* (Banja Luka, 11 June 2004), 35 and 37.
19. Ibid., 38.
20. Letter from High Representative Paddy Ashdown to Javier Solana (High Representative for EU Foreign Policy and Common Security) and Jaap de Hoop Scheffer (general secretary of NATO), summarized in the OHR's 11 June 2004 press release, accessible at http://www.ohr.int.

21. The decision was made by the Government of the RS at its 87th session, 16 July 2004, to prolong the work of the Commission.
22. As remarked by a member of the ICMP's local team who had participated in the Commission's internal work as an assistant to Gordon Bacon.
23. The compilation of Central Records will continue and be carried on by the Missing Persons Institute (MPI), as mandated by the Bosnian law on missing persons.
24. See Republika Srpska Government—The Commission for Investigation of the Events in and around Srebrenica between 10th and 19th July 1995, *Addendum to the Report of the 11th June 2004 on the Events in and around Srebrenica between 10th and 19th July 1995* (Banja Luka, 15 October 2004), 9, accessible at http://www.domovina.net/srebrenica/page_006.php. The A1 list includes the names of 7,108 individuals who went missing between the 10 and 19 July 1995, the A2 list those of 936 individuals for whom information on the date of disappearance is contradictory (i.e., whether or not it took place between 10 and 19 July 1995), the C1 list those of 4,556 individuals for whom the date of disappearance is outside the scope of the Commission's mandate, and the C2 list those of 271 individuals who were listed as missing and who were later revealed to still be living or to have died in circumstances that did not fall under the Commission's mandate.
25. *Addendum to the Report of the 11th June 2004*, 8.
26. Ibid., 33.
27. Government of the Republic of Srpska, *Conclusions*, Banja Luka, 28 October 2004, conclusion no. 2, accessible at http://www.domovina.net/srebrenica/page_006.php.
28. *Oslobođenje*, 24 August 2006, and 25 August 2006.
29. OHR BiH Media Round-up, 9 October 2005.
30. *Oslobođenje*, 26 August 2006; International Criminal Tribunal for the Former Yugoslavia, *ICTY Weekly Press Briefing*, 30 August 2006, accessible at http://www.icty.org/sid/3556, last accessed on 4 February 2010.
31. Intervention at the conference *From Truth to Justice*, held in Pale on 25 March 2005. See *Patriot*, 28 March 2005.
32. FENA, *Oslobođenje, Nezavisne novine*, 30 March 2005.
33. FENA, 30 March 2005.
34. SRNA, 9 June 2005.
35. As remarked by Milan Bogdanić, president of the Commission, during the ICMP conference *Mechanisms for the Research and Documentation of Truth*, held on 20 October 2004 in Jahorina.
36. The Human Rights Chamber for Bosnia-Herzegovina finished its mandate on 31 December 2003.
37. The Commission produced neither a report nor any tangible results. See Sanita Rožajac, "Komisija za Sarajevo čeka odluku Vijeća ministara BiH. Kome je cilj da spriječi istraživanja?" [The Sarajevo Commission Awaits the Decision of the Council of Ministers: Who Wants to Prevent the Investigations?], *Oslobođenje*, 14 February 2007.
38. In fact, the proposal of a Truth and Reconciliation Commission did not go beyond the project phase.
39. See http://ictj.org/news/truth-seeking-western-balkans-initiative-regional-truth-commission.
40. For more explanations of these programs, see the ICMP site: http://www.ic-mp.org.
41. According to the ICMP's blood-sample database, evidence exists for 7,789 individuals who went missing during the fall of Srebrenica in July 1995. The ICMP expects the final number to be around 8,000 victims.
42. Figures for December 2011; see http://www.ic-mp.org for regularly updated figures.

Chapter 8

FACTS, RESPONSIBILITY, INTELLIGIBILITY
Comparing the Srebrenica Investigations and Reports

Isabelle Delpla

To Sabaheta, Emir, and Emira, who lost their fathers, husband, grandfather, uncles, cousins, friends, and childhood photos in Srebrenica. And to Sabaheta who, before she had even been born, escaped through the woods from Srebrenica.

What does one learn from reading and comparing the investigations of the International Criminal Tribunal for the Former Yugoslavia (ICTY) and reports by the UN, France, the Netherlands, and the Republika Srpska (RS) on the fall of the Srebrenica enclave and the massacre that followed it? Since reading these texts can be a trying experience, no quick response is available. Those who wish to understand the sequence and gravity of those events are better served by the more literary approach taken by investigative journalists: David Rohde, for example, who in *Endgame*[1] intertwines the points of view of his various protagonists to produce what is, in its unity of place, time, and action, like a modern-day tragedy without fate, or Chuck Sudetic's family novel, *Blood and Vengeance*.[2] In these works, the reader finds ample information, a chronologically precise reconstruction of events, dramatic intensity, and a sense of development, all of which make them landmark texts. This is all the more remarkable given that they were written shortly after the events occurred. With a clarity and finesse hardly matched by later or more exhaustive reports, they also offer reflections on the manner in which the events are narrated, the status of testimony, and the role of memory, as well as explanatory hypotheses concerning the abandonment of the enclave and the massacre.

As for the official reports and investigations, on the other hand, their interest lies elsewhere. In the first place, the institutions that carried them

---

Notes for this chapter begin on page 165.

out enjoyed much greater powers than those of ordinary journalists and scholars and, so, were able to contribute greatly to our knowledge of what happened.[3] In the second place, these international or state institutions helped to bring documents and debates concerning Srebrenica into the public sphere.[4] Third, the UN, French, and Dutch reports were issued by international organizations or countries that had direct responsibility in the fall of the enclave. By virtue of the publicity of their debates, they help satisfy the Kantian demand for democratic or republican control over foreign and international policy. They can be seen as striving to address individual and institutional responsibility on a cosmopolitan (or international) level whether we examine them as a citizen of a given country in a given space—Europe—or as a citizen of the world.[5] What matters, from this point of view, is the follow-up and consequences of these inquiries in the public sphere.

Complementing Jean-Louis Fournel's chapter on the "report-form," where the public nature of these reports is examined, the comparison presented here mainly focuses on the manner in which the facts were established and responsibility was determined. As an analysis of the narrative forms and the paradigms for intelligibility adopted in the documents reveals, these two issues cannot easily be separated.

Establishing the Facts and Dividing the (Intellectual) Labor

The most notable contribution made by these reports and the investigations is surely in helping to establish the facts. Without the ICTY's efforts both to reconstruct the execution and corpse-moving operations and to exhume bodies and without the ICMP's (International Commission for Missing Persons) efforts to identify those bodies, it is likely that the number of dead from Srebrenica would still only be a matter of rumor.[6] The figure of more than 7,475 dead, established by the ICTY in 2001 on the basis of ICRC lists, is a minimal estimate allowing for variations.[7] These variations can fuel disbelief, confusion, and even denials as to the extent of the massacre. In order to understand that such variations do not reflect falsifications, it is necessary to analyze the methods used in calculating and identifying the dead.[8] It is also important to know how victims are defined. According to the ICTY, the victims included not only the dead but also the women and children who were forcibly displaced and subject to persecution. The Human Rights Chamber even asserts that they were also victims of the crime of forced disappearance.[9] Conversely, not all of the Srebrenica dead were victims in the legal sense of the term. If they died in combat or committed suicide, they were victims of the events but not of direct criminal action.[10]

The ICTY's decisive contribution to reconstructing operation "Krivaja 95" becomes clear when one compares the reports. The factual basis and chronological sequence established by the 2001 Krstić judgment are, in their main lines, reiterated (sometimes verbatim) by the UN, French, and Dutch reports, the Selimović decision of the Human Rights Chamber for Bosnia-Herzegovina and the 2004 RS report. These repetitions in the drafting of the reports reveal how official truths are formed. In fact, only the ICTY had the authority to carry out an investigation, access a site, exhume bodies, and conduct searches and seizures, allowing them to corroborate or go beyond the testimony of victims in order to shed light on the vast military operation that had been launched to eliminate men and, several months later, move their corpses.

The relationship between judicial truths and historical truths (or truths of historians) is also clarified by comparing the ICTY inquiry with the monumental report drafted over a seven-year period by the NIOD, a large historical research institution in the Netherlands. The NIOD team had considerable resources at its disposal and extensive access to confidential governmental and international sources. Despite its self-proclaimed historical positivism and desire for objectivity, the method and results of the NIOD are often weak and would hardly stand up to cross-examination in a court of law. Thus, the NIOD often uses second hand, inaccessible, and sometimes very questionable sources and uncritically adopts the actors' points of view.[11] In contrast to the patient effort on the part of the ICRC, ICTY, and ICMP to calculate the number of missing and dead, for example, appendix IV on the history of Srebrenica uncritically endorses a figure supplied by local sources of a thousand Serb deaths in the Srebrenica region between 1992 and 1994, even despite the fact that none of these sources were considered reliable by the aforementioned international organizations.[12] More prudently, in a valuable study on what became of the column of Bosniaks who fled Srebrenica (which was not specifically investigated by the ICTY[13]), Dick Schoonoord[14] presents the difficulties of exactly reconstructing its route given the imprecise recollections of witnesses. But these difficulties are also indicative of the lack of resources available to historians. Unlike the ICTY investigators, they cannot verify testimony on site or film the sites to help witnesses clarify their statements. Schoonoord's skepticism also reflects a difference between the profession of historian and that of police officer: the latter is more familiar with frequenting criminals and reconstructing their logic. For Schoonoord, the fact that the dissimulation operation was carried out is a mystery given that the massacre was known through testimony and aerial images[15]; Jean-René Ruez, by contrast, explains why one might want to destroy evidence in this context.[16]

This comparison leads us to a more general observation about the divergences among the reports.[17] One important difference is that of their respective origin. Given that Srebrenica was a safe area and that the UN-integrated command chains brought together a plurality of national and international agents, these reports were above all exercises in self-reflection and self-critique.[18] Their diversity is also a matter of the approach adopted: there are considerable disparities of format and working and drafting methods among them,[19] particularly in what concerns the relationship to scientific expertise.[20]

Despite these variations, however, the reports are very similar in their narrative style and aim. This is, of course, due to the status of these texts, which respond to official questions formulated by state or international institutions, but it also holds for the work of journalists, such as that of David Rohde in *Endgame*. These texts reconstruct a detailed chronology of the events. Their style consists of a series of observational statements, the subjects of which are individual or institutional agents who did this or that on a given date in a given place. They resemble classic military or political history in which the main actors are military personnel, diplomats, international officials, or heads of state, with NGO members and ordinary people, for example, only coming afterward. Although the reports benefited from confidential information and, in some cases, vast resources, they differ quantitatively but not qualitatively from good investigative journalism. The NIOD report is no exception in this respect. Even appendix IV, which sketches a long-term history of Srebrenica and seems to borrow its analytical tools from the "new history," often follows the narrative thread of *Blood and Vengeance,* a work which explicitly approaches its subject from the perspective of family narratives and makes no claim to providing a comprehensive history of the events. This relative convergence is also found in the objects that are addressed: the establishment of safe areas, the (mal)function of UNPROFOR, the respective role of each country within it, the fall of the enclave, the executions, and the aftermath and consequences of Srebrenica.[21]

The very similarities among the various reports are what distinguish them, however, from the ICTY's investigations. These investigations allowed decisive progress to be made in understanding the massacre, not only by virtue of police expertise but also because these inquiries were where archives, documents, and testimony (all of a linguistic nature) found a material reference in the work of the scientific police (ballistic and forensic analyses, etc.). The legal investigation is the privileged site where historical narrative is anchored in the world of physical reality.[22] At this stage, the most significant division of labor in the creation of knowledge is not that separating the historian from the journalist or MP but rather that separating disciplines rooted in language and representation (including testimony) from those bringing physical and technical science to bear on the human factor.[23] We usually expect the social sciences to provide the means of reaching beyond the point of view of witnesses and actors by means of long-term history or statistical and economic analyses. In this case, however, it was the physical and medical sciences that performed this role.[24] Indeed, forensic experts played a decisive role in the Krstić trial by turning corpses into witnesses "from beyond the grave"—that is, reconstructing a portion of the events on the basis of autopsy reports when no testimony existed.[25]

In keeping with their reflexive and self-critical dimension, the second significant difference between the reports is linked to national context. Their descriptive and analytical frameworks are historically and geographically dictated by the role played by the institutions that ordered the reports. The RS report only deals with Serb responsibility in the massacre. The Bosnian parliamentary debate deals mainly with Bosniak responsibility in the fall of the enclave. The UN report deals with the role of UNPROFOR in Bosnia. The French report contributes no new information concerning the war in Bosnia and deals with the role of France in UNPROFOR and that of General Janvier in the fall of the enclave. The Dutch parliamentary report and that of the NIOD give priority to the role of Dutch officials in UNPROFOR and the *Dutchbat* (Dutch battalion) in Srebrenica and the run-up to and aftermath of the enclave's fall in Dutch politics. This (inter)national orientation explicitly determines the data collected and the object of study but also—and more insidiously—shapes the analyses. It is on this point that the search for facts and the assignment of responsibility mutually determine one another.

The Search for Intelligibility and the Assignment of Responsibility

The various reports are characterized by the type of intelligibility they offer, which oscillates between an ever more exhaustive examination of the details, sequence of events or causes, and the determination of responsibility. The search for intelligibility proceeds by contextualization (relative to the history of the conflict in Bosnia or the operation of the institutions involved), establishing relationships between a systemic explanation and the interpretations of individual agents. Taken together, the reports and investigations all focus on chronology and differentiate among several types of responsibility (though they all agree on the criminal responsibility of Serb forces). However, in what concerns the relationship between intelligibility and responsibility, they diverge on two main points. On the one hand, though they agree that the decision to capture the town seems to have been taken after the onset of the "Krivaja 95" operation, there is disagreement concerning the manner in which the decision to carry out the massacre was made and the reasons for doing so apart from a consensual and rather vague reference to ethnic cleansing. On the other hand, while the UN, French, and Dutch reports agree that the international community had neither foreseen nor wished for the enclave's fall and the ensuing massacre, they diverge concerning the manner in which criminal and political, local and international, individual and institutional responsibility is to be distributed and inter-related.[26]

In the first place, the considerable importance placed on chronology by the various reports and investigation may lead one to wonder what intelligibility results from this ever greater and more detailed accumulation of facts. This accumulation is as much a matter of attempting to establish narrative credibility in explaining the incredible mistakes and failures of international actors in terms of a conjunction of disparate factors and causalities as it is an effort to establish the facts. It is thus the opposite of conspiracy theory—the favored mode of interpretation in Bosnia—in which the abandonment of the enclave is presented as an intentional deed, a matter of secret agreements and thus, de facto, of complicity in genocide. Although the Bosniaks believe that the blue helmets should be judged in the same way as the Serbs, they distinguish this criminal responsibility from the responsibility of Bosniak politicians and soldiers as echoed in the parliamentary debate in Bosnia.[27] In a yet more direct way, the defense of General Krstić argued that the massacre had been organized by the French secret services with the aim of discrediting the Serbs. By contrast, the inquiries and reports distinguish (criminal) responsibility for the massacre from (political and moral) responsibility for the fall of the enclave. The ICTY investigations and the RS report only deal with the former whereas the UN, French, and Dutch reports mainly deal with the latter. Yet the question of whether or not the massacre and the fall of the enclave were foreseeable shows the difficulty of separating these types and degrees of responsibility.

While all of these texts strive to establish a credible narrative that does not entail international criminal intention, each one puts its detailed reconstruction of events to the service of very different types of intelligibility. For ICTY investigators, who sought to establish individual criminal responsibility, the evidence needed to be as detailed as possible to stand up to cross-examination by the defense. And, given the depths of horror, cruelty, and suffering revealed by the crime scenes, the devil was indeed in the details. For the NIOD, by contrast, detailed research was carried out in the interests of an objective, dispassionate, and non-judgmental history. As a matter of fact, such a mass of information ultimately wages a war of attrition on the critical spirit of the reader, rendering the course of events as unreadable as the report itself. In this way, it dilutes the responsibility of the various actors.

The UN report is all the more remarkable for the balance it establishes between readability and intelligibility in retracing the action of UNPROFOR in Bosnia over the course of a hundred or so clear and synthetic pages. David Harland, the report's principal author,

> did not really consider it my role to assign responsibility at all but rather to provide a comprehensive report of what happened from the establishment of the safe area in 1993 to the conclusion of the peace agreement in 1995. In other words, I saw myself mainly as trying to make a coherent narrative of events. I believe that this is what was asked by the Bosnian-Jordanian-Slovenian resolution which called for the report. ... I regret that the report was eventually called "The Fall of Srebrenica" as it deals, in large part, with events prior to the fall of Srebrenica and after and with the other "safe areas," particularly Žepa.[28]

The choice of these chronological and geographical limits sought to set the fall of Srebrenica in a larger context. In this respect, it corresponds to a type of analysis that, without clearing individuals of responsibility for their failings and errors, presents the fall of the town, not as a simple accident, but rather as the logical consequence of the (mal)function of UNPROFOR, the structural defects of its mandate, and the definition of safe areas. This is why Harland sought to reconstruct the fall of the Žepa enclave a few days after that of Srebrenica. Indeed, while it was known that General Mladić had decided to finish with Žepa and that the enclave would likely fall, with the fate of the men of Srebrenica still uncertain, General Janvier decided to do nothing to defend the enclave, deliberately abandoning it to its fate.

Although the UN report is mainly based on internal archives, it gives a sense of how the events developed. In this respect, it is similar to *Endgame*, where the actions of each actor—from the blindest to the most clearsighted, from the most reluctant to those most determined to use force against the Serb army—contribute to accelerating a catastrophe that could have been avoided.[29] The fact that Harland, director of the UN Civil and Political Affairs in Sarajevo from 1993 to 1999, had been a direct witness both of the war and of Serb efforts to take Goražde in 1994 and was an actor in negotiations surrounding the fall of Žepa certainly contributed to his understanding of the dynamic of events. In fact, Harland had been "a little surprised to be chosen, given that [he] was a vigorous critic of the UNPROFOR policy of minimum use of force."[30] The tone of the report is in sharp contrast with UNPROFOR's search for compromise and appeasement. This firm stance is also found in the report's conclusion, which was not written by Harland. Here, both Serb crimes and the UN policy that allowed them to take place are unambiguously condemned. In this, the report marks a break with the principle that had up till then guided the action of UNPROFOR. It was "a philosophy of impartiality" holding that "the parties were equally responsible for the transgressions that occurred,"[31] that led Serb war aims to be underestimated. And it was in a culture of peace hostile to any and all uses of force—even that of the Bosniaks in self-defense—that the report sees the origin of the UN's errors of judgment, mistakes, and responsibility.[32]

With significant variations—the variations being just as interesting as what is repeated—this general analysis is reiterated in the French and Dutch reports. The French report underscores a flaw (or a policy) that was common to all international actors: that of never making a priority of protecting civilian populations, especially considering the measures taken to protect the blue helmets. The report sees this as a continuity that clarifies the failures and mistakes which the UN report mainly attributes to a culture of impartiality. This attention to the victims, however, does not remedy a very significant lacuna in the French report, which fails to address the fall of Žepa and Janvier's deliberate refusal to defend it, though both are discussed in the UN report.[33] This lacuna, which detracts from the reader's understanding of the dynamic of events, is all the more regrettable given that the role of French soldiers was decisive in Žepa at various levels of the UNPROFOR hierarchy from Janvier's refusal to defend the enclave to the courageous initiative of General Gobilliard to travel to Žepa to save its population to the inaction of French blue helmets when fifteen Bosniak men were pulled off a bus, then disappeared.[34]

The NIOD report's epilogue, for its part, presents the UNPROFOR's getting stuck in a quagmire as a consistent feature of its involvement and shifts the question of Dutch responsibility: where the prologue insists on reconstructing the realistic alternative options that were available to the protagonists, in the epilogue, the question seems to have become "how and why did the Dutch government send troops on an impossible mission?" In fact, the report reproaches the Dutch government in rather severe terms for having given in to an ethic of conviction to the detriment of an ethic of responsibility. Indeed, this challenge to the Dutch government led it to resign. No sanctions, by contrast, accompanied the UN report,[35] the final version of which makes a purely rhetorical mea culpa, taking shelter behind a vague, collective "we," rather than designating UNPROFOR and UN officials by name.[36] Likewise, the French report had all the less impact given that it did not formulate explicit recommendations, even with regard to the victims.

The favorable impression that one may have of the NIOD report on account of its political consequences[37] nevertheless rapidly fades and is often replaced by dismay. By virtue of its claim to produce a systematic history and its thousands of pages of text, the NIOD report certainly invites criticism in a way that the much less ambitious UN and French reports do not. Yet the many criticisms that have and can be made of the NIOD report are not simply a reflection of the extensive scope of its analysis.[38] It is of course impossible to bring a global judgment to bear on such a disparate and uneven collection. In addition to its opaque and sometimes uncritical use of sources, the "historical-analytical investigation" at which the NIOD report aims tends to reproduce the complexity of the real. In this mass of information, the analytical framework is barely explicit, with the result that the reader is often led down the wrong track (and sometimes into contradiction).[39] Unlike the UN report, there is neither a well-defined framework of analysis nor a clear narrative; unlike the French report, there is no democratic presentation of disagreements among the various contributors.

The drafting of the report seems to have been guided by a culture of compromise, governing relations between members of the NIOD as well as the manner in which the events were interpreted. The culture of equivalence between the warring parties, which the UN report saw as the source of its blindness, broadly permeates the NIOD report. With the academic ethos of nuance and impartiality seeming to have taken up where the diplomatic ethos of appeasement and neutrality left off, the NIOD report strives to evenly balance the various points of view. In this effort at dispassionate distance, it resumes the stance taken by some UNPROFOR protagonists during the war and adopts the idea of "a tyranny of victimology." According to the NIOD, this tyranny was spread and encouraged by media coverage of the war and was both excessively emotional and biased in favor of the Bosniaks.[40] This perhaps explains the susceptibility of NIOD researchers to Serb nationalist arguments. Thus, in part I, chapter 6, and the epilogue, the analysis of photos of the Prijedor camp in 1992 often de facto amounts to endorsing Serb nationalist critiques of their authenticity. Similarly, the explanation of the massacre as revenge—put forward on several occasions in the report—repeats that of the Serbs.[41]

This aspect of the report's view of the conflict reaches its acme in the epilogue, which was cited in the press release, and thus was the most visible and public part of the report. Blom, the NIOD's director, wrote it without consulting the other contributors and presents the problem as largely an issue of how the parties handled their public image. According to the epilogue, "while the Bosnians conducted the international propaganda war with efficiency and skill, the Serbs did anything but ... they created a predominantly negative impression and showed little concern for their own 'public relations.'" One of the main problems facing *Dutchbat*, according to Blom, was also that it failed to supply a positive image of its action and the epilogue closes with a discussion of the harm caused abroad to the image of the Netherlands by Srebrenica. Although the massacre itself is presented as an undeniable reality, the epilogue sets it against a backdrop of ethnic cleansing and revenge. The massacre, on this account, was triggered by the departure of the Bosniak column into the woods. By thwarting the plans of the Serb army in its advance on Žepa, Blom claims, the column presented the Serbs with an unexpected "problem." This argument is made explicit in part IV, chapter 2, section 20, which is devoted to examining the executions and the decision to carry out the massacre. According to Schoonoord, the Serb army expected the men to give themselves up at Potočari but the unforeseen departure of the column disrupted its plans. Confronted with an unmanageable number of prisoners, the Serbs decided to kill them in a massacre requiring vast organization. The blue helmets only followed the rules of armed conflict by allowing the Serb forces at the Potočari base to lead the men away. The decision to carry out the massacre came later in any case, with evidence for this claim being found in the fact that there was nothing threatening in the remarks of Mladić and Karadžić.[42]

Should such an astonishing interpretation be seen as an unjustified and decontextualized projection of the functionalist historiography of Nazism—the NIOD historians' initial domain of competence—or rather an obvious case of bad faith? Either way,[43] the fact that historians should have produced such an extremely gullible (or disingenuous?) report should be a matter of concern for the scholarly community. At once receptive to the criminals' point of view and deferential toward political power, this interpretation assigns indirect responsibility for the massacre to the victims themselves since the departure of the column "may even be regarded as the unintentional and unforeseen *trigger* of the mass murders which followed" (epilogue). Moreover, it is internally incoherent and inconsistent with the known facts of the massacre. On the one hand, if it was indeed the number of prisoners that led to the decision to carry out the massacre, it is difficult to see how this number would have been lower if all of the Bosniaks surrendered at Potočari, given that part of the column actually succeeded in escaping.[44] Moreover, even if the Serb forces were incontestably in the minority,[45] as Rohde underscores with finesse, the fact that "the Muslim prisoners around Bratunac that night were [seen] as things that 'bred' too quickly" is a mater of "classic, deep-rooted racism"[46] and not just of arithmetic. On the other hand, the explanation offered by the report is not consistent with other, well-established facts: the men who surrendered at Potočari, many of whom were elderly, were also executed; furthermore, military forces were withdrawn from the front to the detriment of combat operations in order to carry out the executions.[47] What is more, Serb forces never made arrangements for keeping the prisoners. In taking the town, their only real options were to rush to make such arrangements (they did not), let the men go (why then prevent them from leaving by bus or through the forest?), transfer them to nearby camps, such as that at Batkovići (no attempt was made to do so), let them die of hunger and thirst, or kill them.[48]

By contrast, the NIOD's explanation fails to observe the rules of scientific method for evaluating the validity of an explanatory hypothesis relative to the available data and alternate hypotheses. In positing that the departure of the column and the number of prisoners were the unforeseen triggers of the decision to carry out the massacre, the NIOD's explanation is based on a form of logistical determinism. It is probably inspired by the functionalist interpretations of the processes that led the Nazis to settle on the "final solution," although the analogy is not made explicit. It might also be more broadly inspired by the Arendtian conception of the banality of evil, which sees the driving force of participation in mass crimes, not as some diabolical penchant on the part of the perpetrators, but as residing in bureaucratic considerations about how to manage technical issues of logistics.[49] In this way, the NIOD's interpretation minimizes and even obfuscates the plurality of subjective and objective options, the criminals' freedom of choice, and their possible consciousness of the moral gravity and "historic" importance of their decisions. Paradoxically, the NIOD explanation, which seems to echo Serb claims that the column presented a military threat, nevertheless presupposes a ridiculously distorted vision of the Serbs. In order to claim that it was the flight of the column, the large number of prisoners and the logistical problems posed by these unforeseen elements that triggered the decision to carry out the massacre, one must suppose that Serb leaders were incapable of anticipating that capturing the town would either result in thousands of prisoners or in efforts to resist or escape and that they were also incapable of organizing the logistics for keeping the prisoners.

In fact, the logistical dimension to which the NIOD report appeals was far from decisive in the context of Srebrenica.[50] Indeed, NGOs and international organizations, such as the HCR and the ICRC, were present in the region and actually sought to take supplies to the refugees and have access to the prisoners, but were not allowed to do so.[51] Furthermore, the mass executions posed enormous "logistical problems" of their own. These were only gradually resolved over several phases[52] and by using international resources—gasoline, in particular. To suppose that logistical considerations led the ill-prepared Serb forces to forego holding the prisoners, who could have represented a precious bargaining chip, yet did not dissuade or prevent them from successfully organizing a vast operation to eliminate them, amounts to supposing that the Serbs only excelled in the organization of mass crimes! Paradoxically, when pushed to its extreme, the banality of evil ultimately produces what it seeks to avoid, demonizing the criminals.

Their national bias is thus clear: given that this explanation presents the massacre as unforeseeable and its preparation and realization as beyond the control of the blue helmets, the only thing to be gained through it, is absolving them of wrongdoing.[53] More generally, the only explanations NIOD puts forward for the decision to carry out the massacre—as motivated by the column's departure or by revenge—are exclusively focused on relations between Serbs and Bosniaks and do not include the international presence among the possible factors. In fact, the tensions and weaknesses of the NIOD report are clarified by this national bias. On the one hand, it enables one to see the coherence in the approach taken by the report: several of the report's chapters are devoted to the role of representations and the text itself is an exercise in reputation management, with the date of its publication scheduled to allow the Dutch government to resign at the right moment, thereby reinstating the image of the Netherlands.[54] On the other hand, this national orientation throws light on both the tensions underlying how responsibilities are assigned and the question of whether the massacre could have been predicted. While the epilogue insists on the unpredictable character of the massacre, appendix IV of the report seeks to explain the massacre in terms of local-level relations between Serbs and Bosniaks. In according such importance to local revenge, the author of appendix IV, the anthropologist Ger Duijzings (who later indicated his disagreement with the report's conclusions) seems to have a twofold concern: that of an anthropologist seeking the significance of the massacre in anthropological practices and that of a Dutch researcher and citizen who, by underscoring the predictability of the massacre, increased Dutch responsibility for the failure to prevent it.

This national bias may also help in explaining the noticeable omissions in the NIOD report, which devotes such effort to being systematic and asserting its own scientific character. Concerning the decision to carry out the massacre, it is astonishing that three other explanations are not discussed, at least as hypotheses potentially competing with the "logistical" argument centering on the column's departure. Let us first consider a short-term explanation: according to Rohde's hypothesis, the decision was made at the last moment and motivated by a variety of considerations, but it was the euphoria that followed the Serbs' victory that enabled it. The ease with which the Serbs advanced came as such a surprise that it gave Mladić a feeling of divine omnipotence, including having the power of the life and death all around him.[55] This credible, short-term interpretation, though partial, converges with Mladić's numerous statements, the factual chronology, the exhaustivity with which the men were massacred, and Mladić's sudden change of attitude in Žepa. Indeed, the latter remained inflexible concerning the surrender of the men of Žepa up until the Croatian offensive—a major defeat for the Serbs—following which the men of Žepa ceased being his priority.[56] This interpretation refers the effective decision to carry out the massacre to its very *possibility* and the absence of resistance from UNPROFOR, *Dutchbat*, and NATO,[57] which may explain why the NIOD report has so little to say about this hypothesis.

Given the type of political and military history produced by the NIOD report, it is also astonishing that no substantial consideration is devoted to the hypothesis that the massacre fits with the modus operandi of the Serb army in the earlier episodes of the war,[58] as well as the strategy and service record of General Mladić, who made no effort to hide his desire to eliminate the Muslims.[59] Such a middle-term analysis would have shown that, even if *this* massacre was not predictable,[60] *a* massacre and various exactions were.[61] In fact, there had already been cases of systematic execution in the Bosnian war, particularly in 1992, and Mladić had threatened to kill everyone in Goražde in 1994.[62] Such an omission is also to be regretted in the other reports, where a study of the career path of the principal decision-makers—Mladić, Janvier, and Akashi, among others—might have shed light on their actions in July 1995.

Finally, there is no consideration given to the issue of gender, which is particularly unfortunate because the separation of men and women touches on the heart of the events as well as the question of whether the massacre might have been predicted following the separation of the men from the women and children. This absence may be a result of the "report-form," which favors a more event-centered and less cultural style of history. By contrast, it underscores the gap between the reports, which are marked by a certain "classicism," and the judicial decisions, which are richer in conceptual innovation. Indeed, the gendered dimension of violence is at the heart of the ICTY's Krstić judgment, which effects a transition from *gendercide* (execution of the men) to *genocide* (the intention to destroy the group in whole or part). While this move aroused debates among legal experts,[63] it succeeded in singling out the specificity of the massacre.

Frame of Reference and Interplay of Scales[64]

It is through comparison of the various reports that one gets a true sense of the specificity of what took place at Srebrenica: the massacre of populations under international protection. A central issue involved at various levels in such comparison is that of the frame of reference and the choice of scale adopted. Two types of variation are observable in the different accounts of the same event: that of point of view (the UN in New York, France, and the Netherlands) and that of scale. The scale can be local (relations "on the ground" among Serbs, Bosniaks, and blue helmets), regional (UNPROFOR office in Tuzla), national (UNPROFOR office in Sarajevo), international but nearby (UNPROFOR headquarters in Zagreb), and international and geographically far removed (UN headquarters in New York), in accordance with the various levels of UN hierarchy and the plurality of its members.

The singularly "international" character of the Srebrenica events hardly emerges in the theories about international relations referred to in the reports. These theories draw on various forms of the traditional opposition between idealism (the UN pacifist culture) and realism (the use of force). They are based, however, on a conception of sovereignty and national independence according to which each state has the right to defend itself or be defended. This notion is in keeping with the foundational principles of the UN. Relative to these principles, safe areas and the arms embargo on Bosnia (following that on Yugoslavia in 1991) represent deviations, if not outright exceptions.[65] This particularity of Srebrenica especially stands out when we take into account the different levels adopted to describe the events. The problematic relationship between sovereignty, the right to defend oneself, and protection may be described in the conflicts between the blue helmets, who abandoned the town's defensive positions, and the Bosniaks who tried to prevent them from doing so, in the conflicts between the Sarajevo government and the leaders of UNPROFOR, in debates at UN headquarters in New York, and so on. These levels of description show the empirical and conceptual porosity of the national and the international, from the most local and infra-national scale to the most global and supranational one.

These variations also reflect the difficulty of defining the relevant scale for analyzing Srebrenica. Is the specificity of this massacre in the war in Bosnia quantitative or qualitative? Can it be understood by means of comparison with smaller-scale massacres that also eliminated men in large numbers as well as a few women and children, such as those of 1992 in Biljani[66] (Ključ municipality) or in Grabovica (Kotor Varoš municipality) in northwestern Bosnia? Which historical and geographical scale is relevant?

It is interesting to observe how the questions raised vary according to the frame of reference that has been chosen. The NIOD and UN reports make two major contributions to explaining the specificity and reasons for the massacre by treating the question of "why Srebrenica?" as one that may be analyzed by means of contextualization and comparison rather than as an undecidable metaphysical and moral conundrum like the question, "why does evil exist?" The issue thus becomes "why Srebrenica and not somewhere else?" or "why Srebrenica and not Žepa?" Appendix IV of the NIOD report seeks the causes or reasons for the massacre in the history of Srebrenica while Harland's analysis of the fall of Žepa, which is summarized in the NIOD report,[67] insists on the regional dynamic of events.

The obvious difficulty presented by the first approach is the disproportionality between the scale of causes and the scale of consequences. While it cannot be denied that revenge played a decisive role in the participation of the Serbs from Srebrenica and Bratunac in the massacre and in the choice of certain execution sites, like Kravica, it is difficult to understand how this interpretation can go beyond the local scale and explain how it is that the VRS commander of main staff decided to go there in person along with army and police units from other regions of Bosnia and even Serbia for the purposes of local revenge against Naser Orić and his men.[68] This interpretation also raises the difficulty of defining the local dimension of Srebrenica. Was it geographical, historical, or political? This difficulty is particularly brought out by Jacques Sémelin's use of Ger Duijzings' work in *Purify and Destroy*.[69] Sémelin presents this interpretation as continuing along the same line as the analyses of the anthropologist Cornelia Sorabji concerning the organization of municipal authorities into "franchises" for carrying out the work of ethnic cleansing.[70] The local and municipal paradigm applied by Sorabji is very relevant for 1992 given that the victims, the armed forces, and the police for the most part came from the same municipalities. By 1995, however, this paradigm had lost its relevance for Srebrenica. For, by then, the local was no longer defined, as had been the case in 1992, by coincidence between a geographical delimitation, municipal power structures, and the population's home. In 1995, the Srebrenica enclave as a geographical site contained refugees from throughout the region, chased from their homes during the ethnic cleansing of 1992. The local paradigm was operative neither for the victims nor for the Serb troops, most of whom were drawn from the surrounding area rather than from the municipality itself,[71] with some coming from other regions of Bosnia. Above all, in 1995, the soldiers were directly commanded at the national level by Mladić. The local dimension was still a decisive factor in events, but this was for very different reasons than those exposed by Sorabji for 1992. On the one hand, as Rohde rightly underscores, tensions between the inhabitants of Srebrenica and the refugees explain the latter's lack of determination in defending Srebrenica, which was not their home. On the other hand, the refugees were neither familiar with the terrain nor with one another, a state of affairs that constituted a major obstacle to the column's escape, with the Bosniaks getting lost along the way and being (or believing themselves to be) infiltrated by Serbs. As Ruez has explained, this also accounts for why the survivors had such difficulty in locating the sites.

A direct transposition of the municipal paradigm from 1992 to 1995 is thus misleading. There is no guarantee that examining local relations in Srebrenica rather than in Zvornik or northeast Bosnia sheds light on the massacre if the fact that it occurred in Srebrenica rather than elsewhere is due to a plurality of factors. This path of reflection was opened by Harland in his reconstruction of the fall of Žepa, an enclave neighboring Srebrenica that was attacked by Serb forces several days after the fall of Srebrenica but without similar massacres taking place. In information supplied after the UN report was released, Harland offered a multifactor analysis that took the regional, national, and international dynamics of the war into account, something that had often been neglected due to the focus on Srebrenica.[72] Harland's work constitutes an important contribution to the etiology of mass killings. He held that at least six factors were combined, the details of which are explained in the UN report.

> At least six factors combined to save Žepa from the fate of Srebrenica:
>
> (1) the very different dynamics that had developed between the besiegers and the besieged in each phase since 1992, epitomized by the different roles of Orić and Palić; (2) the anxieties of the Pale Serbs (particularly Karadžić) about the need to break off the Žepa action in order to prepare for the impending Croatian attack in the West; (3) the much greater defensibility of Žepa, which made the Serbs so reluctant to push troops and equipment into the Žepa enclave even when they had a huge numerical advantage; (4) less disorganized and passive international response to the attack on Žepa, epitomized by the Gobilliard expedition[73]; (5) the role of Sarajevo, where there is a dramatic contrast to be made between Izetbegović's interaction with Suljić and Muratović's interaction with Palić and the Serbs; and (6) the fact that, because of its proximity to the border across wooded land, it was inherently easier to escape from Žepa.[74]

There would be little point in rewriting the history of Srebrenica on the basis of "what if" scenarios, above all from the point of view of the accumulation of factors that contributed to destroying or might have saved so many lives. Yet the geographical and temporal proximity between the fall of Srebrenica and that of Žepa allows comparisons similar to those of counter-factual history. One may thus seek the factors explaining why thousands of men disappeared in Srebrenica as compared with around a hundred in Žepa.[75] One may also fear that the horror of the massacre might lead us to forget the shared destiny of these two enclaves, both of which were abandoned to the Serbs in every respect, from the decision not to defend them to their inclusion in the RS by the Dayton agreements. For the surviving inhabitants, displaced and made refugees, their sole consolation is the fact that they were not killed.

All in all, reading these reports and investigations reveals a gap between how they treat "doing" and how they approach "letting be done," between how they cast the establishing of facts and the seeking of responsibility and intelligibility concerning the massacre, on the one hand, and how they present the international abandonment of the enclave, on the other. Though they are incomplete, these documents are quite clear when speaking about the course of the massacre, the determination of criminal responsibility, and the punishment of the guilty by arrests and judgments. Much remains to be desired, however, when it comes to how they interpret and assign blame for international responsibility. Neither the citizen of this or that country nor the citizen of the world will find the Kantian demands for cosmopolitan responsibility and republican control over foreign policy satisfied. Furthermore, one may note with dismay how the overlapping of responsibility and intelligibility are handled. Not only do concerns about responsibility orient the search for intelligibility—even at the risk of deforming it—but also the very effort to provide intelligibility seems to relieve the parties of all responsibility, at least if one is to judge by the meager political consequences produced by these reports.[76]

What is more, the reports do not propose the same register of intelligibility for "letting do"[77] and for "doing": they ultimately refer to moral and political philosophy in order to clarify international responsibility, whether it be the pacifist UN philosophy or the opposition between a morality of conviction and a morality of responsibility. Readers of Kant and Weber will be astonished to learn that the ideal of a society of nations governed by law (Kant) or the critique of the morality of conviction (Weber) might clarify Srebrenica given how little conviction is to be found in *Dutchbat* and how little the Kantian principal of autonomy was respected in the demilitarization of the safe areas. Perhaps one should no longer read these reports as a form of political or moral reflection and instead see them as reactivating a now obsolete philosophical genre, the theodicy, which posed the question "why is there evil?" at the most metaphysical level. Defending the cause of God against the accusation that the existence of evil represents, the theodicy similarly justifies inaction on the part of a more powerful and virtuous body faced with evil on the basis of its very goodness or the (moral) norms governing its action. Ultimately, it is perhaps this literature more than the guarded style of the reports that best captures the chasm between justificatory claims—of which these reports are a variant—and accusatory arguments. According to the Bosniaks, a more powerful body that fails to halt a preventable evil has the same moral status as the perpetrators of that evil.[78] In these philosophical debates about evil, at least, one finds an echo of the existential collapse of the Bosniaks after being let down by those whom they expected to save them, culminating in the profound sense that their lives had lost all value in those days in July 1995 when Mladić believed he was the only God.[79]

Translated from French by Ethan Rundell

Notes

1. David Rohde, *Endgame: The Betrayal and Fall of Srebrenica* (Boulder, CO, 1997).
2. Chuck Sudetic, *Blood and Vengeance: One Family's Story of the War in Bosnia* (London, 1998).
3. On these points, for the French parliamentary report, see Pierre Brana's chapter. For the Dutch parliamentary reports, see Christ Klep's chapter. For the Dutch NIOD report, see Pieter Lagrou's and Christ Klep's chapters. For that of the RS, see Michèle Picard and Asta Zinbo's chapter. Concerning the drafting of the UN report, its principal author, David Harland, sent me this information in the course of a 2005 e-mail exchange: "1. On access to sources, the UN was entirely open: let me speak to anyone, and let me look at any document—though I could not quote from those documents if they were confidential. National governments did not give me access to archives. Governments varied in terms of how open they were to my requests for interviews: Yugoslavia and the United States were not very forthcoming; France was originally not forthcoming but then let me speak to Janvier and others at length; Bosnia was similar, but eventually gave me a lengthy interview with Izetbegović and others (the Federation authorities were obviously much more open than the RS ones, though Biljana Plavšić and General Milovanović both gave long interviews); the UK was a bit better, and the Dutch were the best of all. I was given about nine months to do the job (that was decided by a General Assembly resolution), and I was given an excellent colleague to do the mainly archival research in New York and to help with the drafting, Salman Ahmed, and I was given full authority within the organization to get what I needed, and an adequate travel budget. 2. I selected the people to interview, with complete freedom. Only Yugoslavia and the US directly sought to limit access to individuals. At my own decision, I decided not to speak to people who were openly indicted by ICTY, for fear of interfering with juridical processes. So I did not seek to question Karadžić or Mladić, even indirectly, though I did speak at length with their close associates, including Zametica." (Email sent to the author, 20 June 2005). Some of this information was given in David Harland's testimony in the Slobodan Milošević trial before the ICTY on 18 September 2003: http://www.icty.org/x/cases/slobodan_milosevic/trans/en/030918ED.htm, last accessed 8 December 2011.

4. The ICTY made public its basic documents, bills of indictment, rulings, and retranscriptions of hearings. The French and Dutch parliamentary reports gave access to the sources and hearings on which they drew. For the UN report, which did not make public the documents and interviews it used, Harland gave me the following information in an e-mail: "Interviews were given on the basis of confidentiality, unless specifically stated that they were for the record. Many of the records were later taken by the International Criminal Tribunal for the Former Yugoslavia. To be honest, most of the interviews were not very useful—the people who knew the most were all being too careful." (Email sent to the author, 21 June 2005).
5. On the definition of cosmopolitan responsibility and its various forms, see Thomas Pogge, *World Poverty and Human Rights: Cosmopolitan Responsibilities and Reforms* (Cambridge, 2002), 169 onward.
6. Even before the ICTY was able to access them, the execution sites were found by the journalist David Rohde in 1996—which got him arrested and imprisoned in the RS. Afterward, Rohde also found several survivors of the executions, enabling him to get a general idea of this phase of the massacre. But his investigative work did not permit him to retrace the body-moving and reburial operation nor was he able to gain access to most of the primary and secondary mass graves or supply detailed proofs of what had occurred.
7. The ICTY adopted a twofold approach to evaluating the number of victims. First, they used a nominal approach, cross-checking the ICRC missing persons lists with pre-war census lists and post-war electoral lists to rule out the possibility of fictitious missing persons. On this subject, see Helge Brunborg, Torkild Lyngstad, and Henrik Urdal, "Accounting for Genocide: How Many Were Killed in Srebrenica?" *European Journal of Population,* no. 19 (2003): 229–248. This list was then cross-checked with the results of the exhumations. This approach involved a degree of uncertainty, because some missing persons could not be registered with the ICRC and the cause of death was not known in all cases. Then, they applied a material approach, using both counts of the dead that were found in the mass graves and autopsy reports supplying the cause of death, which constituted the factual basis for charging and judging indictees. But this material count also left room for uncertainty: not all of the mass graves or bodies were found and, given the dispersion of human remains, it was sometimes difficult to piece bodies together and count the cadavers (see the chapter by Michèle Picard and Asta Zinbo). The results of this twofold process were presented in the Krstić trial. The remaining uncertainties have since been addressed in subsequent trials at the ICTY and have opposed expert witnesses from the prosecution and the defense. For a very clear presentation and discussion of the methods used and the difficulties encountered in establishing the number of dead and, among them, the number of victims of the July 1995 executions, see ICTY, *Prosecutor vs. Popović et alii (Case IT-05-88-T),* judgment, 10 June 2010, volume I, part III, section J, "Total Number of Deceased: Forensic and Demographic Evidence," 242–265, accessible at http://www.icty.org/x/cases/popovic/tjug/en/100610judgement.pdf, last accessed 8 December 2011.
8. See Michèle Picard and Asta Zinbo's chapter in this volume. The number of victims is estimated at more than 7,475 according to the ICTY (Krstić judgment of 2001), more than 8,000 according to the Federal Commission for Missing Persons, between 7,000 and 8,000 according to the RS report, and 10,000 according to the victims associations. These variations are due to differences in the manner in which victims are defined, the aims of the respective organizations and the time period selected for the enumeration. Thus, taking into account the uncertainty about the cause of death in some cases, especially for surface remains where it cannot be excluded that the victims died in combat

or from suicide, the judges in the Popović et al. trial, in June 2010, cited 5,336 identified individuals as the minimum number for those killed in the executions following the fall of Srebrenica, while indicating that the number could be as high as 7,826. The Federal Commission's list of missing persons may contain the names of individuals killed in combat because its aim is humanitarian, not judicial—that is, it seeks to determine the identity of the victims but not the causes of their deaths. Inversely, the list of victims established by the RS uses Bosnian army data to deduct Bosniak soldiers killed in combat. As for the temporal limits that have been chosen, the ICTY indictments concern the events of July 1995 and the subsequent attempts at covering up the massacre and those of the RS are also very precise. But for families, a loved one is no less dear if he died in earlier months or years of the war, which brings the number of missing persons to more than 13,000 according to the data supplied by the RS commission for the entire war in Srebrenica (see the chapter by Michèle Picard and Asta Zinbo).
9. See the text of Michèle Picard in the present volume.
10. See the interview with Jean-René Ruez in the present volume.
11. Dutch historians sharply criticized the NIOD report in *"Het Drama Srebrenica,"* a special number of *Tijdschrift voor Geschiedenis* 66, no. 2 (2003). In particular, they reproached it for skirting the debate via recourse to sources that could not be consulted by the scholarly community, drawing on historical novels and so on. In fact, this recourse to confidentiality was particularly problematic when it involved such questionable assertions as the claim that a larger number of UNPROFOR troops were killed around Sarajevo by the Bosnian army than by Serb forces (part I, chapter 6, section 1, note 11). Moreover, a good part of the NIOD's analysis is based on articles that appeared in the press, despite the fact that NIOD criticizes the press for having given an emotional and biased representation of the war. As for the adoption of the point of view of actors who lack critical distance, it is clear in the case of General Mac Kenzie (part I, chapter 6) but the same holds for many other parts of the report concerning local explanations of the massacre or the Dutch battalion of blue helmets, *Dutchbat*'s point of view.
12. In this summary of local sources, the appendix's author, Ger Duijzings, nevertheless remarks in a note that the data supplied by the Serb authorities is to a certain extent misleading to the degree that it presents civilians and soldiers alike—including the soldiers and paramilitaries killed in action—as victims of "Muslim terror" without distinction. Yet this reservation does not prevent him from drawing on these sources to claim that the Serbs suffered "a huge number of human casualties" in support of his interpretation of the 1995 massacre as strongly motivated by revenge for Bosniak attacks on Serb villages. In this way, the author neglects to take account of the eminently dubious character of the list of Serb victims in the Srebrenica region. In addition to the names of the soldiers and paramilitaries killed in action in the region of Srebrenica, this list may also contain the names of those killed in the environs of Sarajevo or elsewhere in Bosnia (see the Sarajevo Research and Documentation Center study "The Myth of Bratunac: A Blatant Number Games": http://www.idc.org.ba. This study can also be accessed at http://srebrenica-genocide.blogspot.com/2006/05/myth-about-serb-casualties-around .html, last accessed on 8 December 2011). While the presentation of the massacre as a case of revenge is in this respect based on Bosniak attacks on Serbian villages, such as Kravica and Zalazje, the contrast between the global figures of a thousand Serb victims for the Srebrenica region and the number of victims of attacks on Serb villages—a matter of dozens (not hundreds), soldiers and civilians included—is at the very least perplexing.
13. Even though the fate of the column has not been the focus of ICTY investigations, information concerning the column, its attempt to break though Serb lines, the fight-

ing around Zvornik, and the fate of individual Bosniaks fleeing Srebrenica through the woods can be found in the ICTY trials and judgments. See for example the trial of Obrenović (see reference below, note 47), or that of Pandurević, who allowed the passage of the column on 16 July (see ICTY, *Prosecutor vs. Popović et al.*, 220–223).

14. See NIOD, *Srebrenica—A "Safe" Area: Reconstruction, Background, Consequences and Analyses of the Fall of a Safe Area* (Amsterdam, April 2002), part IV, chapter 1, section 1.
15. See ibid., part IV, chapter 2, section 15.
16. Similarly, Schoonoord concludes from the failure of ballistic analyses that the troops in question were not involved in the executions (part IV, chapter 2, section 11) and not, as Jean-René Ruez has it, that this could just as well be evidence of the extensive circulation of weapons during the war.
17. The large number of inquiries and reports concerning the massacre is not particular to Srebrenica. Ethnic cleansing in Prijedor, for example, was also the object of many legal investigation and reports but, given that no international force was present, there are not as many international points of view concerning Prijedor as there are concerning Srebrenica.
18. It is thus the large number of international reports on the genocide in Rwanda that should be compared with those on Srebrenica rather than those concerning ethnic cleansing in 1992, including the Bassiouni expert commission report on violations of human rights in the former Yugoslavia. On this subject, see Marc Le Pape, "Vérités et controverses sur le Génocide des Rwandais tutsis. Les rapports (Belgique, France, ONU)," in *Crises extrêmes. Face aux massacres, aux guerres civiles et aux génocides,* eds. Marc Le Pape, Johanna Siméant, and Claude Vidal (Paris, 2006), 103–118.
19. While the UN report was for the most part prepared and drafted over a nine-month period by David Harland and Salman Ahmed—two individuals with a solid grasp of the terrain and the language—the French and Dutch reports were collective works in which the writing process and the final conclusions reflected the constraints of compromise or conflicts between the contributors. Another significant difference involves the amount of time given for carrying out the inquiries and writing up the reports: several months in the case of the UN, French, Dutch parliamentary, and RS reports as compared to several years in that of the NIOD (on this subject, see Jean-Louis Fournel's chapter in the present volume).
20. Scientific expertise is almost totally absent from the UN, French, and Dutch parliamentary reports, plays only a secondary role in the RS report, which was written with the assistance of legal experts and historians (see Michèle Picard and Asta Zinbo's chapter in this volume), figures decisively in the ICTY inquiries, which draw heavily on scientific police methods, and is omnipresent in the report of the Dutch historians, for whom, faced with the possibility of political pressure, scientific rigor is a sufficient guarantee of independence.
21. By contrast, the RS report does not deal with the question of international responsibility for the massacre but only that of criminal responsibility. On the temporal and thematic limitations imposed on this report, see Michèle Picard and Asta Zinbo's chapter in this volume as well as that of Jean-Louis Fournel.
22. On condition, of course, that the inquiries are properly conducted. Not all of the ICTY investigation has the same solidity as that concerning the 1995 Srebrenica massacre. This is particularly the case concerning the investigation into Naser Orić, the Bosniak commander of the Srebrenica enclave. In this case, most of the charges were dropped from the initial indictment or in the course of the trial for lack of credible evidence and witnesses.

23. As evidenced in the chapter by Jean-René Ruez in this volume, the technical and human elements are equally indispensable.
24. At this stage, events were mainly known through the victims. This remains largely true even today, though Serb participants have provided valuable information during ICTY proceedings. It is possible that the publication of the confidential annexes of the RS report or the documents found in the course of its preparation—according to one of the individuals who participated in the RS commission's work, these contain orders given to the police and army and data on the number of individuals executed—would allow us to move beyond the present state of knowledge established by the ICTY.
25. On the role of forensic experts in "making the dead speak," see Christopher Joyce and Eric Stover, *Witnesses from the Grave: The Stories Bones Tell* (Boston, MA, 1991); Eric Stover and Gilles Peress, *The Graves: Srebrenica and Vukovar* (Zurich, 1998). See also ICTY, *Prosecutor vs. Popović et alii*, vol. I, part III, section J.
26. The French and Dutch reports tend to put the burden of responsibility for the events on the other's shoulders, with each also underscoring the failures and errors of other countries' UNPROFOR troops. The NIOD report, for its part, insists on Bosniak responsibility for the column's departure and disorganization.
27. See Xavier Bougarel's chapter in this volume.
28. Email sent by David Harland to the author, 21 June 2005.
29. In this regard, Harland, like Rohde, stresses the tragic aspect of General Rupert Smith's decision to bombard the Serbs around Sarajevo in May 1995, which led to the hostage crisis and consequently undermined the position of those in UNPROFOR who wished to use force against the Serb military.
30. Email sent by David Harland to the author, 21 June 2005. The firmness of Harland's point of view is clear in his testimony for the prosecution in Milošević's trial before the ICTY on 18 September 2003 (http://www.icty.org/x/cases/slobodan_milosevic/trans/en/030918ED.htm) and 5 November 2003 (http://www.icty.org/x/cases/slobodan_milosevic/trans/en/031105ED.htm), last accessed on 8 December 2011.
31. *Report of the Secretary-General Pursuant to General Assembly Resolution 53/35: The Fall of Srebrenica*, 107.
32. In order to take account of the fact that the Srebrenica tragedy indirectly contributed to a resolution of the conflict by means of the Dayton agreements, the UN report speaks of "tragic irony" (105) and does not find evidence of a conspiracy in this turn of events.
33. Even though the French report uses the term *error* in regard to Janvier, it remains very elliptical about his role and precise responsibility in the fall of Srebrenica. Nor does the report reconstruct the continuity of Janvier's decisions from Srebrenica to Žepa or his desire to abandon Goražde as well, and this despite UNPROFOR's mandate not to allow the eastern enclaves to fall. In this, Janvier only followed the line of conduct that he had defended in May before the UN Security Council, where he had urged that UNPROFOR troops be brought together and argued for abandoning the eastern enclaves, a proposition that was specifically rejected.
34. On the initiative of Gobilliard and the role of the blue helmets, see below. The absence of any reference to the fall of Žepa in the French report is all the more astonishing given that Gobilliard's gesture could have served as an occasion for glorifying the role of France—according to Harland (see below), it contributed to saving Žepa from the fate of Srebrenica. Indeed, the report makes much of the recapture of the Vrbanja bridge in Sarajevo, which also took place on the initiative of Gobilliard. Moreover, General Gobilliard's remarks before the French parliamentary mission include several allusions to the Žepa episode, which the MPs did not explore in even a cursory fashion. Whatever

the explanation, this lacuna strengthens the feeling that the French report fails to probe deeply into the events.
35. The principal leaders of the UN suffered no sanction for their role in Srebrenica; in fact, Yasushi Akashi was promoted under-secretary general to humanitarian affairs in March 1996.
36. The decision to give job titles in place of proper names took place after the report was drafted by Harland and significantly detracted from the report's clarity for the reader is obliged to consult the end of the report in order to determine which individual held a specific post at a particular time. Individual responsibility is thus attenuated and absorbed (especially in the conclusion) by a rhetorical "we" and a clumsy stance of moral repentance. Thus, for example, the report declares that no one regrets and deplores the failures of the international community in Bosnia and Srebrenica more than "us" (108).
37. See Pieter Lagrou's and Christ Klep's chapters in this volume.
38. For criticism of the Dutch historians, see *"Het Drama Srebrenica,"* a special number of *Tijdschrift voor Geschiedenis* 66, no. 2 (2003). In particular, the NIOD report is reproached for being contradictory and deterministic in its approach, for being written by historians who are not specialists of the subject and for giving an inadequate analysis of the massacre's causes, settling for a weak reference to nationalism and an irrelevant use of the Second World War, which is evoked in a "revisionist" manner. Rik Peters, in particular, criticizes the NIOD report for committing errors at three levels: the level of description (believing that the accumulation of detail produces intelligibility); the level of explanation (not analyzing the options available to actors despite what is announced in the prologue); the level of judgment (condemning the Dutch government for the consequences of its actions but excusing the *Dutchbat* on the basis of its good intentions).
39. It is only a hundred pages into part I, chapter 6 on "the emotionalization of the debate" (which analyzes at length the 1992 photos of the Prijedor camps, the context in which they appeared and the question of their authenticity, all the while leaving the reader perplexed as to their relevance for Srebrenica) that a first substantive issue appears: that of the effect of media representations on decision-making in foreign policy, otherwise known as the "CNN effect." Ultimately, the chapter concludes that these images did not have a decisive effect on Dutch foreign policy. Seeming to run counter to the conclusions of this chapter, however, the epilogue accords a significant place to these photos in the Dutch decision to intervene in Bosnia and in discrediting the Serbs and calls into question their authenticity while chapter 6 remains cautious on this last point.
40. See NIOD, *Srebrenica—A "Safe" Area: Reconstruction,* part I, chapter 6, section 6. This chapter borrows the expression "the tyranny of victimology" from the journalist Paul Moorcraft. Moreover, it largely adopts General Mac Kenzie's views on the equivalence between the various parties to the conflict, all of whom are seen as criminal, and on Bosniak ingratitude toward UNPROFOR. The NIOD report similarly repeats rumors according to which the Bosniaks bombarded themselves in Sarajevo in order to cast the blame on the Serbs and provoke an international intervention (part I, chapter 6, section 6, and epilogue).
41. The fact that this explanation was that of the Serbs does not, of course, render it invalid ipso facto, but it does require one to present it as such (which the report does not do), that is, less as an obvious fact than as part of a discourse intended to justify the massacre and minimize its gravity. Indeed, vengeance, as a form of retribution, supposes a principle of equivalence that can make it an anthropologically acceptable form of regulating violence. Speaking of vengeance is thus implicitly equivalent to challenging the categories of mass crime and genocide, which lose any relationship to proportionality

and can no longer be considered as justifications for or "acceptable" forms of regulating social relations.
42. See NIOD, *Srebrenica—A "Safe" Area: Reconstruction*, part IV, chapter 2, section 3.
43. Many reasons explain the position of the NIOD. These are presented in Pieter Lagrou's and Christ Klep's chapters and Ger Duijzings's remarks at a colloquium entitled "Srebrenica (1999–2005): facts and responsibility," which was held at the University Paris 8 and the Ecole Normale Supérieure on 24 and 25 June 2005. Thus, the NIOD had already worked on an official history of the Second World War that provided Dutch authorities with a critical but acceptable narrative of the Dutch role in the course of that war; it remained dependent on public funding; the research scholars could be both seduced by frequenting the higher reaches of power and discouraged by their experience in the field (with which trained historians have no experience) with Bosniak refugees from Srebrenica who were miserable and angry at the Netherlands; the organization of the NIOD forbid public expression of disagreement among the researchers, etc.
44. According to this line of reasoning, it would have been just as imperative to eliminate them in Potočari. In another version of the reasons for the massacre, the NIOD report also indicates that it was the excessively large number of prisoners in general—and not just in the column—that prevented the Serbs from verifying whether the men were or were not war criminals, thus leading the Serbs to kill them all. Another explanation given is that of ethnic cleansing in the broad sense of the term, and a history of past conflict in which, in seeking a solution, the region's warring parties did not hesitate to massacre the enemy (part IV, chapter 2, section 20).
45. The numerical superiority of the Bosniaks, like the Serb supremacy in weaponry, was obvious and played a significant role in the war in Bosnia, in general, and in Srebrenica, in particular. But the large number of Bosniaks was not a new fact that the Serbs discovered upon the departure of the column and the capture of prisoners.
46. Rohde, *Endgame*, 374.
47. The fact that soldiers had been withdrawn from the front in order to be assigned to the executions appears in the ICTY judgments, in particular in Obrenović's guilty plea, who noted a lack of men and reinforcements in his battles with the 28th Bosnian Division, which he feared would attack Zvornik (http://www.icty.org/x/cases/obrenovic/custom4/en/facts_030520.pdf, last accessed 8 December 2011). Beyond that, the question arises as to whether the executions could have been part of a middle-term military strategy to reduce the number of potential Bosniak soldiers by definitively eliminating those of Srebrenica or whether, obsessed by his mission to eradicate the Muslims of Bosnia, Mladić mobilized considerable human and material resources in Srebrenica and Žepa, losing sight of his military objectives and thus failing to anticipate the Croatian attack in the west.
48. These various options seem to have been considered. According to his guilty plea, Obrenović requested that a corridor be opened to allow the column to pass. According to the testimony of Miroslav Deronjić before the ICTY during the trial of Momir Nikolić, the idea of transferring the prisoners to Bijeljina and the Batkovići camp had been entertained (testimony given 28 October 2003, http://www.icty.org/x/cases/nikolic/trans/en/031028ED.htm), 1550. See ICTY, *Prosecutor vs. Popović et alii*, concerning a corridor for the passage of the column on 16 July (220 et seq.) and the discussion and possibilities of transferring prisoners in surrounding camps like Batkovići (235 et seq.). Few of them were actually sent there. Finally, the question of the fate of the Bosniaks of Srebrenica had come up even before the enclave's fall and, according to Deronjić, Karadžić had told him on 8 or 9 July 1995: "'Miroslav, those people there must be killed.' That was his previous sentence. And then he said, 'Whatever you can, you have to kill.'" (ibid, 1565).

49. This would be the transposition of the bureaucratic or logistical interpretation given by Hannah Arendt to Eichmann's participation in the "final solution," which Arendt presents in *Eichmann in Jerusalem* as one manifestation of the "banality of evil." Arendt contrasted this banality with the effort to demonize Eichmann by the Jerusalem trial prosecutor, Gideon Hausner. On this vision of Eichmann and of the banality of evil, see: David Cesarani, *Becoming Eichmann. Rethinking the Life, Crimes and Trial of a "Desk Murderer"* (Rayleigh, Essex, 2006) for an historical perspective, and Isabelle Delpla, *Le mal en procès. Eichmann et les théodicées modernes* (Paris, 2011), for a more philosophical perspective.

50. From that point on, the process of local radicalization that the NIOD report emphasizes following the model of the functionalist historiography of Nazism (see Pieter Lagrou's chapter) becomes rather mysterious. While this process extended over several months in the case of the German army, it is supposed to have taken place over one or two days in Srebrenica. Furthermore, the situation—in particular, the supply situation—was much more extreme on the eastern front in 1941 and 1942 than in Srebrenica in July 1995. For a survey and analysis of the historiography on this issue, see Christian Ingrao's article, "Conquérir, aménager, exterminer. Nouvelles recherches sur la Shoah," *Annales. Histoire, sciences sociales* 58, no. 2 (March–April 2003): 417–438. I would like to express my warm thanks to Christian Ingrao for his clarifications and the discussions we have had on this subject.

51. Moreover, according to the testimony of Momir Nikolić, it is precisely because the ICRC knew of the Batkovići camp's existence that the prisoners were not transferred there. Indeed, the ICRC and the commander of that camp had prepared food and accommodation in anticipation of the arrival of the prisoners (ICTY, *Prosecutor vs. Popović et alii*, 235).

52. See the interview with Jean-René Ruez in this volume.

53. Indeed, the NIOD report insisted on the fact that the *Dutchbat* knew nothing of the column's departure and had not been involved in the decision to flee the enclave. Even if one accepts this line of reasoning, it is difficult to conclude from it that the *Dutchbat* had no responsibility for its departure: among other considerations, it seems to have been motivated by the belief that the blue helmets would not defend the city and the fact that the NATO strikes announced by the *Dutchbat* leaders to the authorities of Srebrenica did not take place.

54. In the very act of (what it believed to be) taking its distance by providing a history of representations, NIOD adopted one of the most typical stances in the area of international policy, which consists in always supporting our troops and believing that the image of our country and its prestige must regulate its foreign policy. The French report also ends with an encomium of its military and the French soldiers, who paid a high price in Bosnia and did not let fall any of the enclaves in which they were physically present (Bihać, for example). This patriotic defense of the French army would seem less out of place in the report on Srebrenica if the role of Janvier and his hierarchical superiors in the fall of Srebrenica and Žepa had been better established.

55. Rohde mentions many declarations made by Mladić to the crowd of Bosniaks in Potočari and when he appeared before prisoners, according to which he was their only God. For a similar interpretation of Mladić's behavior in Potočari, see Emir Suljagić's autobiographical account, *Postcards from the Grave* (London, 2005). Such an interpretation might, mutatis mutandis, be similar to Christopher Browning's interpretation of the decision to carry out the genocide of the Jews as a "utopian" expression of the euphoria of victory. See *The Path to Genocide: Essays on Launching the Final Solution* (Cambridge,

1992); and *The Origins of the Final Solution: The Evolution of Nazi Jewish Policy, September 1939–March 1942* (Lincoln, NE, 2004).

56. In this connection, Rohde draws on the testimony of an unnamed UN officer. This officer was Edward Joseph, who was a civil affairs officer in UNPROFOR and was sent to Žepa in July 1995. He supplied me with the following information in an email on 9 November 2006: "Mladić was apparently quite taken by surprise with the developments by the Croats and abruptly departed Žepa after those attacks started and escalated. So, the key point was that Mladić, who up to this point, had seemed quite content to stay physically in and around Žepa, and whose demeanor had been even triumphal (he seemed to enjoy being able to dominate the proceedings in Žepa), abruptly departed the scene once the Croats attacked." According to Joseph, Mladić did not then return to Žepa. For Edward Joseph's account on the fall of Žepa, see *Prosecutor vs. Popović et alii* (227 et seq.). Joseph testified at the ICTY on 22, 23, and 24 August 2007.

57. By arguing that the massacre took place because it was *possible*, Rohde joins with the interpretation offered at his appearance before the French parliamentary fact-finding mission by General Gobilliard, who feared the worst in the event of the enclave's fall. According to Gobilliard, Mladić was a shrewd chess player and only understood the language of force. Concerning Srebrenica, Gobilliard made it clear: "I do not think that he [Mladić] had premeditated it from the start but I think that he felt that the will of the Bosniaks was very vulnerable as well, perhaps, as that of the international community. He seized the opportunity and took advantage of it to give the most brutal expression to his exacerbated nationalism. Mladić is a chess player, that is how I figured him out. He only attacks when he feels that his adversary's defense is weak" (hearing of General Hervé Gobilliard, Thursday, 1 March 2001, in *Evénements de Srebrenica. Rapport d'information déposé par la Mission d'information commune sur les événements de Srebrenica*, Paris, 22 November 2001, volume II, 341).

58. The second hypothesis is compatible with that of Rohde. One can simultaneously maintain that the effective decision to carry out the systematic and complete execution of the men took place after the fall of the city *and* that the (or *a*) massacre was predictable or likely in the broader context of Serb nationalist politics during the war in Bosnia.

59. The first part of the NIOD report contains several sections on the careers of Karadžić (chapters 3, 4) and Mladić (chapters 5, 8) and on ethnic cleansing in Bosnia (chapters 5, 6), but these passages give rather superficial treatment to these issues, despite their importance for understanding Srebrenica. Moreover, the psychological profile of Mladić found in section 8 of chapter 5 is inadequately developed—his desire for vengeance, his megalomania, cruelty, and vision of European powers as being gods are not examined more thoroughly in the analysis of the motives for the executions (part IV, chapter 2, section 3).

60. I am referring here only to the predictability or obvious likelihood of the massacre and not to the intelligence available to secret service agencies. For the questions raised by this "secret" knowledge, see appendix II of the NIOD report and Sylvie Matton, *Srebrenica, un génocide annoncé* (Paris, 2005).

61. The reports unanimously claim that the massacre was not predictable and that such a large scale elimination of men had never before taken place in the war in Bosnia. This seems to imply that the massacre of several dozen or even hundreds of people might somehow be "acceptable."

62. On this subject, see David Harland's 18 September 2003 testimony before the ICTY during the Milošević trial. There, Harland indicates that, as early as 1994, Mladić wanted to finish off the enclaves in eastern Bosnia—he only backed off under pressure from

Milošević—and that, when the son of one of his colleagues was taken prisoner by the Bosniaks, Mladić threatened to kill everyone if he were not liberated.

63. While the initial Krstić judgment stuck closely to the investigation's narrative and had the merit of attempting to reconstruct the logic of the events, the Krstić appeal judgment left one altogether skeptical. There, the latter's international bias is every bit as unfortunate as the national bias of the reports. Thus, in order to respond to the objection that the genocide presupposed an exhaustive, as opposed to selective, murder of the men, the appeal judgment argued that the women and children would probably also have been killed, if the blue helmets had not been present. This argument, which a lawyer for the defense could have challenged as pure speculation, reflects deference toward the UN Security Council, upon which the ICTY depends.

64. On this notion, see Jacques Revel, ed. *Jeux d'échelles. La micro-analyse à l'expérience* (Paris, 1996).

65. Exceptions from the point of view of principle but not from that of history: there is nothing exceptional about situations of limited sovereignty or protectorate status, particularly in the Balkans.

66. There are many points of similarity between the Srebrenica massacre and that which took place in the village of Biljani on 10 July 1992, including the modus operandi of the Serb army in separating men and women and transporting men by bus to the site of execution as well as the flight of surviving men through the woods. On this massacre which produced at least 144 victims, see the ICTY's Brđanin, Krajišnik, and Milošević judgments and the Samardžija judgment of the State Court of Bosnia-Herzegovina (http://www.sudbih.gov.ba/?opcija=predmeti&id=18&zavrsen=1&jezik=e, last accessed 8 December 2011). On the idea that "village genocides" or small-scale killings can clarify the mechanisms of larger-scale massacres, see Daniel Chirot and Clark Mc Cauley, *Why Not Kill Them All? The Logic and Prevention of Mass Political Murder* (Princeton, NJ, 2006).

67. See NIOD, *Srebrenica—A "Safe" Area*, part IV, chapter 9.

68. One might conceive of the Srebrenica massacre as a more general case of historical or political vengeance but this is not the interpretation advanced by the NIOD.

69. Jacques Sémelin, *Purify and Destroy: The Political uses of Massacre and Genocides* (New York, 2007).

70. Cornelia Sorabji, "A Very Modern War: Terror and Territory in Bosnia-Hercegovina," in *War, a Cruel Necessity? The Bases of Institutionalized Violence*, eds. Robert A. Hinde and Helen E. Watson (London, 1995), 80–95.

71. In this connection, it is to be noted that the proportion of non-locals (Yugoslav army's soldiers, Arkan and Šešelj's militiamen, etc.) in the offensives and massacres of 1992 was no doubt higher than in Srebrenica in 1995. The difference between 1992 and Srebrenica in 1995 seems to reside in the greater role played by municipal authorities in 1992 (in the form of "Crisis staff") in the conduct of operations at the local level. The lesser importance of the municipal factor in Srebrenica in 1995, for both the victims and the criminals, had a major consequence: compared to many of 1992 crimes, the Srebrenica massacre was much less a case of murder among neighbors who knew one another.

72. For a better understanding of the relationship between the fall of Srebrenica and that of Žepa, see ICTY, *Prosecutor vs. Popović et alii*, 266–306. The trial of General Zdravko Tolimir, who has been indicted for crimes in Srebrenica and in Žepa, began in February 2010.

73. During an interview on 25 November 2006, General Gobilliard supplied me with the following information concerning this expedition. In July 1995, he was the head of UNPROFOR for the Sarajevo sector. Žepa was under its aegis but not Srebrenica. Tem-

porarily replacing General Rupert Smith at the moment of the attack on Srebrenica and its fall, he immediately passed on the *Dutchbat*'s request for air strikes, unsuccessfully attempted to persuade Janvier of the urgent need for these strikes and ordered the *Dutchbat* to take all necessary measures to defend the population. Familiar with Mladić from his time in Sarajevo, Gobilliard decided to firmly oppose the Serb forces in Žepa following the fall of Srebrenica. The Ukrainian unit on site in Žepa was one hundred men strong. On 25 and 26 July 1995, two detachments of reinforcements of 130 and 150 troops, respectively, accompanied by 30 and 15 armored vehicles, reached Žepa from Sarajevo. In the night of the 26th to the 27th, General Gobilliard joined them with nine men and two armored cars. While en route, he received Admiral Lanxade's order to return to Sarajevo, an order that he ignored on the grounds that he was better placed than his superiors to judge the situation. In Žepa, he met with General Tolimir (since Mladić, who was on the scene, refused to meet him following the recapture of the Vrbanja bridge in Sarajevo). Gobilliard had French and Ukrainian blue helmets placed in the buses that evacuated the population and deplores the fact that fifteen or so men had been taken off a bus by Serb soldiers. Given this information, the international response in Žepa seems to have been more firm than in Srebrenica, as Harland notes, but hardly "better organized" to the degree that Gobilliard acted on his own initiative and disobeyed orders. Moreover, chapter IX of the UN report clearly shows that the less disastrous results of international intervention in Žepa were not the outcome of a more coherent policy response. On the contrary, to judge from the analyses of Harland, Joseph, and Gobilliard, it was the initiative of individuals (UN soldiers and civil affairs officers) that helped save the population of Žepa.

74. Email from David Harland to the author, 22 June 2005. One can also find information concerning the factors that allowed the men of Žepa to be saved in Rohde's *Endgame*, which underscores the importance of Avdo Palić's command. Palić organized the departure of men by groups of three hundred, each of which was accompanied by soldiers and people familiar with the neighborhood in contrast with the (dis)organization of the Srebrenica column, which left civilians in the rear. Harland and Rohde emphasize Palić's heroism and talent as a leader, as well as his tragic end: following negotiations in the presence of the UN, he was assassinated by the Serbs. Edward Joseph, to whom Rohde and Harland refer, underscores that Palić was a hero, insufficiently recognized by the Bosnian government, who succeeded in winning time and sacrificed himself to ensure that the men of Žepa could escape: "But it was Avdo Palić who stalled for time, and who ultimately gave up his life in order to save the men of Žepa. He was a hero, and has never been properly acknowledged as such by the Bosnian government" (Edward Joseph in an email on 9 November 2006). For more details on Palić's action and disappearance, see ICTY, *Prosecutor vs. Popović et alii*, 266 et seq. Other factors and information were offered in the NIOD report (part IV, chapter 9) and in Harland's ICTY testimony during the Milošević trial, which for example underscored Milošević's role in ensuring the survival of the men of Žepa who had crossed the border into Serbia.

75. In particular, hypothetical variations on several points are possible: one may ask what would have happened if the Bosniak defense of Srebrenica had been better organized and more effective. Probably the same thing, at least in what concerns the defense of the enclave by UNPROFOR and NATO, if one considers that, in Žepa, the Bosniak resistance held out longer without the enclave having been more extensively defended by an international intervention.

76. This division is clear in the UN report, which adopts the ICTY's condemnatory tone toward crimes and their authors or instigators—i.e., the UN's interlocutors during the

war. But, in the end, it seems that its support for the ICTY in judging crimes was the only action taken by the UN in the area of punishing those responsible.
77. The reports represent a particularly rich source for reflection on the attributions of "rational" beliefs to others and the role played by tacit and implicit considerations in determining how the actors interpreted one another. This material is hardly analyzed by the reports. Yet it is precisely the manner in which each protagonist implicitly regulated his action or inaction vis-à-vis that of the others that renders Srebrenica a tragic chain of events or "passive conspiracy" on Rohde's interpretation.
78. It is striking to note the similarities between the denunciations of the international community that I have often heard voiced by the Bosniaks of Srebrenica and the arguments of the philosopher and historian Pierre Bayle against theodicy. All believe that a superior being who has responsibility for certain individuals and a superior power of action and intervention but nevertheless allows crimes to be committed is just as guilty of those crimes as is the immediate perpetrator. On this comparison, see *Le mal en procès. Eichmann et les théodicées modernes,* epilogue, 213–215.
79. During my field work in Bosnia, I noticed that the Bosniaks who had experienced the war in the enclaves where there was a strong international presence—and this is particularly true of those who survived Srebrenica—were profoundly troubled by a feeling that their lives had lost value. It is fairly common to hear that Bosniak lives are "worth nothing." Yet I never heard such remarks among the Bosniaks of Prijedor, where the war's violence was terrible but where there had been no international presence. It seems to me that this sentiment is due less to the violence of war in itself than to the presence of international forces, as a more or less passive witness to the violence. On this subject, see my article, "Moral Judgments on Foreign Interventions: A Bosnian Perspective," in *Rethinking Ethical Foreign Policy: Pitfalls, Possibilities and Paradoxes,* eds. David Chandler and Volker Heins (London, 2007), 137–157.

BIBLIOGRAPHY

Allcock, John. *Explaining Yugoslavia*. New York, 2000.
Ambos, Kai. "International Criminal Procedure: 'Adversarial', 'Inquisitorial' or Mixed?" *International Criminal Law Review* 3, no. 1 (2003): 1–37.
Ankersmit, Frank, et al. Dossier "Het drama Srebrenica: geschiedtheoretische beschouwingen over het NIOD-rapport" [The Tragedy of Srebrenica: Historical-Theoretical Reflexions on the NIOD-Report]. *Tijdschrift voor geschiedenis* 116, no. 2 (June 2003).
Andjelic, Neven. *Bosnia-Herzegovina: The End of a Legacy*. London, 2003.
Arendt, Hannah. *Eichmann in Jerusalem: A Report on the Banality of Evil*. New York/London, 1994 [1963].
Aron, Raymond. *Peace and War: A Theory of International Relations*. New Brunswick, NJ, 2003 [1966].
Bass, Gary J. *Stay the Hand of Vengeance: The Politics of War Crimes Tribunals*. Princeton, NJ/Oxford, 2000.
Bassiouni, Cherif. *Crimes against Humanity in International Criminal Law*. Dordrecht/Boston, MA/London, 1992.
———. "Former Yugoslavia: Investigating Violations of International Humanitarian Law and Establishing an International Criminal Tribunal." *Security Dialogue* 25, no. 4 (December 1994): 409–423.
Baubérot, Jean. "Le dernier des Curiace. Un sociologue dans la Commission Stasi." In *La nouvelle question religieuse. Régulation ou ingérence de l'Etat? / The New Religious Question: State Regulation or State Interference?* eds. Pauline Côté and Jeremy T. Gunn. Frankfurt am Main, 2006, 247–272.
Bećirević, Edina. *Na Drini genocid. Istraživanje organiziranog zločina u istočnoj Bosni* [The Genocide on the Drina: The Investigation of an Organized Crime in Eastern Bosnia]. Sarajevo, 2009.
Bensa, Alban, and Éric Fassin, eds. Dossier "Qu'est-ce qu'un événement." *Terrain*, no. 38 (March 2002).
Bieber, Florian. *Post-War Bosnia: Ethnicity, Inequality and Public Sector Governance*. Basingstoke, 2006.
Biserko, Sonja, ed. *Srebrenica: od poricanja do priznanja* [Srebrenica: From Denial to Admission]. Beograd, 2005.

Blom, J. C. H. (Hans). "Het NIOD-rapport onevenwichtig en intellectueel gemakzuchtig? Een kwestie van lezen" [The NIOD-Report, Unbalanced and Intellectually Lazy? A Question of Reading]. *Internationale Spectator* 56, no. 9 (September 2002): 448–453.

———. "Une recherche historique entre science et politique. Le cas 'Srebrenica.'" In *L'historien dans l'espace public*, ed. Guy Zelis. Loverval, 2005, 93–108.

Bloxham, Donald. *Genocide on Trial: War Crimes Trials and the Formation of Holocaust History and Memory*. New York/Oxford, 2001.

Bose, Sumantra. *Bosnia after Dayton: Nationalist Partition and International Intervention*. London, 2002.

Both, Norbert. *From Indifference to Entrapment: The Netherlands and the Yugoslav Crisis 1990–1995*. Amsterdam, 2000.

Bougarel, Xavier. *Bosnie: anatomie d'un conflit*. Paris, 1996.

———. "The Shadow of Heroes: Former Combatants in Post-War Bosnia-Herzegovina." *International Social Science Journal*, no. 189 (September 2006): 479–490.

———. "Du cope pénal au mémorandum: les usages du terme 'génodide' dans la Yougoslavie communiste." In *Peines de guerre. La justice pénale internationale et l'ex-Yougoslavie*, eds. Isabelle Delpla and Magali Bessonne. Paris, 2010, 67–84.

Bougarel, Xavier, and Nathalie Clayer, eds. *Le nouvel Islam balkanique. Les musulmans, acteurs du post-communisme 1990–2000*. Paris, 2001.

Bougarel, Xavier, Elissa Helms, and Ger Duijzings, eds. *The New Bosnian Mosaic: Identities, Memories and Moral Claims in a Post-War Society*. Aldershot, 2007.

Brayard, Florent, ed. *Le génocide des Juifs entre procès et histoire 1943–2000*. Brussels, 2000.

———. *La "Solution finale de la question juive". La technique, le temps et les catégories de la décision*. Paris, 2004.

Bringa, Tone. *Being Muslim the Bosnian Way: Identity and Community in a Central Bosnian Village*. Princeton, NJ, 1995.

Brouwer, J. W. L. et al. Dossier "Discussiedossier Srebrenica" [Dossier on the Srebrenica Discussion]. *Bijdragen en mededelingen betreffende de geschiedenis der Nederlanden* 118, no. 3 (2003).

Browning, Christopher. *Ordinary Men: Reserve Police Battalion 101 and the Final Solution in Poland*. New York, 1992.

———. *The Path to Genocide: Essays on Launching the Final Solution*. Cambridge, 1992.

———. *The Origins of the Final Solution: The Evolution of Nazi Jewish Policy, September 1939–March 1942*. Lincoln, NE, 2004.

Brunborg, Helge, Torkild Hovde Lyngstad, and Henrik Urdal. "Accounting for Genocide: How Many Were Killed in Srebrenica?" *European Journal of Population* 19, no. 3 (September 2003): 229–248.

Burg, Steven L., and Paul S. Shoup. *The War in Bosnia-Herzegovina: Ethnic Conflict and International Intervention*. New York, 1999.

Cabanes, Bruno, and Guillaume Piketty. Dossier "Sorties de guerre au XXe siècle." *Histoire@politique*, no. 3 (November–December 2007), available at http://www.histoire-politique.fr/index.php?numero=03&rub=dossier.

Čekić, Smail, ed. *Srebrenica 1995. Zločini nad Bošnjacima u Srebrenici za vrijeme agresije na Republiku Bosnu i Hercegovinu 1991–1995* [The Crimes Against Bosniaks in Srebrenica During the Aggression Against the Republic of Bosnia-Herzegovina 1991–1995], 3 vols. Sarajevo, 1997.

Chirot, Daniel, and Clark Mc Cauley. *Why Not Kill Them All? The Logic and Prevention of Mass Political Murder.* Princeton, NJ, 2006.

Cohen, Lenard. *Serpent in the Bossom: The Rise and Fall of Slobodan Milosevic.* Boulder, 2001.

Cohen, Lenard, and Jasna Dragović-Soso, eds. *State Collapse in South-Eastern Europe: New Perspectives on Yugoslavia's Disintegration.* West Lafayette, IN, 2008.

Combs, Nancy A. *Guilty Pleas in International Criminal Law: Constructing a Restorative Justice Approach.* Stanford, 2007.

Cooper, Belinda, ed. *War Crimes: The Legacy of Nuremberg.* New York, 1999.

Corsellis, John, and Marcus Ferrar. *Slovenia 1945: Memories of Death and Survival after World War II.* London/New York, 2005.

Couzy, Hans. *Mijn jaren als bevelhebber* [My Years in Command]. Amsterdam/Antwerp, 1996.

Dedijer, Vladimir, and Antun Miletić. *Genocid nad Muslimanima* [The Genocide Against Muslims]. Sarajevo, 1990.

De Leeuw, Marc. "A Gentlemen's Agreement: Srebrenica in the Context of Dutch War History." In *The Post-War Moment: Militaries, Masculinities and International Peacekeeping,* eds. Dubravka Žarkov and Cynthia Cockburn. London, 2002, 162–181.

Delpla, Isabelle. "Incertitudes publiques et privées sur les disparus en Bosnie-Herzégovine." In *Crises extrêmes. Face aux massacres, aux guerres civiles et aux genocides,* eds. Marc Le Pape, Johanna Siméant, and Claudine Vidal. Paris, 2006, 287–301.

———. "In the Midst of Injustice: The ICTY in the Perspective of some Victim Associations." In *The New Bosnian Mosaic: Identities, Memories and Moral Claims in a Post-War Society,* eds. Xavier Bougarel, Elissa Helms, and Ger Duijzings. Aldershot, 2007, 211–234.

———. "Moral Judgments on Foreign Interventions: A Bosnian Perspective." In *Rethinking Ethical Foreign Policy: Pitfalls, Possibilities and Paradoxes,* eds. David Chandler and Volker Heins. London/New York, 2007, 137–157.

———. "La preuve par les victimes. Bilans de guerre en Bosnie-Herzégovine." *Le mouvement social,* no. 222 (January–March 2008): 153–183.

Delpla, Isabelle, Xavier Bougarel, and Jean-Louis Fournel, eds. Dossier "Srebrenica 1995. Analyses croisées des enquêtes et des rapports." *Cultures et conflits,* no. 65 (Spring 2007).

Delpla, Isabelle and Magali Bessonne, eds. *Peines de guerre. La justice pénale internationale et l'ex-Yougoslavie.* Paris, 2010.

Dimitrijević, Bojan. "Slučaj likvidacije zarobljenika posle zauzimanja Srebrenice jula 1995" [The Case of the Liquidation of Prisoners after the Capture of Srebrenica in July 1995]. *Istorija 20. veka* 22, no. 1 (2004): 131–157.

Dimitrijević, Vojin, and Marko Milanovic. "The Strange Story of the Bosnian Genocide Case." *Leiden Journal of International Law* 21, no. 1 (March 2008): 65–94.

Donia, Robert J. "Encountering the Past: History at the Yugoslav War Crimes Tribunal." *The Journal of the International Institute* 11, no. 2–3 (Winter–Spring/Summer 2004), available at http://quod.lib.umich.edu/cgi/t/text/text-idx?c=jii;cc=jii;q1=4750978.0011.2 percent2A;rgn=main;view=text;idno=4750978.0011.201.

Donia, Robert J., and John V. A. Fine, *Bosnia and Herzegovina: A Tradition Betrayed*. London, 1994.

Dragović, Soso. *"Saviors of the Nation": Serbia's Intellectual Opposition and the Revival of Nationalism*. London, 2002.

Duijzings, Ger. "The Road to Hell is Paved with Good Intentions: The Srebrenica Report of the Netherlands Institute for War Documentation (NIOD)." *South-East Europe Newsletter*, no. 54 (June 2003): 1–7.

———. "Commemorating Srebrenica: Histories of Violence and Politics of Memory in Eastern Bosnia." In *The New Bosnian Mosaic, Identities, Memories and Moral Claims in a Post-war Society*, eds. Xavier Bougarel, Elissa Helms, and Ger Duijzings. Aldershot, 2007, 141–166.

Evans, Richard J. "History, Memory, and the Law: The Historian as Expert Witness." *History and Theory* 41, no. 3 (October 2002): 326–345.

Faber, Mient Jan. *Srebrenica. De genocide die niet werd voorkomen* [Srebrenica: The Genocide That Was not Prevented]. The Hague, 2002.

Farber, Daniel A. "Adjudication of Things Past: Reflections on History as Evidence." *Hastings Law Journal* 49 (April 1998): 1009–1026.

Final Report of the United Nations Commission of Experts Established Pursuant to Security Council Resolution 780 (1992)—document S/1994/674, available at http://www.ess.uwe.ac.uk/comexpert/REPORT_TOC.HTM.

Friedman, Francine. *The Bosnian Muslims: Denial of a Nation*. Boulder, CO, 1996.

Gagnon, Valère P. *The Myth of Ethnic War: Serbia and Croatia in the 1990s*. Ithaca, NY, 2004.

Garms, Ulrich, and Katharina Peschke. "War Crimes Prosecutions in Bosnia and Herzegovina (1992–2002): An Analysis through the Jurisprudence of the Human Rights Chamber." *Journal of International Criminal Justice* 4, no. 2 (May 2006): 258–282.

Gerlach, Christian. *Kalkulierte Morde. Die Deutsche Wirtschafts- und Vernichtungspolitik in Weissrussland, 1941 bis 1944*. Hamburg, 1999.

Ginsburg, George, and Vladimir N. Kudriavtsev. *The Nuremberg Trial and International Law*. Dordrecht/Boston, MA/London, 1990.

Ginzburg, Carlo. *Wooden Eyes: Nine Reflections on Distance*. New York, 2001.

———. *The Judge and the Historian*. London/New York, 2002.

Golstone, Richard J., and Rebecca J. Hamilton. "Bosnia v. Serbia: Lessons from the Encounter of the International Court of Justice with the International Criminal Tribunal for the Former Yugoslavia." *Leiden Journal of International Law* 21, no. 1 (March 2008): 95–112.

Gow, James. *Triumph of the Lack of Will: International Diplomacy and the Yugoslav War*. New York, 1997.

———. *The Serbian Project and Its Adversaries: A Strategy of War Crimes*. London, 2003.

Habermas, Jürgen. *Perpetual Peace: Essays on Kant's Cosmopolitan Ideal*. Cambridge, MA, 1997.
Hadžić, Miroslav. *The Yugoslav People's Agony: The Role of the Yugoslav People's Army*. Aldershot, 2002.
Hagan, John. *Justice in the Balkans: Prosecuting War Crimes in the Hague Tribunal*. Chicago, IL, 2003.
Hall, Jean G., and Gordon D. Smith. *The Expert Witness*. Chichester, 1997.
Halpern, Joel M., and David A. Kideckel, eds. *Neighbors at War: Anthropological Perspectives on Yugoslav Ethnicity, Culture and History*. University Park, PA, 2000.
Hayden, Robert. "Recounting the Dead: The Rediscovery and Redefinition of Wartime Massacres in Late- and Post-Communist Yugoslavia." In *Memory, History and Opposition under State Socialism*, ed. Rubie Watson. Santa Fe, NM, 1994, 167–188.
Hećimović, Esad. *Kako su prodali Srebrenicu i sačuvali vlast* [How They Sold Srebrenica and Kept Power]. Sarajevo, 1998.
Hoare, Marko A. *How Bosnia Armed: The Birth and Rise of the Bosnian Army*. London, 2004.
Honig, Jan Willem. "Strategy and Genocide: Srebrenica as an Analytical Challenge." *Southeast European and Black Sea Studies* 7, no. 33 (September 2007): 399–416.
Honig, Jan Willem, and Norbert Both. *Srebrenica: Record of a War Crime*. London, 1996.
Horne, John, and Alan Kramer. *German Atrocities, 1914: A History of Denial*. New Haven, CT/London, 2001.
Human Rights Watch. Dossier "The Fall of Srebrenica and the Failure of UN Peacekeeping." *Human Rights Watch Publications* 7, no. 13 (October 1995): 1–80.
Ibišević, Besim. *Srebrenica (1987–1992)*. Amsterdam, 1999.
Ingrao, Christian. "Conquérir, aménager, exterminer. Nouvelles recherches sur la Shoah." *Annales. Histoire, sciences sociales* 58, no. 2 (March–April 2003): 417–438.
Institut d'histoire du temps présent. *Ecrire l'histoire du temps présent*. Paris, 1993.
Jaspers, Karl. *The Question of German Guilt*. Bronx, NY, 2001 [1948].
Jouhanneau, Cécile. "'Si vous avez un problème que vous ne voulez pas régler, créez une commission.' Les commissions d'enquête locales dans la Bosnie-Herzégovine d'après-guerre." *Mouvements*, no. 53 (2008): 166–174.
Jović, Dejan. *Yugoslavia: A State that Withered Away*. West Lafayette, IN, 2009.
Joyce, Christopher, and Eric Stover. *Witnesses from the Grave: The Stories Bones Tell*. Boston, MA, 1991
Jurovics, Yann. *Réflexions sur la spécificité du crime contre l'humanité*. Paris, 2002.
Kant, Immanuel. *Perpetual Peace and Other Essays*. Indianapolis, IN, 1988.
Karremans, Thom. *Srebrenica. Who Cares?* Nieuwegein, 1998.
Kennan, George F., ed. *The Other Balkan Wars: A 1913 Carnegie Endowment Inquiry in Retrospect*. Washington, DC, 1993
Kerr, Rachel. *The International Criminal Tribunal for the Former Yugoslavia: An Exercise in Law, Politics, and Diplomacy*. Oxford, 2004.

Kévonian, Dzovinar. "L'enquête, la délit, la preuve: les 'atrocités' balkaniques de 1912–1913 à l'épreuve du droit de la guerre." *Le mouvement social*, no. 222 (January–March 2008): 13–40.

Klep, Christ. *Somalië, Rwanda, Srebrenica. De nasleep van drie ontspoorde vredesmissies* [Somalia, Rwanda, Srebrenica: The Aftermath of Three Peace Operations Gone Wrong]. Amsterdam, 2009.

Klep, Christ, and Richard van Gils. *Van Korea tot Kabul. De Nederlandse militaire deelname aan vredesoperaties sinds 1945* [From Korea to Kabul: Dutch Military Participation in Peace Operations Since 1945]. Den Haag, 2005.

Klep, Christ, and Donna Winslow. "Learning Lessons the Hard Way: Somalia and Srebrenica Compared." In *Peace Operations between War and Peace*, ed. Erwin A. Schmidl. London, 2000, 93–137.

Kreß, Claus. "The International Court of Justice and the Elements of the Crime of Genocide." *The European Journal of International Law* 18, no. 4 (2007): 619–629.

Krieg-Planque, Alice. *Purification ethnique. Une formule et son histoire*. Paris, 2003.

Krulic, Joseph. "La fin de la Deuxième Guerre mondiale en Yougoslavie 1944–1945." *Revue d'histoire de la Deuxième Guerre mondiale et des conflits contemporains*, no. 149 (January 1988).

Kulovac, Šaban. *Žepa 1992–1995*. Sarajevo, 2007.

Lagrou, Pieter. "Het Srebrenica-rapport en de geshiedenis van het heden" [The Srebrenica-Report and the History of the Present]. *Bijdragen en Mededelingen betreffende de Geshiedenis der Nederlanden* 118, no. 3 (2003): 325–336.

———. "L'histoire du temps présent en Europe depuis 1945, ou comment se constitue et se développe un nouveau champ disciplinaire." *La Revue pour l'histoire du CNRS*, no. 9 (November 2003): 4–15.

———. "De l'actualité de l'histoire du temps présent." *Bulletin de l'Institut d'histoire du temps présent*, no. 75 (June 2000): 10–22.

Lampe, John. *Yugoslavia as History: Twice There Was a Country*. Cambridge, 2000.

Langbein, John H. *The Origins of Adversary Criminal Trial*. Oxford, 2003.

Lemkin, Raphael. *Axis Rule in Occupied Europe*. Washington, DC, 1944.

———. "Le crime de génocide." *Revue de droit international de sciences diplomatiques et politiques* 24 (October–December 1946): 213–222.

Le Pape, Marc. "Vérités et controverses sur le Génocide des Rwandais tutsis. Les rapports (Belgique, France, ONU)." In *Crises extrêmes. Face aux massacres, aux guerres civiles et aux génocides*, eds. Marc Le Pape, Johanna Siméant, and Claudine Vidal. Paris, 2006, 103–118.

Le Pape, Marc, Johanna Siméant, and Claudine Vidal, eds. *Crises extrêmes. Face aux massacres, aux guerres civiles et aux génocides*. Paris, 2006.

Leydesdorff, Selma. *De leegte achter ons laten: een geschiedenis van de vrouwen van Srebrenica* [To Leave the Emptiness Behind Us: A History of the Women of Srebrenica]. Amsterdam, 2008.

Lippman, Matthew. "The 1948 Convention on the Prevention and the Punishment of the Crime of Genocide: Forty-Five Years Later." *Temple International and Comparative Law Journal* 8, no. 1 (Spring 1994): 1–84.

Lorenz, Chris. "Het 'Academisch Poldermodel' en de 'Westforschung' in Nederland" [The "Academic Polder-Model" and the "West Research" in the Netherlands]. *Tildschrift voor Geschiedenis* 118, no. 2 (2005): 252–270.

Lupis, Ivan. "Human Rights Abuses in the Wake of the Collapse of the United Nations-Designated 'Safe Area' of Srebrenica and the International Community." *Helsinki Monitor* 7, no. 1 (1996): 65–72.
Mac Donald, David B. *Balkan Holocausts? Serbian and Croatian Victim-Centered Propaganda and the War in Yugoslavia*. Manchester, 2002.
Maguire, Peter. *Law and War: An American History*. New York, 2001.
Maison, Rafaëlle. *Coupable de résistance? Naser Oric, défenseur de Srebrenica, devant la justice internationale*. Paris, 2010.
Malcolm, Noel. *Bosnia: A Short History*. London, 1994.
Martin, Jonathan D. "Historians at the Gate: Accommodating Expert Testimony in Federal Courts." *New York University Law Review* 78 (October 2003): 1518–1549.
Mašić, Nijaz. *Istina o Bratuncu. Agresija, genocid i oslobodilačka borba 1992–1995* [The Truth About Bratunac: Agression, Genocide and Liberation Fight 1992–1995]. Tuzla, 1996.
Mašić, Nijaz. *Srebrenica: agresija, otpor, izdaja, genocid* [Srebrenica: Agression, Resistance, Betrayal, Genocide]. Srebrenica, 1999.
Matton, Sylvie. *Srebrenica, un génocide annoncé*. Paris, 2005.
May, Larry. *Crimes Against Humanity: A Normative Account*. Cambridge, 2005.
Mesnard, Philippe. "Srebrenica, entre mission et commission." *Mouvements*, no. 20 (2002): 146–151.
Moine, Nathalie, ed. Dossier "Enquêter sur la guerre." *Le mouvement social*, no. 222 (January–March 2008): 3–183.
Mustafić, Ibran. *Planirani haos 1990–1996* [A Planned Chaos 1990–1996]. Sarajevo, 2008.
Nettlefield, Lara. *Courting Democracy in Bosnia and Herzegovina: The Hague Tribunal's Impact in a Postwar State*. New York, 2010.
Neuffer, Elizabeth. *The Key to My Neighbor's House: Seeking Justice in Bosnia and Rwanda*. London, 2001.
Nice, Geoffrey, and Vallieres-Roland Philippe. "Procedural Innovations in War Crimes Trials." *Journal of International Criminal Justice* 3, no. 2 (May 2005): 354–380.
Nora, Pierre. "Le retour de l'événement." In *Faire de l'histoire. Nouveaux problèmes*, eds. Jacques Le Goff and Pierre Nora. Paris, 1974, 210–228.
Nuhanović, Hasan. *Pod zastavom UN-a. Međunarodna zajednica i zločin u Srebrenici* [Under the UN Flag: The International Community and the Crime in Srebrenica]. Sarajevo, 2005.
Orić, Naser. *Srebrenica svjedoči i optužuje. Genocid nad Bošnjacima u istočnoj Bosni april 1992–septembar 1994* [Srebrenica Testifies and Accuses: The Genocide Against Bosniaks in Eastern Bosnia April 1992–September 1994]. Srebrenica, 1995.
Osiel, Mark. *Mass Atrocity, Collective Memory and the Law*. New Brunswick, NJ, 1997.
Pargan, Mehmed. *Srebrenica. Dokumenti o genocidu* [Srebrenica: Documents About the Genocide]. Tuzla, 2004.
Peskin, Viktor A. *International Justice in Rwanda and the Balkans: Virtual Trials and the Struggle for State Cooperation*. Cambridge, 2008.
Petrović, Vladimir. "Juridical Memory Making and the Transformation of Historical Expert Witnessing: Contextualizing the Eichmann Case and the Frank-

furt Auschwitz Trial." In *Remembering and Forgetting/Erinnern und Vergessen. Yearbook of Young Legal History*, vol. 2, eds. Oliver Brupbacher et al. Munich, 2007, 326–346.

———. "Weltgericht ohne Weltgeschichte: Historians as Expert Witnesses in the ICTY." *Ab Imperio*, no. 3 (2007): 195–217.

Pohl, Dieter. *Nationalsozialistische Judenverfolgung in Ostgalizien 1941–1944: Organisation und Durchführung eines staatlichen Massenverbrechens*. Munich, 1996.

Pollack, Creg E. "Burial at Srebrenica: Linking Place and Trauma." *Social Science & Medicine* 56, no. 4 (February 2003): 793–801.

———. "Intentions of Burial: Mourning, Politics, and Memorials Following the Massacre at Srebrenica." *Death Studies* 27, no. 2 (February 2003): 125–142.

———. "Returning to a Safe Area? The Importance of Burial for Return to Srebrenica." *Journal of Refugee Studies* 16, no. 2 (June 2003): 186–201.

Quinche, Nicolas. "Reiss et la Serbie: des scènes de crime aux champs de bataille, l'enquête continue". In *Le théâtre du crime: Rodolphe A. Reiss (1875–1929)*, eds. Christophe Champod et al. Lausanne, 2009, 289–306.

Revel, Jacques, ed. *Jeux d'échelles. La microanalyse à l'expérience*. Paris, 1996.

Ricoeur, Paul. *The Just*. Chicago, IL, 2003.

———. *Memory, History, Forgetting*. Chicago, IL, 2004.

Rohde, David. *A Safe Area: Srebrenica, Europe's Worst Massacre since the Second World War*. New York/London, 1997.

Rousso, Henry. *The Haunting Past: History, Memory and Justice in Contemporary France*. Philadelphia, PA, 2002.

Rozemond, Sam. "Het NIOD en de intellectuele gemakzucht" [The NIOD and the Intellectual Laziness]. *Internationale Spectator* 56, no. 6 (June 2002): 289–301.

Runia, Eelco. "'Forget About It': Parallel Processing in the Srebrenica Report." *History and Theory* 43, no. 3 (October 2004): 295–320.

Shklar, Judith N. *Legalism: Law, Morals and Political Trials*. Cambridge, 1986.

Siméant, Johanna et al., eds. Dossier "Le modèle de l'enquête judiciaire face aux crises extrêmes." *Critique internationale*, no. 36 (2007).

Sion, Liora. "'Too Sweet and Innocent for War', Dutch Peacekeepers and the Use of Violence." *Armed Forces & Society* 32, no. 3 (April 2006): 454–474.

Sorabji, Cornelia. "A Very Modern War: Terror and Territory in Bosnia-Herzegovina." In *War, a Cruel Necessity? The Bases of Institutionnalized Violence*, eds. Robert A. Hinde and Helen E. Watson. London, 1995, 80–95.

Stover, Eric. *The Witnesses, War Crimes and the Promise of Justice in The Hague*. Philadelphia, PA, 2007.

Stover, Eric and Harvey M. Weinstein, eds. *My Neighbor, My Enemy: Justice and Community in the Aftermath of Mass Atrocity*. Cambridge, 2004.

Stover, Eric and Gilles Peress. *The Graves: Srebrenica and Vukovar*. Zurich, 1998.

Subotic, Jelena. *Hijacked Justice: Dealing with the Past in the Balkans*. Ithaca, NY, 2009.

Sudetic, Chuck. *Blood and Vengeance*. London, 1998.

Suljagic, Emir. *Postcards from the Grave*. London, 2005.

Tardy, Thierry. *La France et la gestion des conflits yougoslaves (1991–1995)*. Paris, 1999.

Teitel, Ruti G. *Transitional Justice*. Oxford/New York, 2000.

Tieger, Alan, and Milbert Shin. "Plea Agreements in the ICTY: Purpose, Effects and Propriety." *Journal of International Criminal Justice* 3, no. 3 (July 2005): 666–679.
UG Žene Srebrenice. *Samrtno srebreničko ljeto '95. Svjedočanstvo o stradanju Srebrenice i naroda Podrinja* [The Deadly Summer of Srebrenica in 1995: Testimonies about the Suffering of Srebrenica and the People of the Drina Valley]. Tuzla, 1998.
Vasiljević, Vladan. "La responsabilité pour crimes contre l'humanité perpétrés en Yougoslavie de 1941 à 1945." *Jugoslovenska revija za međunarodno pravo* 38, no. 3 (1991): 314–338.
Veyne, Paul. *Writing History: Essay on Epistemology*. Middletown, CT, 1984.
Vidal-Naquet, Pierre. *Assassins of Memory: Essays on the Denial of the Holocaust*. New York, 1993.
Vujadinović, Željko. "Fenomenologija Srebrenice." *Istorija 20. veka* 24, no. 2 (2006): 147–163.
Wagner, Sarah E. *To Know Where He Lies: DNA Technology and the Search for Srebrenica's Missing*. Berkeley, CA, 2008.
Wilson, Richard A. "Judging History: The Historical Record of the International Criminal Tribunal for the Former Yugoslavia." *Human Rights Quarterly* 27, no. 3 (August 2005): 908–942.
———. "Humanity's Histories Evaluating the Historical Accounts of International Tribunals and Truth Commissions." *Politix*, no. 80 (2007): 31–58.
———. *Writing History in International Criminal Trials*. Cambridge, 2011.
Woodward, Susan L. *Balkan Tragedy: Chaos and Dissolution after the Cold War*. Washington, DC, 1995.
Žarkov, Dubravka. *The Body of War: Media, Ethnicity, and Gender in the Break-Up of Yugoslavia*. Durham, NC, 2007.
Žarkov, Dubravka, and Cynthia Cockburn, eds. *The Post-War Moment: Militaries, Masculinities and International Peacekeeping*. London, 2002.

Notes on Contributors

Xavier Bougarel is researcher at the French Centre national de la recherche scientifique (UMR 8032 Centre d'études turques, ottomanes, balkaniques et centrasiatiques). He is working on the wars of the 1990s and their aftermath in former Yugoslavia and on the transformations of Islam in the post-Communist Balkans. Among his publications are *Bosnie, anatomie d'un conflit* (Paris, 1996); *Le nouvel islam balkanique. Les musulmans, acteurs du post-communisme 1990–2000* (Paris, 2001), co-edited with Nathalie Clayer; *The New Bosnian Mosaic: Identities, Memories and Moral Claims in a Post War Society* (Aldershot, 2007), co-edited with Elissa Helms and Ger Duijzings.

Pierre Brana is a former MP in the French National Assembly (Socialist parliamentary group). He was a member of the Srebrenica Fact-Finding Mission, rapporteur of the Rwanda Fact-Finding Mission and—from 1988 to 1993 and, again, from 1997 to 2002—a member of and then secretary to the Foreign Affairs Committee (rapporteur on the cooperation funding and, later, on the Ministry of Foreign Affairs' budget).

Isabelle Delpla is assistant professor of philosophy at the University Montpellier 3 and member of the UMR 5206 "Triangle" (Ecole normale supérieure de Lyon – University of Lyon); she has worked in philosophy of language and philosophy of international justice. Over the last years, she has directed a research program on international justice (ACI 67110) and conducted fieldwork in Bosnia with victim associations, Hague witnesses, and convicted war criminals. She has published several books on those issues. Among them, *Quine, Davidson: Le principe de charité* (Paris, 2001); *L'Usage anthropologique du principe de charité* (Paris, 2002); *Peines de guerre. La justice pénale internationale et l'ex-Yougoslavie* (Paris, 2010), co-edited with Magali Bessone; *Le mal en procès. Eichmann et les théodicées modernes* (Paris, 2011)

JEAN-LOUIS FOURNEL is professor at the University Paris 8 and a member of the UMR 5206 "Triangle" (Ecole normale supérieure de Lyon – University of Lyon). He is a specialist in the history of the warfare, political thought, and rhetoric of the Italian Renaissance. In collaboration with Jean-Claude Zancarini, he has published several articles, translations of important texts from Machiavelli, Savonarola, and Guicciardini, and two books on Florentine republican thought (*La politique de l'expérience* [Alessandria, 2003]; and *La grammaire de la République* [Genève, 2009]). Between 1997 and 2001, he directed several European cooperation programs with the universities of Bosnia-Herzegovina. In 1994, with the city under siege, he co-organized the initiative to twin his university with that of Sarajevo.

CHRIST KLEP ws till 2011 lecturer at the Department of International Affairs of the University of Utrecht. He is currently a freelance historian and publicist. In 1995, he was employed at the History Research Department of the Dutch Ministry of Defense and was one of the Defense historians who went to Zagreb to interview the *Dutchbat* soldiers who had just returned from Srebrenica. In the following years, he served both as an advisor and witness to several inquiry commissions, including the Interim Parliamentary Commission and the NIOD-report. He left the Ministry of Defense in 2000. Among his publications are *Somalië, Rwanda, Srebrenica. De nasleep van drie ontspoorde vredesmissies* [Somalia, Rwanda, Srebrenica: The Aftermath of Three Peace Operations Gone Wrong] (Amsterdam, 2009).

PIETER LAGROU is professor of contemporary history at the Université libre de Bruxelles (ULB) and researcher at the Institut d'histoire du temps présent (IHTP) in Paris. Among his publications are *The Legacy of Nazi-Occupation: Patriotic Memory and National Recovery in Western Europe 1945–1965* (Cambridge, 2000); "Europe as Place for Common Memories? Some Thoughts on Victimhood, Identity and Emancipation from the Past," in *Clashes in European Memory. The Case of Communist Repression and the Holocaust,* eds. Muriel Blaive, Christian Gerbel and Thomas Lindenberger (Innsbrück, 2010), 281–288; "'Historical Trials': Getting the Past Right—or the Future?," in *The Scene of the Mass Crime. History, Film and International Tribunals,* eds. Christian Delage and Peter Groodrich (London, 2012).

MICHÈLE PICARD is currently judge at the ICTY. She is former vice-president of the District Court of Paris. She served as president of the Human

Rights Chamber for Bosnia-Herzegovina from November 1997 to December 2003. Having served as an independent expert advisor to the United Nations for Uzbekistan, she has been appointed to the Human Rights Advisory Panel in Kosovo by the special representative of the UN Secretary General in Kosovo. She contributed to the edited volume *La Convention européenne des droits de l'homme. Commentaire article par article*, eds. Emmanuel Decaux, Pierre-Henri Imbert, and Louis-Edmond Petiti (Paris, 1999).

JEAN-RENÉ RUEZ is a police commissioner working currently for the French Ministry of Interior. He led the ICTY investigations into the Srebrenica massacre from 1996 to 2001, has testified in the trials of all those charged by the ICTY in this case, and continues to do so. Several writings, documentaries, and movies have been dedicated to his work in Srebrenica, among them chapter five of John Hagan's book, *Justice in the Balkans* (Chicago, IL, 2003); Morad Aït-Habbouch's documentary film *Srebrenica, plus jamais ça* (2006); and Giacomo Battiato's fictional movie *Résolution 819* (2008).

ASTA M. ZINBO is currently a democracy specialist with the US Agency for International Development. She was director of the Civil Society Initiatives Department of the International Commission on Missing Persons (ICMP) for the former Yugoslavia from 1998 to 2008. From 1997 to 2000, she was deputy director of the regional office of the NGO *Freedom House* in Hungary. She holds an MA in International Relations from the Georgetown School of Foreign Service in Washington, DC, a BA in Political Science from the University of Michigan, and a degree in Political Science from the Institut d'études politiques (IEP) in Aix-en-Provence (France).

Name Index

A
Ahmetović, Ćamil, 118, 125n
Ajanović, Ekrem, 104, 112, 117, 123n, 124n
Ajanović, Irfan, 112, 114, 115, 125n, 128n
Akashi, Yasushi, 113, 115, 126n, 160, 170
Albright, Madeleine, 33, 34
Amsterdam, 69, 71, 92, 99, 102n
Andjelic, Neven, 19n
André, René, 62
Arendt, Hannah, 157, 172n
Arsović, Marko, 138
Ashdown, Paddy, 137, 146n
Aubert, Marie-Hélène, 46, 63
Avdić, Sead, 124n

B
Bacon, Gordon, 138, 139, 147n
Bajalica, Nevena, 102n
Bakker, Bert, 72–74, 76–77, 81, 83n
Balkenende, Jan Peter, 77
Banja Luka, 4, 5, 8, 140, 142, 146n, 147n
Bassiouni, Cherif, 168n
Batkovići, 158, 171n
Baubérot, Jean, 55n
Bayle, Pierre, 176n
Beara, Ljubiša, 36, 38, 39n
Behmen, Alija, 128n
Belgium, 20n, 168n
Belgrade, 38, 113

Bensa, Alban, 55n
Berberović, Ljubomir, 123n
Bihać, 6, 7, 54n, 125n
Bijeljina, 171n
Biljani, 161
Blagojević, Vidoje, 36
Block, Robert, 82n
Blom, Hans, 73, 84n, 91, 92, 94, 102n, 156, 157
Bloxham, David, 22n
Bogdanić, Milan, 138, 146n
Bolkestein, Frits, 71
Borovčanin, Ljubomir, 36–38, 39n
Bossenbroek, Martin, 102n
Both, Norbert, 82n
Bougarel, Xavier, 18, 19n, 20n, 22n, 101n, 123n, 129n, 130n, 169n
Boutros Ghali, Boutros, 113, 115
Brana, Pierre, 17, 43, 46, 47, 63, 84n, 165n
Branjevo, 27, 36
Bratunac, 24–27, 32, 34–36, 38, 40, 125n, 135, 143, 157, 162, 167n
Braudel, Fernand, 18
Brayard, Florent, 92, 103n
Brčko, 3
Brđanin, Radoslav, 174n
Browning, Christopher, 92, 103n, 172n
Broz-Tito, Josip, 49, 119
Burg, Steven, 19n
Brunborg, Helge, 166n
Bukejlović, Pero, 141
Butler, Richard, 32

C

Čampara, Avdo, 112, 125n
Carmichael, Cathie, 20n
Čavić, Dragan, 137, 138, 142
Cazeneuve, Bernard, 58
Čekić, Smail, 138, 139, 141
Cero, Muharem, 112, 125n, 128n
Cerska, 24, 26, 28
Cesarani, David, 172n
Cohen, Lenard, 19n
Couzy, Hans, 72, 78, 83n
Croatia, 2–5, 15, 19n, 21n

D

Đapo, Mirsad, 125n
Delić, Rasim, 107, 112–114, 125n, 126n, 127n, 129n
Delpla, Isabelle, 18, 19n, 20n, 23–39, 53n, 55n, 101n, 103n, 129n, 172n, 176n
Deronjić, Miroslav, 35, 38, 171n
Dervišbegović, Hasan, 112, 113, 125n, 126n
Dimitrijević, Vojin, 21n
Donia, Robert, 19n
Doorn, Jacobus van, 102n
Drina (river), 3, 24, 107, 108, 116, 122n, 124n
Duijzings, Ger, 22n, 49, 102n, 129n, 159, 162, 167n, 171n
Duraković, Nijaz, 106

E

Edward, Joseph, 173n, 175n
Erdemović, Dražen, 120n, 128n

F

Faber, Mient Jan, 20n, 70, 71, 83n
Fassin, Eric, 55n
Fine, John, 19n
Fisk, Robert, 68, 82n
Foča, 3, 11, 143
Fournel, Jean-Louis, 8, 84n, 101n, 149n, 168n
France, 2, 9, 20n, 40–43, 47, 53n, 56–66, 69, 148, 152n, 161, 165, 168n, 169n
Frankfort, Titia, 102n

G

Gagnon, Valère, 19n
Ganić, Ejup, 112, 123n
Gerlach, Christian, 92, 103n
Ginzburg, Carlo, 22n, 54n
Gobilliard, Hervé, 155, 163, 169n, 173n, 174n, 175n
Gojer, Gradimir, 123n
Goldstone, Richard, 22n
Goražde, 6, 7, 54n, 105, 125n, 126n, 154, 160
Gow, James, 20n
Graaf, Bob de, 102n
Grabovica, 161
Grave, Frank de, 70, 75
Grbavci, 27
Grbo, Ismet, 123n
Great Britain, 9, 48, 165n
Greece, 20n, 21n
Gvero, Milan, 36–38, 39n

H

Hadžić, Hasan, 117, 122n, 123n, 128n, 129n
Hadžić, Izet, 109
Hadžić, Miroslav, 19n
Haglund, Bill, 27, 31
Halilović, Sefer, 121, 129n
Hamilton, Rebecca, 22n
Harland, David, 17, 18, 42, 43, 53n, 54n, 154, 155, 162, 163, 165n, 166n, 168n, 169n, 170n, 173n, 175n
Hausner, Gideon, 172n
Hećimović, Esad, 120, 123n, 129n
Heljić Bećir, 105, 124n
Hoare, Marko, 20n, 123n
Honig, Jan Willem, 82n
Hoop Scheffer, Jaap de, 146n
Husejnović, Alosman, 124n

I

Ibrahimpašić, Smail, 112, 117
Igman (mount), 125n
Ingrao, Christian, 172n
Isović, Safet, 112
Ivošević, Milorad, 138, 139

Izetbegović, Alija, 106, 109, 119, 121, 123n, 124n, 125n, 128n, 129n, 130n

J
Jadar (river), 26
Jahić, Fikret, 124n
Janvier, Bernard, 45, 46, 60, 62, 63, 113, 115, 126n, 152, 154, 155, 160, 165n, 169n, 172n, 175n
Jaspers, Karl, 128n
Jokić, Dragan, 36
Jong, Louis de, 88–90, 100, 102n
Joseph, Edward, 173n, 175n
Joyce, Christopher, 169n
Juppé, Alain, 80

K
Kadić, Rasim, 125n
Kafedžić, Mujo, 109
Kamp, Henk, 78, 86
Kant, Imanuel, 164
Karadžic, Radovan, 9, 35, 37, 38, 63, 111, 128n, 142, 157, 165n, 171n
Karremans, Thom, 72, 83n, 98
Kemenade, Wim van, 70, 72, 83n
Keraterm, 3
Kersten, Albert, 102n
Kladanj, 126n
Klep, Christ, 17, 19n, 21n, 84n, 165n, 170n, 171n
Koedijk, Paul, 84n, 102n
Kok, Wim, 71, 74–77, 82
Konjević Polje, 25, 26
Kosovo, 8, 15, 34, 50, 55n, 89
Koštunica, Vojislav, 15
Kozluk, 27
Krajišnik, Momčilo, 174n
Kravica, 26, 27, 37, 39n, 162, 167n
Kress, Claus, 22n
Krstić, Radislav, 2, 9, 23, 36, 39n, 46, 63, 79, 128n, 134, 135, 142, 150, 152, 153, 160, 166n, 174n

L
Lagrou, Pieter, 18, 54n, 82n, 102n, 103n, 165n, 170n, 171n, 172n
Latić, Nedžad, 129n
Lazović, Miro, 125n, 129n

Léotard, François, 62
Le Goff, Jacques, 55n
Le Pape, Marc, 20n, 129n, 168n
Lorenz, Chris, 103n

M
Maguire, Peter, 94, 103n
Malcolm, Noel, 19n
Mašović, Amor, 109, 146n
Matanović, Tomislav, 132
MacKenzie, Lewis, 167n, 170n
Meholjić, Hakija, 106, 119, 121, 129n
Mierlo, Hans van, 80
Mikerević, Dragan, 138
Miletić, Dejan, 138
Miletić, Radivoje, 36–38, 39n, 138, 146n
Milošević, Slobodan, 14, 39n, 50, 121, 130n, 165n, 169n, 173n, 174n, 175n
Milanović, Marko, 21n
Milovanović, Miloš, 165n
Mlaćo, Dževad, 110, 112, 127n
Mladić, Ratko, 1, 7, 9, 15, 23, 24, 26, 34, 36, 37, 46, 55, 61–63, 78, 98, 111, 126n, 128n, 142, 154, 157, 160, 162, 165n, 171n, 173n, 174n
Moorcraft, Paul, 170n
Morillon, Philippe, 6, 46, 54n
Mostar, 143
Muminović, Šemsudin, 112
Muratović, Hasan, 112, 113, 126n
Mustafić, Ibran, 110–112, 118, 119, 121, 124n, 129n, 137

N
Naimark, Norman, 20n
Netherlands, 2, 9, 10, 21, 33, 40, 43, 46, 48, 67–85, 86–103, 148, 150, 157, 159, 161, 171n
New York, 13, 19n, 31, 71, 87, 95, 161, 176n
Nicolaï, Cees, 62
Nikolić, Drago, 36–38
Nikolić, Momir, 36, 171n, 172n
Nora, Pierre, 55n
Norton-Cru, Jean, 98
Nova Kasaba, 24–26, 34

Nuhanović, Hasan, 146n
Numanović, Sead, 123n

O
Obrenović, Dragan, 36, 168n, 171n
Ogata, Sadako, 60, 61
Omarska, 3
Orahovac, 24, 27
Orić, Naser, 3, 103n, 105, 107–109, 112, 113, 119, 122n, 124n, 126n, 129n, 162, 168n
Owen, David, 6, 121, 129n

P
Palić, Avdo, 175n
Pandurević, Vinko, 36–38, 39n, 168n
Pargan, Mehmed, 123n, 128n
Peress, Gilles, 169n
Peters, Rik, 170n
Petkovci, 24, 27
Picard, Michèle, 17, 21n, 53n, 54n, 145n, 165n, 166n, 167n, 168n
Pilica, 24, 27, 36
Plavšić, Biljana, 165n
Pogge, Thomas, 166n
Pohl, Dieter, 92, 103n
Pollack, Creg, 129n
Popović, Vujadin, 36, 38, 39n, 166n, 167n, 168n, 169n, 171n, 172n, 173n, 174n, 175n
Popper, Karl, 99
Potočari, 24, 25, 30, 95, 136, 137, 145, 157, 158, 171n, 172n
Prijedor, 3, 11, 35, 132, 170n
Prlić, Jadranko, 124n
Pronk, Jan, 75

Q
Quilès, Paul, 58

R
Rajner, Igor, 112, 114, 117, 118, 124n, 125n, 127n
Reiss, Rodolphe, 10, 20n
Revel, Jacques, 55n, 174n
Roćević, 27
Rogatica, 143

Rohde, David, 82n, 130n, 148, 151, 157, 160, 162, 165n, 166n, 169n, 171n, 172n, 173n, 175n, 176n
Romijn, Peter, 102n
Rousso, Henry, 22n
Ruez, Jean-René, 16, 17, 42, 50, 53n, 151, 163, 167n, 168n, 169n, 172n

S
Šabić, Veiz, 125n
Salihović, Zulfo, 124n, 125n
Salman, Ahmed, 165n
Sanski Most, 3, 8
Sandići, 25, 26
Sarajevo, 3–9, 37, 40, 42, 54n, 63, 105–111, 113, 115, 119–121, 122n, 123n, 124n, 125n, 126n, 127n, 128n, 129n, 142, 143, 147n, 154, 161, 163, 167n, 169n
Savić, Cvjetko, 138
Schomburg, Wolfgang, 35
Schoonoord, Dick, 102n, 150, 157, 168n
Šehović, Mustafa, 112, 118
Sejmenović, Mevludin, 127n
Sémelin, Jacques, 162, 174n
Serbia, 2–6, 9, 13–15, 19n, 21n, 22n, 24, 51, 110, 133, 139, 162, 175n
Shoup, Paul, 19n
Silajdžić, Haris, 106, 107, 116, 118
Siméant, Johanna, 20n, 129n, 168n
Skoković-Tomić, Biljana, 128n
Slatina, Senad, 128n
Smith, Rupert, 60, 79, 84n, 126n, 169n, 175n
Solana, Javier, 146n
Sorabji, Cornelia, 162, 174n
Stojaković, Đorđe, 138, 139
Stoltenberg, Thorvald, 6, 121, 129n
Stover, Eric, 169n
Sudetic, Chuck, 148, 162n
Šušnjari, 24, 25

T
Tadić, Boris, 15, 128n
Tardy, Thierry, 20n, 53n
Tešanj, 124n

Tihić, Sulejman, 142
Tokača, Mirsad, 30
Tolimir, Zdravko, 36, 37, 174n, 175n
Torkid, Lyngstad, 166n
Trbić, Milorad, 36
Tuzla, 4–6, 8, 23, 30, 54n, 91, 95, 105, 106, 108, 109, 111, 112, 117, 122n, 123n, 124n, 125n, 126n, 128n, 144, 145, 161

U
United Kingdom. *See* Great Britain
United States, 6, 7, 9, 50, 64, 69, 165
Urdal, Enrik, 166n
Uye, Rolf van, 102n

V
Vance, Cyrus, 6, 9
Vasilj, Pero, 125n
Veyne, Paul, 22n
Vidal, Claudine, 20n, 129n, 168n
Vidal-Naquet, Pierre, 22n
Viewiorka, Annette, 22n
Višegrad, 3, 11, 143
Vlasenica, 143
Vogošća, 130n
Voorhoeve, Joris, 68, 71, 72, 75, 83n

Vukotić, Gojko, 138, 139
Vujadinović, Željko, 139

W
Weber, Max, 164
Wiebes, Cees, 102n
Wind, Onno van der, 83n
Woodward, Susan, 19n

Y
Yugoslavia, 2, 15, 19n, 48, 57, 60, 134, 144, 145, 161, 165n, 168n

Z
Zagreb, 17, 62, 73, 85n, 87, 95, 161
Zalazje, 167n
Zametica, John, 165n
Zeleni Jadar, 127n
Žepa, 6, 7, 21n, 38, 42, 54n, 105, 108–110, 115, 121, 125n, 126n, 127n, 129n, 154, 155, 157, 160, 162–164, 169n, 171n, 172n, 173n, 174n, 175n
Zinbo, Asta, 17, 19n, 21n, 53n, 54n, 131, 145n, 146n, 165n, 166n, 167n, 168n
Zvornik, 3, 11, 24–27, 32, 34, 36–38, 63, 118, 122n, 125n, 163, 168n, 171n

SUBJECT INDEX

A
aerial images, 28, 29, 33, 34, 39, 95, 151
AID (Agency for Information and Documentation), 30
air strikes, 6, 7, 23, 62, 63, 71, 108, 175n
annexes (of the reports), 11, 44, 88, 102, 139, 143, 169
archives, 11, 39, 53n, 89, 94, 99, 100, 151, 154, 165n
  access to, 93, 94, 149, 151, 165n
  of the ICTY, 14
  of the Nuremberg trials, 29
  Serbian, 50
  See also document and evidence
arm embargo, 6, 161
ARBiH (Bosnian army), 3–6, 8, 20n, 29, 32, 108, 120, 121, 122n, 167n

B
Balkan wars, 10, 49
black market, 98, 103n
blue helmets, 1, 6, 9, 25, 43, 62, 65, 67, 97, 113, 153, 155, 157, 159, 161, 167n, 169n, 172n, 174n, 175n
Bosnian Parliament. *See* Parliament
Bratunac brigade (of the VRS), 26, 32, 36, 38

C
camps, 3, 89, 98, 110, 156, 158, 170n, 171n, 172n
causality, 96, 113, 164–166
civil society, 17, 29, 144, 145
civilians, 6, 25, 35, 39n, 95, 114, 127n, 135, 155
column (heading toward Bosnian-held territories), 24, 25, 38, 107, 111, 113, 122n, 150, 157–159, 163, 167, 168n, 169n, 171n, 172n, 175n
combatants (vs. non-combatants), 23, 25–28, 105, 108, 123n
commemoration (of the massacre), 15, 21n, 86, 95
competence (vs. incompetence), 17, 51, 54n, 70, 72, 77, 90, 157
comparison
  between the reports and the ICTY investigations, 99, 151, 161, 162, 176n
  of the reports, 10–12, 17, 18, 20n, 21n, 40–49, 54n, 87
consensus, 11, 46, 60, 74, 79, 87–91, 96, 100, 101, 114, 138
conspiracy theories, 11, 120, 130n, 153, 169n, 176n
Court of Bosnia-Herzegovina, 36, 37, 39n, 132, 139, 141, 143, 174n
crimes against humanity, 36, 51, 93, 128n, 138
Croatian army, 3, 7
chronology, 27, 32, 49, 54n, 92, 113, 151, 153, 160

D
Dani (newspaper), 120, 121, 122n, 137

Dayton agreements, 7, 27, 50, 51, 108, 109, 122n, 132, 134, 135, 137, 145n, 154, 155, 164, 169n
death toll (number of victims), 19n, 25, 27–29, 33, 43, 94, 166n
demilitarization (of Srebrenica), 61, 164
denial (of the massacre), 9, 20n, 11, 12, 36, 49, 80, 142–143
dissimulation (of the bodies), 9, 27, 28, 150
Dnevni Avaz (newspaper), 137, 146n
document, 10, 13, 14, 16, 20n, 28, 32, 37, 57–59, 61, 64, 72, 75, 83n, 90, 99, 102n, 125n, 128n, 135, 139, 140, 149, 151, 164, 165n, 166n, 169n.
See also archives and evidence
Drina Corps (of the VRS), 9, 23, 26–28, 32, 36, 37, 141
Drina Valley Alliance (refugee association), 123n
"Drina Wolves" (military unit), 32
Dutchbat (Dutch bataillon), 1, 7, 13, 17, 43, 45, 49, 61, 67, 70–73, 77, 79–81, 82n, 83n, 85n, 86, 87, 90, 97, 98, 100, 102, 103n, 152, 157, 160, 164, 167, 170n, 172n, 175n
and "Zagreb reception", 73, 83n
debriefing of, 70, 82, 83n
Dutch government, 40, 46, 53n, 67–69, 71, 75–80, 84n, 86–89, 91, 97, 99, 101, 101n, 102n, 155, 159, 170n
Dutch Parliament. See Parliament

E
ECHR (European Court of Human Rights), 132–135
Ecumenical Council for Peace, 21n
elections, 2, 10, 76, 108, 112, 115, 119, 120
enclaves (in eastern Bosnia), 1, 5–7, 21n, 105–109, 112, 113, 121, 126, 164, 169, 172n, 173n, 176n
"ethnic cleansing", 1, 3, 4, 6, 8, 11, 20n, 33, 55n, 113, 153, 157, 162, 168n, 171n, 173n
European Parliament. See Parliament
European Union, 15

event, 10, 18, 40–42, 44, 48, 52, 55n, 56, 58, 77, 91, 112, 143, 173n
epistemology of, 40, 42, 48–50, 53n, 54n, 55n, 160, 161
evidence, 1, 2, 10, 14, 27–32, 35, 37–39, 42, 48, 50, 51, 63, 79, 81, 94, 140, 144, 146n, 147n, 151
destruction of, 153, 157, 166n, 168n, 169n
See also archives and document
executions, 3, 9, 24–27, 30, 34–35, 37–38, 49, 92, 135, 139, 142, 149, 151, 157–159, 166n, 167n, 168n, 171n, 173n
execution sites, 24, 26–28, 31, 34, 162, 166n, 174n
executive and legislative powers, 46, 47, 56, 58, 61–69, 72–76, 81, 117. See also Parliament
exhumations, 12, 27–28, 94, 111, 140
experts
  Balkan experts, 45, 47, 60
  criminal experts, 28, 29, 31
  expert-witnesses, 28, 29, 30, 53, 60, 85n
  legal and political experts, 13
  mixed commissions of, 40, 42, 168n

F
facts/factual, 10, 14, 16, 18, 28, 30–32, 39, 40, 46, 51, 54n, 55n, 57, 60, 63, 64, 70, 81, 84n, 85n, 87, 89, 90, 91, 94–96, 135, 138, 140, 142, 143, 148–165, 166n, 171n, 173n, 175n
FBiH (Federation of Bosnia-Herzegovina), 6, 7, 122n, 123n, 132, 146n
foreign policy, 2, 10, 21n, 56–59, 61, 65, 66, 80, 97, 102n, 112, 124n, 125n, 146n, 149, 172n, 176n
forensic science, 10, 31, 32, 33, 94, 144, 151, 152, 160, 166, 168n, 169n, 152. See also experts
French Parliament. See Parliament

G
gendercide, 139, 160, 173n
Germany, 93

genocide, 9, 14, 15, 20n, 21n, 22n, 31, 36, 45–46, 63, 65, 79, 83n, 84n, 104, 113–115, 134, 142, 143, 160, 166n, 167n, 168n, 170n, 172n, 174n
   Convention on the Prevention and Punishment of the Crime of Genocide (1948), 134
   in Rwanda, 45, 65
   in the ICJ decision, 9,13, 14, 63, 79
   in the ICTY judgments, 9, 36, 63, 79, 142, 160
   in the resolution of the European Parliament, 15
guilty plea, 36, 37, 39, 171n

H

HDZ (Croatian Democratic Community), 3, 124n, 125n
hearings, 42–45, 53n, 57, 59–61, 70–72, 76, 83n, 84n, 85n, 136
historians, 16–18, 22n, 40, 42, 47, 49, 50, 53n, 54n, 85, 90, 99, 101, 150, 152, 176n
history writing, 2, 10, 16–18, 22n, 47, 54n, 80, 81, 87, 93, 94, 100, 150
   and emotion, 98
   and investigation commissions 10
   collective and individual, 100, 168n
   judges and historians, 16, 17, 35, 93, 94
   style, 21n, 87, 90, 100, 151, 160, 165
   See also positivism
historical narrative, 16, 50, 149, 151–154, 156, 171n, 174n
historiography
   of the Nuremberg trial, 22n
   of Nazism, 87, 93, 94, 157, 158, 172n
   of the collapse of Yugoslavia, 94, 95
   See also Event
hostages (blue helmets), 6, 63, 96, 113
Human Rights Chamber for Bosnia-Herzegovina, 132, 133, 135
HVO (Croat Defense Council), 3–6, 8

I

ICJ (International Court of Justice), 13, 14, 15, 127
ICMP (International Commission for Missing Persons), 12, 17, 19n, 40, 131, 132, 137, 138, 144, 145n, 146n, 147n, 149, 150
ICRC (International Committee of the Red Cross), 108, 133, 134, 149, 150, 158, 166n, 172n
ICTY (International Criminal Tribunal for the former Yugoslavia), 8, 9, 12–17, 22n, 20–31, 33, 35, 37, 39n, 41, 46, 48–51, 53n, 63, 79, 87, 89, 93–95, 101, 111, 114–116, 127, 128n, 129n,130n, 132–136, 138, 142, 146n, 147n, 148–151, 153, 160, 165, 166n–169n, 171n–176n
IKV (Interchurch Peace Council), 70
image (and reputation), 43, 58, 63, 64, 81, 96, 102n, 119, 157, 159, 172n
   of France, 48, 63
   of the Netherlands, 43, 46, 99, 157, 159
immunity (of the UN), 13
impartiality
   and academic ethos, 88, 156
   UN philosophy of, 155, 156
international community, 1, 2, 10, 18, 40, 42, 83n, 94, 95, 110, 113–116, 125n, 126n, 127n, 131, 136, 138, 146n, 170n, 173n
interviews, 17, 30, 45, 82n, 99, 124n, 140, 165n, 166n
investigations (and investigators), 1, 2, 8, 9, 10, 11, 16, 17, 23, 25–31, 33, 35–39, 42, 43, 48, 49, 56–59, 64–66, 68–82, 83n, 84n, 85n, 86–88, 93, 150, 153
   by the commission of the RS, 48
   by the French National Assembly Fact-Finding Mission, 9, 41
   by the ICMP, 145, 149, 150, 153
   by the ICTY, 9, 16, 23, 24, 25, 26, 27, 28, 29, 30, 32, 33, 34, 35, 41, 48, 49, 53, 79
"Krivaja 95" (military operation), 23, 139, 140, 150, 153

J

JNA (Yugoslav People's Army), 3, 14, 19n, 20n, 130n, 174n

journalists, 9, 30, 31, 64, 68, 70, 72, 79, 82, 116, 120, 148, 149, 151, 152, 166n, 170n
judgment
  moral, 14, 15, 21, 31, 51, 67, 71, 78, 80, 95, 97, 98, 104, 105, 113, 116, 118, 119, 142, 146n, 155, 164, 170n, 175n, 176n
  political, 43, 52, 62, 76, 155
judgments (and decisions)
  of the ICTY, 2, 9, 13, 14, 31, 89, 101, 132, 168n, 171n, 174n
  Krstić case (ICTY), 39n, 46, 134–135, 142, 150, 160, 166n, 174n
  Matanović case (Human Rights Chamber), 132
  Popović and alii case (ICTY), 39n, 166n
  Samardžija case (Court of Bosnia-Herzegovina), 174n
  Selimović case (Human Rights Chamber), 17, 131, 134
  Unković case (Human Rights Chamber), 133
justice
  and truth, 144, 145, 147n
  criminal, 2, 16, 29, 141, 145
  transitional, 21n

K
knowledge, 2, 11, 13, 16, 33, 38, 47, 78, 81, 100, 149, 152, 169n, 173n

L
legislative power. *See* Parliament and executive and legislative powers
legitimacy (and legitimization), 51, 52, 87, 88, 90, 137, 143
Ljiljan (newspaper), 112, 119, 120, 124n, 129n
local scale (and interplay of scales), 5, 18, 92, 95, 98, 109, 110, 113, 117, 119, 124n, 132, 133, 136, 147n, 153, 159, 161–163, 167n, 172n, 174n

M
mandate
  of the Human Rights Chamber, 147n
  of the ICMP, 145n, 147n
  of the NIOD, 73, 89, 100, 145n
  of the UNPROFOR, 6, 9, 19n, 73, 116, 126n, 154, 169n
mass graves (primary and secondary), 1, 9, 24, 26–28, 31, 34, 94, 111, 135, 138–140, 144, 166n
MBO (Bosniak Muslim Organization), 109, 117, 123n
Médecins sans frontières, 21n
military intervention, 6, 8, 19n, 49, 50, 86, 89, 147n, 170n, 175n, 176n
"Mothers of Srebrenica and Podrinje Association" (victim association), 137

N
nationalist parties, 2, 3, 120
NATO, 1, 6–8, 48, 50, 55n, 60, 62, 71, 89, 108, 110, 125n, 146n, 160, 172n, 175n
NGO, 9, 12, 14, 20n, 21n, 29, 45, 48, 53n, 70, 136, 142, 146n, 151, 158
NIOD (Dutch Institute for War Documentation), 9, 10, 13, 16, 18, 22n, 40–51, 53n, 54n, 55n, 69–82, 82n, 83n, 84n, 85n, 86–104, 150–162, 165n, 167n, 168n, 169n, 170n, 171n, 172n, 173n, 174n, 175n
Nuremberg tribunal, 10, 16, 22n, 29, 93–94, 94, 142, 143, 146n, 147n

O
oath, 57, 59, 84n, 116
objectivity, 41, 42, 150
OHR (Office of the High Representative), 10, 40, 46–49, 53n, 146n, 147n
Oslobođenje (newspaper), 117, 119, 122n, 123n, 124n, 127n, 128n, 129n, 137, 146n, 147n

P
Parliament
  Bosnian Parliament, 11, 18, 104–130, 152
  Dutch Parliament, 10, 17, 40, 43, 53n, 55n, 67–85, 96, 101

European Parliament, 15, 21n
French Parliament, 17, 41, 43–45, 47–51, 53n, 55n, 56–66
Serbian Parliament, 12, 14, 15
Parliamentary inquiry commission
  (Dutch) Interim Commission on Decision Making during Peace Operations, 18, 69, 71–74, 81, 82
  (Dutch) Short Full Parliamentary Inquiry into Srebrenica, 69, 74–78, 82
  (French) Parliamentary Fact-Finding Mission on Srebrenica, 9, 17, 41, 43–45, 47, 56–66
peacekeeping, 1, 8, 67, 69, 72–74, 82, 84n
peace plans (and negotiations), 6, 7, 108, 120, 121, 122n, 129n, 154–155
PIP (Podrinje identification project), 144
positivism (historians), 87, 90, 92, 96, 150
public opinion, 9, 47, 52, 53n, 63–66, 70, 77, 79, 82, 94, 96, 97, 99, 101, 106, 127n, 138, 140, 143, 156, 157, 171n
public sphere, publicity, 2, 11–14, 18, 21n, 40, 41, 44, 45, 47, 49, 51, 52, 58, 64, 71, 84n, 87–89, 91, 105, 120, 130, 136, 141, 142, 149, 156, 166n
publication (of the reports), 14, 49, 55n, 58, 60, 75, 87–89, 91, 92, 100, 102n, 119, 124n, 136, 140, 159, 169n

R

radio communications, 29, 32, 37, 38, 129
raids (against Serbian villages), 4, 80
Ratna Tribina (newspaper), 105–123, 122n
"Realpolitik", 51, 79
refugees, 1, 4, 24, 25, 30, 54n, 60, 71, 75, 78, 107–110, 116, 124n, 158, 162–164, 171n
repentance (or apologies, mea culpa), 12, 15, 51, 64, 75, 101, 141, 155, 170n
reports, 1, 2, 9–13, 16–18, 20n, 21n, 28, 33, 40–52, 53n, 54n, 61, 70, 76, 79, 82, 86, 87, 148, 149, 160, 161, 164, 166n, 168n, 173n, 174n, 176n
  Bassiouni report, 168n
  Bosnian reports, 112, 114, 124n, 125n
  by Amor Mašović (president of the commission for missing persons), 109, 110
  Dutch parliamentary reports, 11, 13, 17, 40, 42–46, 51, 67–85, 149, 152, 153, 155, 165n, 166n, 168n, 169n
  French parliamentary report, 11, 13, 17, 40–49, 51, 54n, 56–66, 80, 149, 150, 152, 153, 155, 156, 166n, 168n, 169n, 170n, 172n
  Greek report, 20n
  NGO reports, 12, 29, 53n, 70, 71
  NIOD report, 13, 16, 18, 22n, 40–45, 47, 49–51, 53n, 54n, 72, 74–76, 78–80, 82, 82n, 83n, 84n, 86–103, 150–152, 155–160, 162, 165n, 167n, 169n, 170n, 171n, 172n, 173n
  of the (Dutch) Interchurch Peace Council, 70
  Republika Srpska report (or RS report), 10, 11, 16, 40, 42–44, 48, 49, 51, 53n, 54n, 55n, 131–147, 150, 151–153, 166n, 168n, 169n
  Rwanda genocide reports, 20n, 61n, 65, 168n
  UN report, 13, 18, 20n, 40–44, 46, 47, 49–51, 53n, 54n, 55n, 61, 79, 128n, 149, 150, 152–156, 162, 163, 165n, 166n, 168n, 169n, 170n, 175n
"report-form", 18, 40, 48
"Republic of Serb Krajina", 3, 7, 139
resolution (on Srebrenica)
  of the Bosnian Parliament, 110, 114, 115, 119, 124n
  of the Canadian Parliament, 21n
  of the Croatian Parliament, 21n
  of the European Parliament, 15, 21n
  of the Macedonian Parliament, 21n
  of the Montenegrin Parliament, 21n
  of the Serbian Parliament, 12, 14, 15
  of the US Senate and Congress, 21n

responsibility (questions of), 1, 2, 9–13, 16, 18, 31, 41, 43, 45, 47, 48, 55n, 56, 61, 63, 64, 75, 84n, 86–88, 105–121, 131, 132, 143, 148–176
  cosmopolitan responsibility, 164, 166n
  criminal (or penal) responsibility, 2, 9, 10, 13, 23, 38, 42, 43, 48, 115, 153, 164, 168n
  hierarchy of responsibility, 115, 116, 153
  individual responsibility, 18, 35, 38, 55n, 107, 114, 136, 149, 153, 154, 170n
  institutional responsibility, 18, 41, 149, 164
  local responsibility, 100, 114
  moral responsibility, 2, 9, 48, 115, 118, 153
  of General Bernard Janvier, 155, 169n
  of the Dutch authorities, 11–13, 43, 61, 75, 76, 77, 84n, 86, 88, 149, 153, 155, 159, 169n
  of the French authorities, 11, 43, 44, 63, 64, 80, 149, 153, 169n
  of the international community and the UN, 1, 2, 10, 12, 16, 21n, 41, 43, 45, 61, 106, 107, 110, 114, 115, 126n, 149, 153, 155, 166n, 169n, 176n
  of the Sarajevo authorities, 11, 80, 105–121, 128n, 130n, 146n, 153, 169n, 172n
  of the Serbs, 13, 14, 152
  political responsibility, 2, 9, 10, 16, 13, 41–43, 48, 63, 64, 75–77, 79, 115, 116, 118
  types of responsibility, 118, 153, 157
RRF (Rapid Reaction Force), 6, 7
RS (Republika Srpska), 3, 6, 7, 9–11, 15–17, 22n, 40, 42–45, 47–49, 51, 53n, 54n, 55n, 131–148, 150, 152, 153, 162, 164, 165n, 166n, 167n, 168n, 169n
rumors, 67, 73, 105, 120, 133, 134, 170n
  on the number of deaths, 11
  on the abandonment of Srebrenica by Sarajevo authorities, 63, 105, 108, 110
  on an agreement between General Bernard Janvier and Ratko Mladić, 46, 62, 63
  on the former enclave leaders, 119
Rwanda, 17, 20n, 57–59, 61, 63–65, 84n, 168n
  France, Bosnia-Herzegovina and, 20n, 53n, 58, 168n

S

"safe areas", 1, 6, 7, 9, 12, 42, 43, 49, 54n, 55n, 69, 82n, 83n, 102n, 109, 111, 125n, 126n, 151, 154, 161, 164, 168n, 170n, 171n, 174n
Sarajevo (siege of), 3, 5, 7, 197, 121
SBiH (Party for Bosnia-Herzegovina), 111–113, 117, 124n, 125n, 128n
"Scorpions" (military unit), 38, 142
SDA (Party of Democratic Action), 3, 19n, 105–121, 123n, 124n, 125n, 126n, 127n, 128n, 129n, 130n
SDP (Social Democratic Party), 106, 117–119, 123n, 124n, 125n, 128n
SDS (Serbian Democratic Party), 3, 19n
secrecy, 11, 16, 44, 47, 58, 99, 130n, 136, 138, 153, 173n
secret services, 30, 34–37, 69, 93, 95, 102n, 126n, 153, 173n
Serbian Parliament. *See* Parliament
Slobodna Bosna (newspaper), 111, 120, 124n, 128n, 129n
source, 11, 12, 17, 30, 34, 48, 64, 77, 79, 90, 150, 156, 176n. *See also* document and evidence
survivors, 9, 26, 93, 98, 99, 104, 108, 116, 119, 145, 146n, 163, 166n

T

temporalities, 18, 40–42, 48–52
testimony, 9, 12, 23, 28, 34, 45, 54n, 59, 60, 70, 83n, 84n, 85n, 93, 94, 98, 104, 148, 150–152, 165n, 169n, 171n, 172n, 173n, 175n
translation, 87, 102n, 128n

transparency, 11, 44, 65, 99, 136. *See also* publicity
trial 37, 38, 119
   Eichmann trial, 172n
   Karadžić trial, 36
   Krstić trial, 23, 36, 39n, 79, 142, 150, 152, 166n
   Milošević trial, 9, 14, 121, 165n, 169n, 173n, 175n
   Mladić trial, 36
   Nikolić trial, 171n
   Obrenović trial, 168n
   Orić trial, 16n
   Popović et alii trial, 36, 38, 39n, 166n, 167n, 168n, 169n, 171n, 172n, 173n, 174n, 175n
   Tolimir trial, 36, 174n
truth, 11, 13, 27, 30, 34, 35, 39, 52, 54n, 56, 59, 64, 66, 76, 91, 117, 129n
   and justice, 144, 145, 147n
   demand for, 105
   public construction of, 40–47, 51, 53n
   truth and reconciliation commissions, 136, 144
28th Division (of the ARBiH), 25, 105, 108, 171

U

UBSD (Union of Bosnian Social Democrats), 117, 122n, 123n, 125n, 127n
UN (United Nations), 1, 2, 6, 8, 9, 12, 13, 15, 20n, 21n, 23–25, 34, 41–51, 53n, 54n, 55n, 58, 62, 64, 65, 70, 71, 73, 80–82, 83n, 84n, 99, 106, 107, 114–116, 126n, 128n, 148–156, 161–164, 165n, 168n, 169n, 170n, 173n, 174n, 175n, 176n
UNHCR (United Nations High Commissioner for Refugees), 60, 61, 110
UNPROFOR (United Nations Protection Force), 6, 7, 19n, 41, 43, 46, 53n, 54n, 60–62, 79, 95, 110, 112, 116, 125n, 126n, 151, 152, 154–156, 160, 161, 167n, 169n, 170n, 173n, 175n

V

vengeance (references to), 121, 129n, 135, 148, 156, 157, 159, 161, 162, 165n, 167n, 170n, 173n, 174n
victims
   and Dutch government, 75, 79, 80
   attention to, 155–157, 169
   identification, 94, 144, 145, 167n
   legal proceedings by, 12, 13, 51, 68, 70, 71, 94, 95
   representation, 45
   status, 131, 133–137, 149, 150
   testimony, 9, 12, 45
   typology, 28, 166n
   See also death toll
victim associations, 17, 45, 61, 80, 129n, 136, 137, 166n
violence, 3, 14, 18, 19, 22n, 46, 54n, 83n, 96, 154, 160, 170n, 173n, 174n, 176n
VRS (Army of the Republika Srpska), 3, 9, 23–25, 32, 36, 37, 46, 139–141
   general staff, 36, 37
   security branch, 36, 37
   special police unit, 37, 38
   See also Drina corps

W

witnesses, 17, 27, 28, 30, 32, 33, 45, 53n, 54n, 60, 72, 76, 77, 79, 80, 84n, 114, 115, 121, 129n, 150, 152, 166n, 168n, 169n. *See also* testimonies
war crimes, 14, 22n, 30, 110, 128n, 136, 141
war crime commission (Bosnian), 30
"Women of Srebrenica" (victim association), 21n, 45, 61
World War I, 10, 98
World War II, 2, 10, 16, 49, 82n, 88–90, 92–94, 98, 100, 130n, 170n, 171n, 172n

Z

Zvornik brigade (of the VRS), 26, 32, 36–38

www.ingramcontent.com/pod-product-compliance
Lightning Source LLC
Chambersburg PA
CBHW072153100526
44589CB00015B/2209